D1431256

MAN IN COMMUNITY

Man in Community

*A Study of St. Paul's Application of
Old Testament and Early Jewish Conceptions
of Human Solidarity*

by

RUSSELL PHILIP SHEDD

WILLIAM B. EERDMANS PUBLISHING COMPANY
GRAND RAPIDS, MICHIGAN

This first American edition published by
William B. Eerdmans Publishing Company
First printing 1964

PHOTOLITHOPRINTED BY CUSHING - MALLOY, INC.
ANN ARBOR, MICHIGAN, UNITED STATES OF AMERICA
1 9 6 4

PREFACE

EVERY writer must seek some justification for the publication of his work. This is doubly true in the event of an addition of another book to the list of over two thousand extant treatments of either the life or teaching of St Paul. In answer to this challenge at the least two things might be said. First of all, current ecumenical discussion attempting to find a common ground upon which to erase the divisions shattering the unity of the Church, has brought the biblical conception of human solidarity into clear focus as a research subject. Secondly, although the stimulation to re-examine the biblical conception of unity has issued in a number of excellent works, to the writer's knowledge there is no specific comprehensive treatment of St Paul's doctrines of human solidarity in relationship to their background.

Although the original manuscript was presented to the Faculty of Divinity at the University of Edinburgh as a partial fulfilment of the requirements for the Doctorate of Philosophy, certain modifications have been considered to be advisable. It is hoped that these changes will not detract from the value of this study, but rather add to the pleasure and understanding of the reader.

My indebtedness to the professors of New College, especially to my advisers, Dr James S. Stewart and Dr William Manson, although gratefully acknowledged, cannot be repaid. Appreciation for the helpful suggestions proffered by Professor W. D. Davies, Dr E. Earle Ellis, the Rev. John Sanderson, and the Rev. John Stam, is gratefully acknowledged.

v

CONTENTS

PART TWO

FOREWORD

By Professor James S. Stewart

HAVING known at first hand the distinguished piece of New Testament research Dr Shedd carried through during his sojourn in the University of Edinburgh, I have much pleasure and confidence in commending this book, based upon the thesis he then wrote. In these days when so much is being spoken and written from one angle and another on the theme of 'Man in Community', and when in reaction from the hyperindividualism of a past generation so many experiments in community are being tried, it is essential to listen to the Biblical witness on this matter. 'Is there any word from the Lord?' The Bible, which starts from the solidarity of the race in the first Adam, goes on to tell of the unity of the people of God under the Old Covenant, and then proclaims the community of the new Israel in the second Adam, the Son of man, the Lord from Heaven. Our divided world's tragic plight and its desperate quest for community make the theme of this book peculiarly relevant and appropriate to the hour in which we live. Dr Shedd's work deserves to be read and pondered deeply.

James S. Stewart

Edinburgh
1958

ABBREVIATIONS

APOT . . .	*Apocrypha and Pseudepigrapha of the Old Testament*, ed. R. H. Charles
ATR . . .	*Anglican Theological Review*
BDB . . .	Brown, Driver and Briggs (*A Hebrew Lexicon of the Old Testament*)
BJRL . . .	*Bulletin of the John Rylands Library*
DSD . . .	*Dead Sea Manual of Discipline*
ExT . . .	*Expository Times*
HBzNT . .	*Handbuch zum Neuen Testament*
HDB . . .	*Hastings Dictionary of the Bible*, ed. J. Hastings
HERE . . .	*Hastings Encyclopedia of Religion and Ethics*, ed. J. Hastings
HUCA . . .	*Hebrew Union College Annual*
IRM . . .	*The International Review of Missions*
ICC . . .	*International Critical Commentary*
JBL . . .	*Journal of Biblical Literature*
JerT . . .	*Jerusalem Talmud*
JE . . .	*Jewish Encyclopedia*
JTS . . .	*Journal of Theological Studies*
LoClL . . .	*Loeb Classical Library edition*
Mek . . .	*Mekilta de-Rabbi Ishmael*, ed. J. Z. Lauterbach
RA . . .	*Rabbinic Anthology*
SASPT . .	*System der Altsynagogalen Palästinischen Theologie*
SDFOS . .	*Sources of the Doctrines of the Fall and Original Sin*
TWBB . . .	*Theological Wordbook of the Bible* (London, 1950), ed. A. Richardson
TWNT . . .	*Theologisches Wörterbuch zum Neuen Testament*, ed. G. Kittel

The common abbreviations for the tractates from the Talmud, Mishna, and other Jewish sources have been employed, as well as those in common use, to designate books of the Bible.

PART I

CHAPTER I

THE CONCEPTIONS OF HUMAN SOLIDARITY IN THE OLD TESTAMENT

THE derivative implications of group solidarity were important elements in Israelite life in the period of Old Testament history. There are few pages in the Chronicle of Sacred History which do not multiply the evidence of a conception of a very strong group unity. Because the consciousness of group solidarity revolved primarily around the family and nation, our major task is to present the aspects of the Hebrew conception of solidarity which by and large refer to Israel alone.

No sustained argument is necessary to justify the assumption that ideas found in the Old Testament are fundamental to the understanding of much of St Paul's teaching. Seventy-eight direct quotations in addition to numerous allusions to the Old Testament are significant in showing the extent to which it determined his thought.[1] Paul's Bible was the final authority for his doctrine (cf. Rom 15⁴, 2 Tim 3¹⁶⁻¹⁷, 1 Cor 10⁶, ¹¹). In limiting the scope of Paul's thought-background to the Old Testament and Jewish sources, we have the unequivocal endorsement of J. Klausner:

There is nothing in all the teaching of Paul, as there is nothing in the teaching of Jesus, which is not grounded in the Old Testament or in the Apocryphal-Pseudepigraphal, and Tannaitic literature of the time.[2]

A comparative study of St Paul's conceptions of human solidarity and those of his Jewish background will reaffirm this general position.

Any investigation into the cultural phenomena which comprise the religious and sociological history of the people of Israel, will posit a marked contrast between ancient Semitic thought and

---

[1] Cf. F. Prat, *The Theology of St Paul*, trans. J. L. Stoddard (London, 1945), I. 41ff; F. C. Porter, 'The Place of Apocalyptical Conceptions in the Thought of Paul', *JBL*, Vol. XLI (1922).

[2] *From Jesus to Paul*, trans. W. F. Stinespring (New York, 1944), p. 482. So also W. D. Davies, *Paul and Rabbinic Judaism* (London, 1948), *passim*.

the modern Western mind. In opposition to the fragmentary individualism of the West since the Renaissance, the thinking of ancient Israel might be characterized as synthetic. It has well been described by the phrase, 'grasping of a totality'.[3] Phenomena were perceived as being parts of some total relationship. This Semitic outlook is evident in the language, laws, worship, and the conception of man. The individual was thought of as a part of some psychic whole such as the nation or some lesser whole.[4]

The term 'corporate personality' has been coined and popularized by H. W. Robinson to describe this conception of human solidarity. Corporate personality involves two basic elements which are used in the definition of a corporation according to English law: (1) a body that is authorized to act as an individual, (2) an artificial person (authorized) and having the capacity of perpetual succession.[5] Thus, the application of the term to a group means that a nation or family, including its past, present, and future members, might function as a single individual through any one of those members conceived as a representative of it.[6] The community was therefore conceived as an interminable continuity. At the same time the group-consciousness was analogous to the idea of a personality. As we proceed with the investigation of this conception, a better understanding of the idea of a single community personality will emerge. The term 'corporate personality', however, is not to be contrasted with the term 'solidarity'. The former defines more precisely the variety of unity evinced in the Old Testament.

At first, the choice of the term 'personality' may appear out of place, especially if Plato's idea of the simplicity of the soul (the 'ego' retaining throughout all changes, the unanalysable awareness of identity) is paramount; but if on the other hand a statement by C. H. Dodd is accepted, the term may pose less difficulty.

In actual fact, human personality, as we know it in ourselves, is not 'simple', but indefinitely complex. In particular it is constituted out of personal relations. From the beginning of our individual existence we

---

[3] A. R. Johnson, *The Vitality of the Individual in the Thought of Ancient Israel* (Cardiff, 1949), p. 7.
[4] E. C. Rust, *Nature and Man in Biblical Thought* (London, 1953), p. 50.
[5] H. W. Robinson, 'The Hebrew Conception of Corporate Personality', *Werden und Wesen, Beihefte Zur Zeitschrift fur die Alttestamentliche Wissenschaft 66* (Berlin, 1936), p. 49.
[6] Ibid. p. 49.

throw out tentacles, as it were, to other persons, and they throw out tentacles to us.[7]

It is primarily in this area of thought that the Hebrew conception of the unity of the community lies. It is a striking recognition of the fact that the individual is more than an atom cut off from his group; rather he as an individual is such because he is part of the group from which he emerges. It might be declared with slight modification that the group is a mass individual living through its constituent members.

The procedure to be followed in this chapter is to examine four general aspects of the Hebrew conception of the group's corporate unity. These aspects are neither progressive nor are they logically dependent. They are no more than convenient titles under which the attempt is made to group the varied evidence to be culled from the Old Testament to both support and explain the Hebrew conception of corporate personality.

THE ASPECT OF THE PERSONAL EXTENSION OF THE GROUP

(1) *The Identification of the Family with its Ancestor*

A number of ideas held by the ancient Hebrews support the contention that the personality of the group transcended both space and time limitations. One of these ideas lies behind the statements which identify a race with its ancestor. There was a very strong sense of solidarity which produced a consciousness of continuous extension crossing the barriers of succeeding generations and uniting the whole group.[8] This unity stemmed directly from the ancestor of the nation. Indeed, the life of the ancestor was conceived as extending itself in his children.

This idea occurs frequently in the Old Testament. For the purpose of illustration we may note Malachi 1[3-4], where Esau and the nation of Edom are equated. Israel as a nation and Jacob as the paternal source are often indistinguishable as in Isaiah 41[8]: 'But thou, Israel, art my servant, Jacob whom I have chosen, the seed of Abraham my friend.' It is particularly difficult to determine in the genealogies of Genesis 9[18] and 10[15-20] whether individuals alone or ancestors and the tribes which came from them are designated.[9] In any case, with relative frequency,

---

[7] *The Communion of Saints* (Cambridge, Mass., 1936), p. 9.
[8] Cf. S. A. Cook, *The Cambridge Ancient History* (Cambridge, 1925), III.438.
[9] Cf. M. Burrows, *An Outline of Biblical Theology* (Philadelphia, 1946), p. 143.

a city or nation bears the name of its founder, which implies more than the mere identity of appellation.

In the same category we may place the conception of a national biography. The nation is treated as an individual. The events and history of the nation are related as though they belonged to the biography of the ancestor. Thus we read in Hosea 11¹: 'When Israel was a child, then I loved him, and called my son out of Egypt.' The mercies of God to Israel in the wilderness are recounted by Moses before the congregation in the second person singular in Deuteronomy 8²⁻²⁰. The nation as a whole forms a corporate personality or collective individual, making the history of the race the biography of the national super-individual.

This conception is well illustrated in the contention that the sons and succeeding generations may share in the experiences of their ancestors. This idea was especially applied to the great events of Israel's history such as the Exodus and the establishment of the covenant. Moses controverts the notion that sons are not involved in the decisions of their fathers. 'The Lord made not this covenant with our fathers, but with us, even us, who are all of us alive here this day' (Deut 5³; cf. 5⁶, 6¹²). The actual generation bound by the covenant at Sinai had perished in the wilderness as had the Jews which were redeemed from Egypt, but Joshua addresses his own generation in the name of the Lord: 'And I brought your fathers out of Egypt: and *ye* came unto the sea; and the Egyptians pursued after your fathers with chariots and horsemen unto the Red sea. And when they cried unto the Lord, he put darkness between *you* and the Egyptians, and brought the sea upon them, and covered them; and *your* eyes have seen what I have done in Egypt: and *ye* dwelt in the wilderness a long season' (24⁶⁻⁷). Throughout the passage there is an apparent confusion of generations which would not have been recognized by the Hebrew mind. That is why hundreds of years after the Exodus, the Lord addresses the nation by Amos in this manner: 'Hear this word . . . O children of Israel . . . which I brought up from the land of Egypt' (3¹). The rationale behind the release of the bond-servant on the year of jubilee is stated thus: 'For they are my servants, which I brought forth out of the land of Egypt . . .' (Lev. 25⁴²). Thus father and son, ancestor and tribe, were identified in a realistic way.

(2) *The Hebrew Conception of a Name*

Closely parallel to the ideas of identification just mentioned was the conception of a name. Rather than thinking of one's name as a convenient aid to distinguish himself from others, the early Israelite viewed his name as bearing character. As the household bore the name of the father, the patriarch's character imbued the house. The son bore the dignity or dishonour of his father because he was called by the parent's name. The passing on of the name meant also the passing on of the life or soul.[10] By giving one's name to a son, in a sense, one does not die. It was for this reason that the Israelite wished for a son more than for anything on earth.[11] The possession of sons to bear the name of their father was desirable because it made the ancestor great. Throughout the Old Testament there is a constant identity of the name with one's seed. They are co-extensive, as Isaiah 66[22] indicates: 'For as the new heavens and the new earth, which I will make, shall remain before me, saith the Lord, so shall your seed and your name remain' (cf. Num. 27[4]). Abraham's name is made great through his progeny. 'And I will make of thee a great nation, and I will bless thee, and make thy name great; and thou shalt be a blessing' (Gen. 12[2]). The great nation which bears the name of Abraham is identified with its ancestor. Although the passage speaks of blessing through Abraham in individual terms, the fulfilment of the promise is carried out through Israel (cf. 12[3]).[12] It is little wonder that David, the king, is not insulted at the expressed wish of his courtiers: 'God make the name of Solomon better than thy name, and make his throne greater than thy throne' (1 K 1[47]). To have a son with a greater name meant simply that one's own honour was increased.[13]

As the Israelite felt that he went on living in his children to a degree that really made their life his own, the name conveyed

---

[10] J. Pedersen, *Israel: Its Life and Culture*, trans. A. Møller (London, 1926), I-II.254. Such an understanding of the name must recognize the soul, not as limited to the ego as the conscious finished personality, but everything that fills it, i.e. renown, property, or realm in which it works. Cf. A. R. Johnson, op. cit. *passim*; Lévy-Bruhl, *How Natives Think*, trans. L. A. Clark (London, 1926), p. 121.

[11] Cf. G. A. F. Knight, *From Moses to Paul* (London, 1949), pp. 37f; M. Burrows, 'Levirate Marriage in Israel', *JBL*, LIX (1940), 31.

[12] It is essential to note that although Abraham had more than one son, it is only Isaac which bears the Patriarch's name and therefore his character (cf. Gen 21[12]).

[13] J. Pedersen, op. cit. I-II.254.

the idea of this life-relationship in an unsevered state. It follows
that 'cutting off of the name from the earth' is more than the
destruction of a single individual. It is, rather, the extermina-
tion of a family-line (cf. Josh 7[9], Deut 29[20], 2 K 14[27], 1 S 24[21-2]).
The institution of Levirate marriage was designed to avoid the
danger of a family line being extinguished through the death of
a childless father. Thus the law states that the first-born of the
new union (wife and the deceased man's brother) was to succeed
in the name of the deceased brother, '. . . that his name be not
put out of Israel' (Deut 25[6]).

The identity of the name with the family life is emphatically
expressed by Bildad in his description of the fate of the wicked:
'His remembrance shall perish from the earth, and he shall have
no name in the street. . . . He shall neither have son nor nephew
among his people, nor any remaining in his dwellings' (Job
18[17, 19]).[14] By way of contrast, David has been elected to the
role of king over Israel for ever (1 Ch 28[4]) in that the 'sons of
David', that is, those that bear his name, will carry on his life.[15]

(3) The Hebrew Conception of the Family

Closely allied to the understanding of a name is the ancient
conception of the family. One cannot easily separate the idea of
a common name derived from an ancestor from the notion of
family participation in a common flesh. Common flesh, like a
common name, makes for a common character.[16] As the flesh
of the son is derived from his father, the ancestor is the source of
the community of flesh which pervades all of his descendants—
those that form his family.[17] The idea will be clarified by
examining the social conception of a single immediate family.

The man of the house was known as the בַּעַל. The significance
of the term extends beyond that of a husband or father to the
idea of lordship. בַּעַל implies not only ownership, but also
complete responsibility for the family.[18] He was the centre from

[14] Cf. A. R. Johnson, *The One and the Many in the Israelite Conception of God* (Cardiff, 1942), p. 8.
[15] Cf. H. W. Robinson, *Religious Ideas of the Old Testament* (London, 1913), p. 91; A. R. Johnson, 'The Role of the King in the Jerusalem Cultus', *The Labyrinth*, ed. S. H. Hooke (London, 1935), p. 75.
[16] J. Pedersen, op. cit. I-II.48.
[17] L. Köhler, *Theologie des Alten Testaments* (Tübingen, 1947), pp. 147f.
[18] See Brown, Driver and Briggs, *A Hebrew Lexicon of the Old Testament* (Oxford, 1952), p. 127; cf. L. Wallis, *Sociological Study of the Bible* (Chicago, 1912), p. 41.

which strength and will emanated.[19] Speaking of the relationship of father to family, C. Ryder Smith says: 'He was responsible for all its members, and his acts bound them; they shared his prosperity or his poverty, his eminence or his doom; they were part and parcel of him.'[20] This relationship, founded on the basis of a blood-bond, established a type of psychic unity. The blood of a living creature contained the life of that organism (cf. Gen 9[4], Deut 12[23]);[21] hence, every member of the family by virtue of a common descent partook of the same blood and consequently of the same life.[22]

It follows that many years after his death Abraham possesses the Land of Promise as Genesis 13[15-17] states: 'For the land which *thou* seest, to *thee* will I give it, and to thy seed forever. . . . Arise, walk through the land in the length of it and in the breadth of it; for I will give it unto *thee*.' When Israel finally possesses the land almost five hundred years later it is equivalent to the fulfilment of this promise, because it is the family of Abraham and the extension of his life.

This manner of thinking makes gaps in genealogy insignificant. Thus Jacob's children are claimed by Laban to be his own (Gen 31[43]), although he was actually their grandfather. Representatives from Israel are not loath to argue with Edomites regarding unrestricted passage through Edom, because Jacob and Esau *are* brothers (Num 20[14]). Matthew's familiar genealogy of Jesus Christ, 'the son of David, the son of Abraham', illustrates the same point (cf. 1[1]).

Involved in the identity of the father and his family is the ancient conception of the blood-bond. Among the earliest bases of kinship was the idea of a common participation in one blood.[23] The blood-bond was the unifying factor of kinship. The kin-group fluctuated in direct response to the strength (recognized) of the blood tie. Therefore, 'to the primitive man all other men fall under two classes, those to whom his life is sacred and those

---

[19] The *baalim* (i.e. Canaanite deities mentioned in the Old Testament) is the plural of *baal*, which signified 'possessor of the land'. C. H. Patterson, *The Philosophy of the Old Testament* (New York, 1953), p. 55; cf. O. S. Rankin, *TWBB*, p. 95.

[20] *The Bible Doctrine of Society* (Edinburgh, 1920), p. 76.

[21] Cf. W. R. Smith, *The Religion of the Semites* (3rd edn, London, 1927), p. 40; L. Köhler, op. cit. p. 131.

[22] W. R. Smith, op. cit. p. 41.

[23] W. R. Smith, op. cit. p. 41; cf. A. Lods, *Israel; From its Beginnings to the Middle of the Eight Century B.C.*, trans. S. H. Hooke (London, 1932), p. 198.

to whom it is not sacred'.[24] This involved the practice of blood-revenge which was the practical test of kinship, in that the whole clan was answerable for the life of each of its members.

In the event that the guilty party could not be seized for punishment, vengeance was satisfied by the son. This principle was enforced in the death of Saul's seven sons. Saul had broken the treaty contracted by Joshua with the Gibeonites (cf. Josh 9[15]). Since redress could not be secured during Saul's life-time, the death of his sons satisfied the Gibeonites' demands for justice (2 S 21[1-14]).[25] Similarly, the guilt incurred by Ahab through his avaricious judicial murder of Naboth was avenged in the death and ignominious burial of Joram, Ahab's son (2 K 9[26]). In a realistic sense the son, through the blood-bond, partook of the life of the father; therefore, the son might inherit the penalty which was in reality the due of the parent. There was no question of injustice involved, since the family or kin-group composed a corporate personality.

From the immediate family and the obvious kinship of the מִשְׁפָּחָה, the unity of the larger community was derived. It was imbued with the common character and spirit which characterized a family.[26] For this reason it was quite proper to refer to a tribe or clan as a family. Therefore, we read that Manoah came from the 'family of the Danites' (Judg 13[2]; cf. 17[7], 18[19]). A passage such as Exodus 6[14], 'The sons of Reuben the firstborn of Israel: Hanoch, and Pallu, Hezron, and Carmi: these be the families of Reuben' (cf. 6[15, 19, 25], Num 3[15]), indicates that the tribal family was itself composed of families which correspond roughly to clans.[27] They are accorded very little prominence in the biblical record in comparison with the tribe.

Since the family was thought of as a psychic community, it is not surprising that occasionally instead of מִשְׁפָּחָה the Hebrews used the word חַי signifying those related as a community of life[28] (cf. 2 S 23[13], Num 32[41], Deut 3[14], Judg 10[4], 1 K 4[13], Ps

[24] W. R. Smith, op. cit. p. 272; cf. W. A. Irwin, *The Old Testament: Keystone of Human Culture* (New York, 1952), pp. 202f.
[25] Cf. H. W. Robinson, *The Religious Ideas of the Old Testament*, p. 88, and *The Christian Doctrine of Man* (Edinburgh, 1911), p. 28.
[26] Cf. J. Pedersen, op. cit. I-II.57; L. Köhler, op. cit. p. 114.   [27] Cf. BDB, p. 1046.
[28] J. Pedersen, op. cit. I-II,50. BDB take 2 S. 23[11], 'assembled into a troop', as dubious on the authority of Ewald, Driver, and others. Of 23[13], however, the rendering, '. . . and a community (וְחַיַּת) of Philistines (i.e. a group of allied families making a raid together) was encamping', is doubtless correct (cf. 1 Ch. 11[15] וּמַחֲנֵה וְחַיַּת). Cf. BDB, op. cit. p. 312.

68[11]).[29] This word is important because it indicates that early Hebrew thought actually conceived of kinship in terms of vital ties. In 1 Samuel 18[18], the incorrectly pointed חַיַּי (to read 'my life')[30] probably should be referred to relatives: 'And David said unto Saul, Who am I? and who are my *kinsfolk*, my father's family in Israel, that I should be son in law to the king?' (so the *RSV*).

In the broader context of the clan, tribe, or even nation, such distinctions of relationship as אָח ('brother'), צָמִית ('kinsman'), and עֵר, רֵעֶה ('fellow', 'neighbour'), become indistinct. The lack of precision is especially evident in Leviticus 19[16-18], where they are used promiscuously and carry the same meaning.[31] Again, David argues for reinstatement to the throne by appealing to the elders of Judah as members of his own family: 'You are my kinsmen (actually אַחַי—'brothers'), you are my bone and my flesh . . .' (2 S 19[12], *RSV*). All the members of the tribe partake of a common brotherhood.[32] So Lot is referred to as Abraham's brother, although in truth he was a nephew (cf. Gen. 14[16] with 11[27, 31]). So also the record calls Laban and his retinue the brethren of Jacob, although in reality they were uncle and nephew (cf. Gen. 31[54]).

Beyond the application of the idea of kinship to the tribe, there are passages of the Old Testament which designate the nation of Israel as a family.[33] Therefore, Moses looks upon the burdens of his *brethren*, for any Hebrew is his brother (Ex 2[11], Heb 11[24-6]; cf. Lev 10[6], 2 S 19[42], Jer 34[14]). All Israelites are brothers and belong to a single household, even though one may be a slave to another (Deut 15[12]). Jeremiah says, 'The Lord has rejected the two families which he chose' (33[24], *RSV*), indicating the divisions of the kingdom following the reign of Rehoboam.[34] In

---

[29] In these passages the *AV* translation 'towns' or 'troops' and the *RSV* rendering, 'villages', 'cities', or 'bands', might well be changed to 'clans' or 'encampments' in the non-permanent Bedouin fashion. The חַיָּה and עִיר 'city' are contrasted (cf. Num 32[36, 42] with [41]).

[30] Cf. *AV* rendering of the Masoretic text.

[31] J. Pedersen, op. cit. I-II.57.　　[32] Ibid. p. 59.

[33] Cf. H. W. Robinson, 'Hebrew Psychology', *The People and the Book*, ed. A. S. Peake (Oxford, 1925), p. 377; J. Pedersen, op. cit. I-II.59.

[34] Jer 2[4], 'Hear the word of the Lord, O house of Jacob, and all the families of the house of Israel' (*RSV*), shows the ambiguity which characterizes the word. C. Lattey is quite correct in saying: 'The solidarity of the clan (מִשְׁפָּחָה) involved of course the solidarity of the larger units containing it, the tribe and the nation.' 'Vicarious Solidarity in the Old Testament', *Vetus Testamentum*, I (Leiden, 1951), 271; cf. G. E. Wright, *The Biblical Doctrine of Man in Society* (London, 1954), p. 49.

Amos 3² the Lord speaks: 'You only have I known of all the families of the earth; therefore I will punish you for all your iniquities.' Israel is but one of the nation-families that people the earth. The same terminology is used in the covenant of Abraham (Gen. 12³, '. . . all the families of the earth . . .') and in the denunciation of the nations by Jeremiah (10²⁵).

Although there is no reference which alludes to the human race as a single family, the old Testament might well have done so. For the idea upon which the conception of the nation as a family was based, was identical to that upon which the unity of the immediate family rested. That basis was the one ancestor who was to the tribe or nation what the בַּעַל was to the household unit. The foregoing discussion indicates a vertical extension of the life of the ancestor. The extension and expansion of the original family of the patriarch was promulgated through his progeny, generation upon generation *ad infinitum*. Man was what he was only as a link in that family.[35]

The Old Testament traces the origin of the human race to one man, Adam (cf. Gen 1²⁶⁻⁷, 2⁷; note also that all men are descended from Noah, Gen 7²³, 9¹). On this basis it is not too much to suppose that, since the whole of mankind had descended from Adam and Eve, all men were considered in the broadest sense as brothers and belonging to the same מִשְׁפָּחָה.[36] Because the solidarity of any group is developed on empirical rather than on theoretical grounds, it cannot be considered strange that this most expanded form of unity did not receive formal adoption. As W. R. Smith has so convincingly argued, the main cause for the strong *consciousness* of psychic unity in the broader community of the clan or tribe was the common danger of obliteration through war and raids.[37]

THE IMPLICATIONS OF CORPORATE EXTENSION IN PUNISHMENT AND BLESSING

(1) *Punishment Extended to Later Generations*

The most obvious consequence of the vertical extension of the personality of the group is the application of merit or demerit

[35] J. Pedersen, op. cit. I-II.259; cf. L. Köhler, op. cit. p. 114; W. Eichrodt, *Theologie des Alten Testaments*, II (Zurich, 1948), p. 91.
[36] Cf. S. A. Cook, op. cit. III.438, where he concludes: '. . . the fundamental principles are the same, and it was possible to extend the limits of the group to all mankind'.
[37] *Kinship and Marriage in Early Arabia* (Cambridge, 1885), p. 56.

to those who did not individually participate in its evoking cause. A succinct statement of this principle is found in Exodus 20[5-6]: '. . . for I the Lord thy God am a jealous God, visiting the iniquity of the fathers upon the children unto the third and fourth generation of them that hate me; and shewing mercy unto thousands of them that love me, and keep my commandments.' Later history gave Israel cause to make frequent reference to the principle involved, even to the extent of giving it a proverbial counterpart. 'The fathers have eaten sour grapes, and the children's teeth are set on edge' found common expression in Ezekiel's day (cf. Ezek 18[2]). As the wickedness of the father stained the history of his children's generations, Jews were forced to give the problem of corporate justice careful consideration. As in the case of the shamelessness of Canaan's father, Ham (Gen 9[20-29]), or the opposition of Amalek to Israel (Ex 17[8-16]), men and women had to suffer because of their descent (cf. 1 S 15[2-33]).[38]

The extension of punishment to the second generation is the most frequent example of the application of the principle of corporate justice in the Old Testament. It may be helpful to examine a few of the more prominent passages in the biblical record where punishment is shown to involve innocent individuals.

The Rebellion of Korah

In the sixteenth chapter of Numbers, an account is given of a rebellion against the autocratic rule of Moses. The ring-leaders of the sedition were Korah, Dathan, and Abiram, who were challenged to produce divine authority for their case by offering acceptable incense before the Lord. The punishment of the two hundred and fifty princes was destruction by a consuming fire 'from the Lord' (cf. 16[35]). But for the three who prompted the challenge to Moses' authority, a more fearful punishment was reserved. Korah, Dathan, Abiram, their families, and all that they had, were swallowed alive into the earth. In contrast with the families of the princes who apparently escaped any implication in the punishment of this group, the households of the leaders are so closely allied to them that they were required to share in their punishment. Here is a clear example of the strength of the bond of solidarity portrayed in the Old Testament. Even where there is no guilt (apparent) there can still be punishment and

[38] S. A. Cook, op. cit. III.438f.

suffering of the consequences of the offence because of a relationship to the offending party.[39]

It must be said in passing that the alarming character of the idea of corporate punishment involving the undeserving tends to draw attention out of proportion to its desert. Very nearly all the provisions of Old Testament law apply solely to individual responsibility.[40] One passage will bear out this point: 'And if a man cause a blemish in his neighbour; as he hath done, so it shall be done to him: breach for breach, eye for eye, tooth for tooth; . . . ye shall have one manner of law as well for the sojourner as well as for the home-born: for I am Jehovah your God (Lev 24[19-22], *RV*; cf. Deut 24[16]: '. . . every man shall be put to death for his own sin.'). Individual justice was applied in practice also. When a man desecrated the Sabbath by doing unlawful work, his punishment was administered individually (Num 15[32-6]). When Nadab and Abihu offered strange fire before the Lord, the principle of sole personal responsibility was applied (Lev 10[1-2]).[41] The application of individual justice greatly exceeds in number the cases involving corporate justice.

The case of Korah, Dathan, and Abiram suggests a possible solution to the intended purpose which underlies the infliction of corporate justice. The record states that the two hundred and fifty princes were punished individually while the leaders were punished corporately. We have discussed above the psychic, almost indivisible, unity of the Hebrew household presupposed in various conceptions which were held. It follows that the destruction of the family would be considered as a more severe sentence than an individual death penalty. The contention is made by A. R. Johnson that the personality (נֶפֶשׁ) of a man extended to the whole of his house[42] just as it did to the members of his own body[43] but with a diminishing intensity corresponding to the decreased awareness of unity. It may be put in this

---

[39] G. B. Gray, *The Divine Discipline of Israel* (London, 1900), p. 78. This practice was indulged in in the interest of precise retaliation, not the transference of guilt. Cf. D. Daube, *Studies in Biblical Law* (Cambridge, 1947), p. 169; A. B. Davidson, *The Theology of the Old Testament* (Edinburgh, 1904), p. 219.

[40] W. Eichrodt, *Man in the Old Testament* (London, 1951), pp. 9-11. Eichrodt mentions the Book of the Covenant (Ex 20[23]) as exemplifying this awareness of the individual.

[41] Cf. G. E. Wright, op. cit. p. 24.

[42] *The One and the Many*, p. 8. Cf. G. A. F. Knight, op. cit. pp. 33f; Lévy-Bruhl, op. cit. p. 121.

[43] Note A. R. Johnson, *The Vitality of the Individual*, p. 39.

manner: the Hebrew conception of *himself* individually as a *unity* involved a stronger awareness of solidarity than of his household as a personal extension of his נֶפֶשׁ. By the same token, the personality of the ancestor was still more sparsely diffused through his succeeding clan or tribe.

More modern ideas see no difficulty in accepting the principles of retribution propounded in the *lex talionis* (Lev 24[17-21]) because they assume that no punishment can be greater than the requirement of the payment of an individual life as a just recompense for any deed or series of deeds. To the Israelite, however, with his strong consciousness of the unity of the household, the requisition of an individual life is but one punishment in an ascending scale in degrees of severity, from the payment of a tooth for a tooth to the destruction of the whole family for the more serious offence. Thus the problem of corporate justice turns on the conception of the unity of the group coupled with an interest in precise retaliation for an offence. Depending on the deed, a just recompense can then be extended far beyond the limits of the single individual to the family, a whole generation, or even to the whole world.[44]

The sin and punishment of Achan

The case of Achan, narrated in the seventh chapter of Joshua, is the classical example of the inclusion of the children in the punishment of the father. Achan's disobedience was the direct contradiction of the command of the Lord that nothing of the city of Jericho should be appropriated personally. The city and that which it contained was either חֵרֶם ('a devoted site') or קֹדֶשׁ ('a holy thing'). Achan's action was a violation of both of these distinctions (cf. Josh 6[18-19] with 7[21]). The direct consequences of the deed were the defeat of the Israelite contingent at Ai (7[5]), the stoning of Achan, his family, and all of his property, which was thereupon burned. Again, the severity of the consequences of this action are bound inseparably with the principle of solidarity.[45] The sacred character of the commandment violated is throughout the passage viewed in the most serious terms. This provides further evidence for the contention already made that

---

[44] Cf. M. Kadushin, *Organic Thinking* (New York, 1938), pp. 10f.
[45] A. R. Johnson, *The One and the Many*, p. 6; cf. also W. Eichrodt, *Theologie des Alten Testaments*, III.110, and A. B. Davidson, op. cit. p. 220.

the death of Achan alone would not have answered for the crime
which he had committed and that consequently, the rest of *him*,
i.e. his family and property, were also destroyed. There is here
no question of the guilt of the rest of the family, although nothing
can be said one way or another. Their inclusion in the punishment of the father partakes of the same character as do the
implicated members of the body in the death of the individual.
They are appurtenances belonging to him in so intimate a way
that they must be included.

Further examples of corporate implication in the judgement
of an ancestor's sin, especially of individuals removed more than
one generation, are very rare in the Old Testament. The fate
pronounced by Elisha on Gehazi to extend 'unto thy seed for
ever' (2 K 5[27]), is disputed by many as Hebrew hyperbole. In
any case the flexibility of the word עוֹלָם indicates only an in-
definite period extending into the future. It could in some cases
mean no longer than the life span (cf. Deut 15[17], Ex 21[16], 1 S
27[12]).[46]

National implication in the sin of an ancestor

On a tribal or national scale, the situation is different. Particularly significant are those instances where the tribal or national
ancestor is involved. Thus, in Genesis we read that Simeon and
Levi (the tribes) are to be scattered in Israel for the cruelty of
the patriarchs from whom they are derived (Gen 49[5-7]). The
tribe of Reuben could never attain to stability because of the sin
which Reuben had committed (Gen 49[3-4]). The exclusiveness of
the blessing given to Jacob means that Edomites (the descendants
of Esau) will be the servants of Israel (cf. Gen 27[37] with Mal
1[3-4] and Ezek 35[5-6]). The ethnic Amalek is to be 'utterly destroyed' because 'he laid wait for him (Israel) in the way, when
he came up from Egypt' (1 S 15[2-3]). Israelites of Ezekiel's day
were sure that they bore the sins of their fathers (Chapter 16).[47]
Jeremiah acknowledged the iniquity of Israel and 'of our fathers'
(Jer 14[20]). Canaan bears the unending curse of Noah because
the original ancestor, Ham, had done evil on the occasion of
Noah's drunkenness (Gen 9[18-29]).

These cases in the Old Testament where the sins of the fathers

---

[46] BDB, pp. 761ff.　　　　　　[47] J. Pedersen, op. cit. I-II.436.

are visited on succeeding generations do not always involve the same issues as the suffering of the innocent children of the immediate family. This difference is evidenced in the history of Levi. Because the tribe took its stand on 'the Lord's side' to help Moses eradicate idolatrous worship from Israel (Ex 32$^{26-9}$), the sentence which had been pronounced against the tribe because of the tribal ancestor's sin (cf. Gen 49$^{5-7}$), was altered from evil to good. The scattering became the means by which the knowledge of the Lord was to be maintained in the nation (cf. Josh 21$^{1-42}$) as well as bearing the burden of the details of the worship system. Here, as in the individual case of Ahab (1 K 21$^{17-29}$), the inclusion in or exclusion from the guilt of the father is dependent on the persistence in or rejection of his ways. This emphasis is very clear in Ezekiel and Jeremiah where although the punishment of the nation has reference to the iniquity of the previous generations (see above), the particular reason for this punishment in *their* day is in consequence to their own wickedness. Amalek might continue for many generations, but the debt is finally paid, presumably at a time when its sinfulness was most odious. Jesus spoke of the blood of previous generations being required of Jews in His day because of the heinousness of their sin and because it was against so great light (cf. Matt 11$^{20-4}$).

The latter passages besides implying the unity of the group, also emphasize the indivisibility of sin. Due to its contagious character, iniquity involves the interrelated members of a community. It is not barred by the line which separates generations. The sons often bear the punishment of their fathers because they follow in their footsteps. They bear the character-type which pervades the life of the family. The Old Testament developed the idea through the observation of empirical phenomena awaiting the full theological development in the New Testament.

(2) *Blessing Extended to Later Generations*

The principle of corporate extension relates to more than corporate punishment. Corporate blessing or merit is the positive side of the issue, involving an even more comprehensive coverage than punishment and demerit.[48] While Exodus 20^5 teaches that the vengeance of God on sin will extend to the fourth generation, His mercy includes thousands of generations in the reward of

[48] Cf. L. Köhler, op. cit. p. 149.

faithful observance of His commandments (Ex 20⁶). Some of the Old Testament examples of corporate blessing will bear out the truth of this declaration.

Although there is no evidence regarding the character of the family of Noah, the emphasis on his singular righteousness and its consequent reward suggests that it was because of their solidarity with him that they were saved (Gen 6⁷). In the record of the preservation of the family of Lot, the unity of the family offers the explanation for the exemption of the group from the destruction of Sodom (Gen 19¹⁻²⁸).⁴⁹ Subsequent behaviour of Lot's wife (Gen 19²⁶), as well as that of his daughters (Gen 19³¹⁻⁸), suggests that their salvation was not dependent upon their own righteousness. It was Solomon's good fortune that he had King David for a father as we find in 1 Kings 11¹¹⁻¹²: 'Forasmuch as this is done of thee, and thou hast not kept my covenant and my statutes, which I have commanded thee, I will surely rend the kingdom from thee. . . . Notwithstanding in thy days I will not do it for David thy father's sake. . . .'

A further concession in the retention of the one tribe (Judah) as a kingdom is made to Rehoboam in regard for the merit of David (1 K 11¹³).⁵⁰ In the same manner, Abijam came under the canopy of David's corporate blessing although he was himself a wicked king: 'Nevertheless for David's sake did the Lord his God give him a lamp in Jerusalem, to set up his son after him, and to establish Jerusalem . . .' (1 K 15⁴). Jerusalem as a city was preserved from the attack of Sennacherib and the mighty Assyrian army for the sake of David, the servant of God (2 K 19³⁴).⁵¹

Still greater periods of time are involved in the corporate blessing of Abraham. In the covenant which God made with this patriarch a strong emphasis is placed on the conception of transferred merit.⁵² Because of his obedience and faith, not only were

⁴⁹ Although the intercession of Abraham for the cities of the plain does not properly belong under the title of this section, the basis of Abraham's plea is relevant to this discussion. His presupposition is that the towns are indivisible units. He invites corporate justice in blessing rather than the expected corporate punishment which would have rightly destroyed the *few* righteous with the *many* wicked.

⁵⁰ S. A. Cook, op. cit. III.439.

⁵¹ Cf. L. Köhler, op. cit. p. 242 note 125.

⁵² By 'transference' the idea of inclusion and relationship is to be understood rather than the more modern conception of imputation. The idea of a measurable quantity of merit, popularized in Roman Catholic theology, is completely foreign to ancient Hebrew thinking.

his progeny to enjoy greatness in numbers and strength, so that they might possess the land of Palestine, but all the families of the earth would also share in his blessing (Gen 12^{1-9}, 15^{5-21}, 17^{1-22}).

The possibility of transferred blessing was frequently made the basis of intercession. If Israel had sinned, God's remembering Abraham, Isaac, and Jacob, was an urgent cause why He should show leniency in judgement for their sakes (Ex 32^{13}).[53] The very election of the nation of Israel to be the people of God rested on the original call of righteous Abraham (cf. Gen 12^2). On such an occasion as the election might be endangered through Israel's idolatry or sin, forgiveness was sought on the basis of the original promise to Abraham. Thus, in the Hebrew conception, the divine dealings with the nation are mediated through its ancestor, for good or for evil.[54] There were modifying factors to be sure, as Israel had to learn, but the grace of God shown to the patriarch invariably affected His dealings with his descendants.

Times of national stress and difficulty tended to convince later generations that the principle of transferred blessing was no longer of any great consequence. This inference may be drawn from such passages as Ezekiel 14^{14-20}, where there is no evidence that the people thought the righteousness of a Noah, Daniel, or Job would actually alleviate or commute their deserved punishment. Rather, says the prophet, even if 'these men were in it, as I live, saith the Lord God, they shall deliver neither sons nor daughters; they only shall be delivered . . .' (14^{16}). No longer is mention made of the gracious remembrance of the fathers of the nation. Later Jewish writers made a great deal of the benefit of the merit of the ancestors (see Chapter 2, pp. 59-66 *infra*), but the conception had its roots in the idea of the corporate unity of the nation with its ancestor(s), a conception evinced in the Old Testament.[55]

(3) *The Implications of Corporate Extension in the Covenant*

The buttress and intermediary of the Old Testament conception of the corporate unity of the nation was the covenant. A covenant between men or tribes bolstered a corporate unity as W. R. Smith has said: 'A covenant means artificial brotherhood, and has no

---

[53] S. A. Cook, op. cit. III.539.
[54] Cf. H. W. Robinson, *Inspiration and Revelation in the Old Testament* (Oxford, 1946), p. 151.
[55] C. G. Montefiore and H. Loewe, *A Rabbinic Anthology* (London, 1938), p. *c*.

c

place where the natural brotherhood of which it is an imitation already subsists.'[56] This statement must be modified in the light of our previous discussion. In the case of Israel, the covenant served as an external frame within which the generic unity of the nation subsisted. This understanding made it possible for Israel to maintain both an inclusivism, through the admission of foreigners which were incorporated into the covenant, and an exclusivism, which the laws of the covenant rigorously maintained.

The basic meaning of בְּרִית is 'pact', or 'compact'. It is used to refer to contracts between men as well as between God and men.[57] It is the latter usage which primarily concerns us in this section. Its derivation from בָּרָה ('to cut'), is maintained by Cremer,[58] but is unrecognized by Brown, Driver, and Briggs.[59] These lexicographers and Quell in the *Theologisches Wörterbuch* prefer to relate בְּרִית to the Assyrian *baru*, *beritu* ('bind', 'bond').[60] The emphasis of the Old Testament idea of the covenant is one of relationship. The accompanying promises are the visible signs. Thus it became used primarily of the covenant between God and Israel as Cremer notes:

In a word, we must affirm that בְּרִית, as a *term. techn.*, signifies primarily the covenant relation in which God has entered, or will enter, with Israel, then the relation into which Israel enters with God (cf. Jer 22[9] with Ex 23[32], Jer 34[18]); and, correspondingly, next, the two-fold and mutual relationship; thus, finally, the stipulations or promises which are given as signs, which set forth and embody the covenant, in which the covenant is expressed.[61]

It is the covenant which is presumed by the history and religion of Israel—a covenant which has bound the nation into a unity and has given continuity to its life. This it could do because it was made with the nation as a unity, not with individuals.[62]

---

[56] *Religion of the Semites*, p. 318; cf. J. Pedersen, op. cit. I-II.285.

[57] BDB, p. 136; J. O. Cobham, 'Covenant', *TWBB*, p. 55.

[58] *Lexicon of New Testament Greek*, tr. by W. Urwick (3rd Eng. edn, Edinburgh, 1880), p. 549; cf. the division of sacrificial victims in the covenant institution in Genesis 15[9-18].

[59] BDB, p. 136.

[60] *TWNT*, II.107f.

[61] H. Cremer, op. cit. p. 551.

[62] A. B. Davidson, op. cit. p. 241. This point is equally applicable to the Davidic Covenant (2 S 7[13,16], 23[5]), the Levitic Covenant (cf. Num 18[6]) and the Abrahamic (Gen 17[19]), the three factors of Israel's religious history. Cf. idem, 'Covenant', *HDB*, I (Edinburgh, 1898), p. 511.

Nor was it necessary to restate the terms of the covenant to succeeding generations because of the national solidarity uniting Abraham and the Israelites of the Exodus. A. Büchler has pointed out this feature in the three normative passages relating to the covenant (i.e. Gen 17^{14}, Deut 31$^{16-20}$, and Jer 11^{10}, 31^{33}):

All the three passages take it for granted that the covenant made by God with Israel at Sinai continued to be binding throughout the centuries, though not renewed; and the same is stated explicitly in Genesis 17$^{9, 12}$, when God imposed circumcision upon Abraham and his descendants throughout their generations expressly as an everlasting covenant (17^{13}), and so also the Sabbath in Exodus 31^{16}, 'to observe the Sabbath throughout their generations, for a perpetual covenant'.[63]

L. Köhler speaks correctly of the People of Israel in the conception of the covenant, as 'above time, timeless'.[64]

Through the covenant the eternity and immutability of God were aligned directly with the nation of Israel. Because He is a party to the contract, the continuity of the nation is guaranteed.[65] Thus, when the prophets speak of the righteousness of Jehovah and consider that it implies that He will save His people, they speak within the frame-reference of the covenant. But since they have broken their side of the contract, appeal is really made to the nature of God. 'Remember the covenant' is 'Remember the past, the old relationship—that with Abraham.'[66] Although it was through Abraham that the original covenant was made (cf. Gen 15$^{12-21}$), its specific provisions have actual application to his seed to which God had 'given this land' (15^{18}). Therefore, it was through the covenant that the immutable God was united to Abraham, and through him to the nation, and through them to the land (cf. Ex 6$^{4, 7-8}$). Thus, there is a strict injunction found in Leviticus against giving up the land: 'The land shall not be for cutting off (lit. Heb.), for the land is mine; for ye are strangers and sojourners with me' (25^{23}; cf. Num 36$^{7-8}$, where a similar law restricts the transference of the land allotted to each tribe).

There are other implications besides the continuity of the nation

[63] *Studies in Sin and Atonement in the Rabbinic Literature of the First Century* (London, 1928), p. 10.
[64] Op. cit. p. 48.
[65] Ibid. pp. 43ff.
[66] A. B. Davidson, op. cit. p. 241.

involved in the covenant. H. W. Robinson has pointed out the fundamental significance of the covenant for the unity of the People of God. 'It is characteristic of the genius and eventual contribution of Israel that its national unity was from the outset based on religion.'[67] This unity was derived from the recognition that Israel was the chosen people, linked to Him by no quasi-physical tie such as that of a nature-god, but a moral act. This חֶסֶד ('mercy, lovingkindness'), shown in God's initiation of the covenant relationship,[68] was the basis of benevolent figures designed to describe it. Thus the covenantal relationship is analogous to adoption and Israel may be called the son of God (Hos. 11[1]). Israel's apostasy was a direct violation of the terms of the covenant; hence, the nation is described as an adulterous wife (cf. Ezek 23).[69] In Deuteronomy 32[6, 18], God is the Father who at once bought, formed (i.e. created) and begat Israel.[70] The preferred position of Israel is compared to the 'firstborn' (Ex 4[22]). Through the promises of the covenant which is Israel's birth-right, she will enjoy the benefits embodied in the promises (Deut 28[1-14]).

Although from one point of view, the emphasis on the covenant made Israel exclusive, the contract itself provided for the inclusion of the גֵּר ('resident alien') within its folds.[71] The distinctive sign or token of the covenant was circumcision (Gen 17[13]; cf. Rom 4[11]). Because it was closely akin to an initiatory ceremony, '. . . it naturally came to be interpreted in a wider sense as an act of admission to a group'.[72] Therefore the law read: 'When a גֵּר shall יָגוּר ('reside') with thee, and will keep the passover to the Lord, let all his males be circumcised, and then let him come near and keep it; and he shall be as one that is born in the land: for no uncircumcised person shall eat thereof'

[67] 'The Group and the Individual in Israel', *The Individual in East and West*, ed. E. R. Hughes (London, 1937), p. 159; cf. A. C. Welch, *Post-exilic Judaism* (Edinburgh and London, 1935), pp. 1, 9, 10.
[68] Cf. Amos 7[20], Deut 7[9, 12], 1 K 8[23]; BDB, p. 339.
[69] Cf. J. Bright, *The Kingdom of God* (New York, 1953), p. 74.
[70] See G. A. Barton, 'The Kinship of Gods and Men Among the Early Semites', *JBL*, XV (1896), pp. 168ff, for parallels in Semitic ideas. Note Jer 2[27-8], where mention is made that idolatrous people claim descent (i.e. filial relationship) to trees and stones; ibid. p. 171.
[71] Cf. W. A. Irwin, op. cit. pp. 194-5; A. Lods, 'Les Antécédents de la Notion d'Église en Israël', *Origine et Nature de l'Église en Israël* (Paris, 1939), pp. 24ff. L. Köhler notes that 'no man of the Old Testament is without a people (*volkslos*)'; op. cit. p. 115.
[72] A. Lods, Israel, p. 198.

(Ex 12⁴⁸). The passover was Israel's distinctive national celebration. For an alien to partake of that feast meant that he realistically included himself in the redemption from Egypt, the foundation of Israel's national existence.

So prominent is the feature of union rather than descent in the original constitution of the nation that K. Mohlenbrink is unwilling that we should use the term 'people' for the group created or led by Moses, nor for that matter a 'state' or a 'race'. According to this author, Israel never formed a genuine people, but an exclusively religious alliance, an amphictyony.[73] In the sense of עַם, the group under Moses was a people, as A. Lods points out: 'The עַם to begin with is a group of men who are descended, or believe themselves descended, from a common ancestor.'[74] While this description would fit the majority of the Israelites in the wilderness wandering, the fact that it was a 'mixed multitude' which came up out of Egypt requires a somewhat broader meaning for עַם. Brown, Driver, and Briggs concur by stating that the probable original meaning of עַם is 'those united, connected, or related'.[75]

As a matter of historical fact, the corporate unity of the nation was not seriously impaired by the inability to prove natural descent from the national ancestor(s). The covenant provided the uniting bond which welded the alien and pedigreed Israelite into one.[76] Thus S. A. Cook is right in suggesting that although blood-relationship might seem to be the more basic and powerful in producing corporate unity, 'The psychical factors are clearly not less powerful than the physiological, and it is convenient to regard all group-units psychologically as systems, the social group of kinsfolk being the most elemental'.[77] This contention is well illustrated in Leviticus 25³⁵⁻⁵⁵, where the גֵּר and the תּוֹשָׁב

---

[73] Noted by A. Lods, 'Origins of the Religion of Israel', *Record and Revelation*, ed. H. W. Robinson (Oxford, 1938), p. 204, from *Die Enstehung des Judentums* (Hamburg, 1936), pp. 17f.

[74] *Israel*, p. 204. So also S. A. Cook: 'Yahweh's dealings with and promises to the patriarchs ensure the welfare of those who regard themselves as their descendants . . .', *The Old Testament: a Reinterpretation* (Cambridge, 1936), p. 118.

[75] Op. cit. p. 766. Cf. G. E. Wright, op. cit. p. 78. This meaning is especially important to the recognition of Israel's self-consciousness as the people of Yahweh. See M. Noth, *Geschichte Israels* (Göttingen, 1950), pp. 1-7.

[76] W. Eichrodt, *Theologie des Alten Testaments*, I.8.

[77] S. A. Cook, 'Notes' appended to W. R. Smith, *The Religion of the Semites*, p. 506. Cf. A. Lods, 'Les Antécédents', p. 12.

('sojourner') are termed, 'thy brother'. Presumably the distinctions between the נָכְרִי ('foreigner') and the 'brother' in Deuteronomy 15³ and elsewhere involve a distinction in the intention of the alien, for he may be treated differently from the homeborn, in the matter of debt payment after the Sabbath year.

Fundamental to the union of the alien and son of Abraham, was the covenant which related a man to his neighbour and God to the whole. Pedersen has emphasized this point well:

This denotes the psychic communion and the common purpose which united the people and its God. It is also expressed by saying that the peace of Yahweh reigns in Israel (Jer 16⁵); therefore, the relation between them is characterized by love, the feeling of fellowship among kinsmen.[78]

Many of the laws of the Pentateuch were designed to maintain this feeling of brotherhood throughout the varied elements of the Israelite community. Thus Jesus significantly put the Shema (Deut 6⁴⁻⁵) and the Golden Rule of the Old Testament (Lev 19¹⁸) together, and commended the scribe for discovering the sum of the Torah in them (Mark 12³⁰⁻⁴).

Through the initiatory ceremony of circumcision,[79] the partaking of Pesach,[80] the observation of the law, and the renunciation of pagan worship, the גֵּר became a 'child of the covenant'.[81] He was not a convert in the sense that proselytes were in later Judaism. It was not so much a change of religion as a complete change of nationality. In a real sense the 'resident alien'

[78] J. Pedersen, *Israel: Its Life and Culture*, III-IV, trans. A. I. Fausbøll (London, 1940), p. 612. Cf. L. Köhler, op. cit. p. 172; G. E. Wright, op. cit. pp. 48, 82.

[79] See E. O. James, 'Initiatory Rituals', in *Myth and Ritual*, ed. S. H. Hooke (Oxford, 1933), pp. 147ff. He claims that in such societies where a corporate attitude of mind prevails, an initiation into tribal society is required, as distinct from that of the family in which he is born; ibid. p. 150. Cf. A. Lods, *Israel*, p. 198.

[80] In the Pesach celebration, there may be involved a conception of the unity which pervades the group through a common meal. A covenant meal produced a bond of a more or less psychic nature which one did not dare violate. Note that Jacob invited his erstwhile enemy Laban to 'eat bread' as a final assurance that their covenant would remain unbroken (Gen 31⁵⁴). Cf. L. Köhler, op. cit. p. 172. Further examples to support this point, would include the treaty which Melchizedek contracted with Abraham by proffering bread and wine (Gen 14¹⁸⁻²⁴). The covenant contracted for Israel with the Gibeonites by the princes was solemnized through partaking of Gibeonite food (Josh 9¹⁴). Obadiah uses 'men of thy confederacy' and 'men of thy bread' as parallel expressions; T. H. Gaster, *Passover; its History and Traditions* (New York, 1949), p. 18. A fuller discussion may be consulted in W. T. McCree, 'The Covenant Meal in the Old Testament', *JBL*, XLV (1926), pp. 120ff.

[81] C. Ryder Smith, op. cit. p. 260.

performed Jewish ritual because of imposition,[82] in that he had joined a theocratic society in which no deviation was tolerated. It was in this realm that Israel's mission to the nations lay. God was the creator and ruler of the whole earth. The ideal was the incorporation of the whole world into the domain of the covenant which defined the boundary of the Kingdom of God. The failure of Israel to capitalize on its mission to the nations[83] proved to the prophets of the classical period that the old covenant was temporary. The message of Isaiah and Micah pointed to a future establishment of an everlasting covenant which would reunite David, the king, and the people under God (Isa 55[3-5]). Because of the wickedness of Israel's kings, the breaking of the old covenant, the the consequent punishment of the nation, the future must bring the radical reintroduction of the ideal embodied in the covenant of David. This involved the mission of the Servant of the Lord which would extend in influence to the whole world. '. . . Nations that knew not thee shall run unto thee because of the Lord thy God' (Isa 55[5]; cf. Micah 4[2f]). In Isaiah 42[6-7] the Servant is designated as לִבְרִית עָם. The scope of this new covenant extends beyond the national boundaries of Israel—a pledge of mercy on God's part to all mankind.[84] We may not necessarily agree with C. R. North that the phrase refers originally to Israel and subsequently to the individual Servant, but the extent of the covenant is clear.[85] It is of the utmost significance that the Old Testament should refer to a person (corporate?) as a covenant. The importance is seen in the New Testament doctrine of the New Covenant mediated by Christ.

This brief discussion is completely inadequate to show how fundamental the covenant is in the Old Testament. W. Eichrodt has made it the interpretative basis of the Hebrew Scriptures in his *Theologie des Alten Testaments*.[86] Unity of race and continuity of history were Israel's through the covenant. The benevolent relationship between God and the nation was everlasting,

---

[82] Cf. M. Kadushin, *The Rabbinic Mind* (New York, 1952), p. 99.

[83] Cf. G. A. F. Knight, op. cit. p. 184.

[84] Cf. C. C. Torrey, *The Second Isaiah* (Edinburgh, 1928), pp. 113, 327f. On the universalism of the prophet, see pp. 111ff.

[85] See C. R. North's careful discussion of the difficulties encountered in this passage: *The Suffering Servant in Deutero-Isaiah* (London, 1948), pp. 131ff.

[86] Cf. H. W. Robinson, 'The Hebrew Conception of Corporate Personality', p. 55.

equivalent to sonship (Isa 63[16], 64[8]),[87] or marriage.[88] Beyond unity
and continuity the solidarity of the nation was strongly intimated.
No individual was a recipient of the benefits of the covenant
except as a member of the nation.[89] Indeed, the Old Testament
conception of the covenant is inseparably linked to the conception of corporate personality.[90] Says A. Lods to this effect:

But the principle [of corporate personality] applies widely in other
less recognizable realms, as well as in the standing example of the
covenant between Yahweh and Israel as a people. It makes a unit
of Israelites, past, present, and future (cf. Ex 20[5-6]), and gives to the
individual Israelite a group consciousness which has no real parallel
in modern conceptions.[91]

Strictly speaking, the covenant is not merely an implication of
the continuous extension of the personality of the group. It is to
a great extent the basis for this extension. It forms an immutable moral tie between the unchanging God and Israel. All the
members of a covenantal community are subordinate to the whole.
To sever oneself from the group is to be cut off from the covenant
and thereby from the covenant-making God.

THE ASPECT OF REALISM

Caution must be observed, warns H. W. Robinson, that the evidence
of solidarity in the Old Testament be not considered figuratively.
It is a true realism—belonging to the realm of anthropology and
archaeology rather than to philology.[92] It is extremely difficult
to determine with assurance what is figurative speech and what
is Semitic realism; hence, the evidence must be weighed carefully.
The first essential is the adoption of an ancient Semitic mental
frame of reference; from this vantage point the possibility of a

---

[87] Cf. A. B. Davidson, 'Covenant', *HDB*, I.511; cf. Lev 24[8] with Jer 33[20f].

[88] C. Chavasse, *The Bride of Christ* (London, 1940), p. 23. In Hosea's prophecy the
idea gains full development. It serves the purpose of revelation well, for the nexus
of the people with God was national and corporate (ibid. p. 29) and at the same time
showed the continuity of the relationship of the 'Choosing God' to the 'Chosen People'
irrespective of the passage of successive generations. The immutability of the covenant
despite the repeated and prolonged unfaithfulness of Israel, the Wife, is the theme of
Isaiah's declaration (61[10], 62[4-5]); (ibid. pp. 133ff). The 'divorce' so movingly
declared by Hosea was but a temporary estrangement (Isa 50[1]). Cf. J. Bright, op. cit.
p. 141.

[89] H. W. Robinson, 'The Group and the Individual in Israel', p. 160.

[90] H. W. Robinson, 'The Hebrew Conception', p. 55.

[91] 'Origins of the Religion of Israel', p. 332.

[92] 'The Hebrew Conception', p. 51.

correct evaluation of many statements in the old Testament will be greatly increased.

First of all it must be recognized that the Israelite thinks in universals rather than atomistically. He seizes the essence, then subordinates the details to it. Pedersen says in a point of clarification:

If, for instance, he calls up the image of a Moabite, then it is not an individual person with a number of individual qualities, which also include the fact of his coming from Moab. The features which make the specially Moabitic character, create a *type* which is the sum and substance of Moabitic features. . . . The individual Moabite, *mo'abhi*, is a manifestation of it.[93]

Thus, it was possible for the whole to be embodied in one or a group of its parts. An oscillation between the group seen as an individual or a plurality is therefore not an isolated phenomenon in ancient semitic writings.

Unification is instinctive to the Hebrew mind.[94] Examples are to be found in all areas of life. The Hebrew language is an excellent area for illustrative purposes. It is full of 'general or totality denomination or denominations of species', which reveal themselves in the individual or individuals in view.[95] Thus, for example עֵץ, which carries the idea of 'tree', may stand equally well for a single tree or a forest (cf. Gen 3³ with Ps 74⁵).[96] אָדָם may signify either a man (Gen. 2⁵⁻²⁵) or mankind (2 S 7¹⁹, Jer 21⁶, 31²⁷, 50³).[97] רֶכֶב stands for chariotry (2 K 13⁷, Ex 14⁷) or for a single chariot (1 K 22³⁵· ³⁸).[98] Another illustration of the same principle is the use of the derivative ending to designate the individual (e.g. מוֹאָבִי, מוֹאָב) 'which implies that the individual is that

---

[93] Op. cit. I-II.109.
[94] H. W. Robinson, 'The Hebrew Conception', p. 51. It is comparable with what R. M. MacIver says of the primitive mind: 'To the primitive man the group is all. He finds himself in a group, but he never finds *himself*. He is not a personality, but one of the bearers of a type personality. He is summed up in the group, the clan or the tribe.'—*Community* (London, 1917), p. 332. Cf. L. Köhler, op. cit. p. 149.
[95] J. Pedersen, op. cit. I-II.110.
[96] Cf. BDB, p. 781, for more examples.
[97] Ibid. p. 9. Cf. C. Lattey, 'Vicarious Solidarity', p. 269; L. Köhler, op. cit. p. 113. The ambiguity is strikingly attested in Deut 4³², where it is impossible to determine whether it is a singular or generic mankind 'that God created on the earth' (cf. Job 31³³). To the Hebrew mind, the problem was non-existent, since they are equivalent or interpenetrative ideas.
[98] BDB, p. 939. Many more illustrations of the point in question might be presented, but those cited will suffice to maintain the contention.

which is derived'.[99] On this basis, no Platonic abstraction was necessary for the Hebrew to see a potential unity existing between the whole and any of its parts.[100] The part was a manifestation of the original totality, the essence of which was diffused through the part.

(1) *The Conception of the Totality of Life*

The realistic conception of universal totalities is of interest to us because it is evident in the Hebrew conception of society. In this category belongs the idea of a totality of life (צְרוֹר הַחַיִּים). When one's life is to be preserved it is rolled up 'in the bundle of life' (1 S 25[39]; cf. Gen 44[30]). For this reason Zedekiah admitted that taking away the life of Jeremiah was to rob him 'of something which he shares with his fellows as a gift from Yahweh "who hath made for us this life" (נֶפֶשׁ, Jer 38[16])'.[101] A common life or נֶפֶשׁ ('soul') in a group is frequently alluded to in the Old Testament. Thus for example, '. . . the soul of thy wives' (2 S 19[6], Heb.), or the '. . . the soul of thy enemies' (1 K 3[11], Heb.), properly expresses the conception of the unity which pervades the psychic group (cf. Isa 3[9], 42[2], Heb.; Jer 31[14], 17[21], Heb.; 2 Ch 1[11], Heb.).

The term הַחַי ('the life') is used as a parallel expression to 'all men' and is a precise synonym in Ecclesiastes 7[2]. The idea of a community of life may explain the origin of the term חַיָּה ('animal, living thing')[102] to distinguish the animate from the inanimate. This totality is vitalized through the breath of God (cf. Gen 2[7]), which the flesh, composed of עָפָר ('dust'), needs for its animation (cf. Ezek 37[8-14]).[103]

Co-terminal with the universal unit of life is the totality of בָּשָׂר ('flesh'). It is also a totality of which any single species such as that of men, birds, or animals is but a manifestation. Therefore Noah takes into the ark two by two from amongst all the creatures, 'of all flesh' (Gen 7[15-16]; cf. 9[15-17], Lev 17[14], Num 18[15]). The horses of Egypt are composed of flesh (Isa 31[3]) as are the

---

[99] J. Pedersen, op. cit. I-II.110. Cf. C. Lattey, op. cit. p. 269; G. E. Wright, op. cit. p. 50.
[100] A. R. Johnson, *The Vitality of the Individual*, p. 8.
[101] Ibid. p. 13. Cf. L. Köhler, op. cit. pp. 129f.
[102] BDB, p. 312.
[103] Cf. E. C. Rust, op. cit. p. 97.

forces (men and cavalry) of Assyria which are described as one of its arms (2 Ch 32⁸).¹⁰⁴ 'Flesh' is frequently used as a totality to denote mankind (cf. Gen 6¹³⁻¹⁴, Num 16³², Deut 5²³, Ps 65³, Isa 66¹⁶, ²³⁻⁴, etc.). J. A. T. Robinson has well said: 'The flesh-body was not what partitioned a man off from his neighbour; it was rather what bound him in the bundle of life with all men and nature.'¹⁰⁵ Therefore, God is the God of the 'spirits of all flesh' (Num 27¹⁶), with the emphasis on the individuation of the רוּחַ, not the totality of 'בָּשָׂר'.

(2) *The Conception of a Corporate Heart*

The Old Testament frequently attributes to the nation a single heart. It may be perfect with Jehovah God (1 K 8⁶¹) or be broken (Num 32⁷, Heb.; cf. further Deut 11¹⁶, Josh 14⁸, 1 S 6⁶, Heb.; Gen 18⁵, 42²⁸, Ex 35²⁹). The very frequent references to the heart of Israel (in the singular) are obviously metaphorical. The term 'heart' refers to the mind. It is therefore Israel's one mind that is signified by this expression.¹⁰⁶

(3) *The Conception of Realistic Representation*

(a) *The Realistic Representation of the National Ruler.* As the individual manifestation or member of the group bears the life of the group in himself, a prominent member may incorporate the essence of the group. The manner in which representation in the Old Testament is depicted throws light on that important 'individual who gathers to himself the force of the whole group'.¹⁰⁷ The most vivid example of realistic representation in the Old Testament is the conception of the king identified with his kingdom.¹⁰⁸ Thus, the prince of Tyre is addressed in the dirge of Ezekiel 28, but the city is included in his destruction (cf. 28⁷⁻¹⁹). It is the precise embodiment of Israel by David that provides the grounds for Joab's retort: 'Why will he (David) be a cause of trespass to Israel' (1 Ch 21³). Israel's responsibility for David's sin in numbering the people cannot be more than the fact that David is acting for them in a realistic way in lieu of the point

¹⁰⁴ Cf. W. Eichrodt, *Theologie des Alten Testaments*, II.74.
¹⁰⁵ *The Body* (London, 1952), p. 15.
¹⁰⁶ Cf. W. A. Irwin, 'The Hebrews', *The Intellectual Adventure of Ancient Man*, ed. H. Frankfort (Chicago, 1946), p. 277.
¹⁰⁷ H. W. Robinson, 'The Hebrew Conception', p. 55.
¹⁰⁸ Cf. N. A. Dahl, *Das Volk Gottes* (Oslo, 1941), pp. 20ff.

that no part of the nation had any actual part in the decision.[109] It is therefore not primarily a question of the personal guilt of those who perished in the pestilence, but the proximity of the relationship of the people to the king. His sinning implicates them in his own punishment. This same corporate unity is evidenced in the warning of God to Abimelech concerning the appropriation of Sarah as his wife: 'And if thou restore her not, know thou that thou shalt surely die, thou and *all that are thine*' (Gen 20[7]). In Abimelech's chiding of Abraham, there is an acknowledgement of the corporate character of the sin which he was about to commit, for it would not have been upon him alone, but also upon his whole kingdom (Gen 20[9]).

The manifestation of the life of Israel in David is depicted figuratively in the use of the term נֵר ('lamp')[110] (2 S 21[17]; cf. Ps 132[17-18]), which would be extinguished in the event of his death (cf. Job 18[6], Ex 18[18-19], where the 'fading' of Moses implies the fading of the people, i.e. Israel). A passage such as Lamentations 4[20], 'The breath of our nostrils, the anointed of the Lord, was taken in their pits . . .', further confirms the contention that the king was identified with the *vitality* of the nation.

There are other passages which describe the 'Anointed', but apply the title almost without distinction to the people. The representation of the king is realistic enough for 'anointed' and 'people' to be synonymous. Note, for example, Habakkuk 3[13]: 'Thou wentest forth for the salvation of thy people, to save thy Christ (i.e. anointed).' Psalm 18[50] speaks of the great deliverance which the Lord effects for His King, showing mercy to His Christ, to David and to his seed continually. But it is not the head distinguished from Israel, his people, as Psalm 28[8] declares: 'The Lord is *their* strength and he is the strength of salvation of his anointed . . .' (cf. Ps 2[2], 20[7], and especially Ps 105[15]).[111]

The solidarity of the king and the nation is particularly obvious in the interaction of religious conditions. The explanation behind the epithet attached to Jeroboam, 'who made Israel to sin' (cf. 1 K 22[52], 15[30], 16[2]), lies in the indivisible unity which must characterize the royal leader and his subjects. The same psychic

---

[109] D. Daube, op. cit. pp. 162-3.

[110] Cf. W. O. E. Oesterley, 'Early Hebrew Festival Rituals', *Myth and Ritual*, pp. 143f.

[111] C. A. A. Scott, *Christianity According to St Paul* (Cambridge, 1939), p 156.

unity explains the possibility of the purification of the nation under Asa, Jehoshaphat, Hezekiah, and Josiah. They were good kings, and the nation under their leadership followed their example in docility. The evil of the king may well have been the result of a national trend, rather than merely an expression of his own individuality. All the same, the representative character of the king inevitably implies for evil or for good, that the nation will partake of that character.

(b) *The Realistic Representation of the Priest.* In the carrying out of the national liturgical worship, the priest was a more important figure than the king. The rationale behind the importance of sacerdotal mediation was the conception of the unity of the nation. It was considered quite impossible for the individual '. . . to become shut up in himself and to achieve a private and isolated relation between God and the soul'.[112] Proximity to God was gained through recognizing the realistic representation of the priest as he incorporated the group in himself and presented himself as a corporate personality to God. The conceptions of sacrifice and the priestly role, bear this point out. He was required to stand as a vicarious substitute for the individual or the community in its relationship to God.[113] In a corresponding manner, '. . . if it is the anointed priest who sins . . .' he will bring guilt upon the people (Lev 4³, *RSV*).

The ritual of the Day of Atonement will serve as an example of the realistic representation of the priest, as well as that of the offered sacrificial victim. The first requirement was that the priest should offer for himself and his family a bullock without blemish (Lev 16⁶, ¹¹). For the congregation he was to offer one goat as a sin-offering to cleanse the 'uncleanness' of the people and to purify the sanctuary (Lev 16¹⁵, ¹⁹). Following this, the officiating high priest was to take the goat offered by the congregation (16⁵) and 'to lay both his hands upon the head of the live goat, and confess over him all the iniquities of the children of Israel, and all their transgressions in all their sins, putting them upon

[112] W. Eichrodt, *Man in the Old Testament*, p. 37; *Theologie des Alten Testaments*, III.51. Cf. J. Bright, op. cit. p. 42; L. Köhler, op. cit. p. 52; S. Mowinckel, *Psalmenstudien* (Kristiania, 1923), V.36f (Exkurs); G. B. Gray, op. cit. p. 81. But note the modifications of this point in O. S. Rankin, *Israel's Wisdom Literature* (Edinburgh, 1936), p. 55.

[113] Cf. S. H. Hooke, 'The Theory and Practice of Substitution', *Vetus Testamentum*, II (Leiden, 1952), p. 11; J. Pedersen, op. cit. III-IV.362.

the head of the goat' (16^{21}). The priest as the realistic representative of the nation, bore the sins of the community; hence
he could transfer them to the scapegoat.[114] The living goat, thus
identified with the sins of the people, was relegated to Azazel,
to symbolize the entire removal of the sins and the consequent
guilt of the Congregation.

(c) *The Realistic Representation of One Tribe for the Nation.* The
choice of the tribe of Levi to be a permanent vicarious substitute
for the nation rests on the corporate unity of the group. Israel
in its entirety was the Lord's possession and domain (cf. Ex 19^{5-6}).
When the authority of the Lord had been challenged by the
nation, the tribe of Levi took the part of the Lord; hence, it was
appointed as the national representative in the place of the first-
born (cf. Ex 32^{28-9} with Deut 33^{8-11}). The latter were chosen
by the Lord to represent the nation, an obligation indicated in
their peculiar sanctification (cf. Ex 13^{2}). The responsibility of
the first-born representing the individual family was transferred
to the tribe of Levi for practical efficiency (cf. Num $3^{11-13, \, 41,}$
$^{45-51}$, 8^{14-18}). Throughout, the transfer of the responsibility of the
nation to the first-born, and from them to the Levites, the principle of solidarity is in play.[115]

(d) *The Realistic Representation of a Righteous Intercessor.* A conception parallel to that which allowed the transfer of the responsibility of the nation to a part, or even a single member, is found
in the representative role of the righteous intercessor. We may
consider, for example, the prayer in Nehemiah: 'Howbeit thou
art just in all that is brought upon us; for thou hast done right,
but *we* have done wickedly' (9^{33}). There is the same appreciation of a corporate unity found in Daniel's prayer of confession:
'*We* have sinned, and have committed iniquity, and have done
wickedly, and have rebelled, even by departing from thy precepts and from thy judgements . . .' (9^{5-19}). The solidarity of the
nation was of such a character that all of its members were implicated in the sin of any major or minor part. By the same

---

[114] W. O. E. Oesterley and T. H. Robinson note that the unit is Israel (hence,
the sacrifice is in actuality equivalent to individual sacrifice). The individual Israelite
approached God as a sub-unit. *Hebrew Religion* (2nd edn, London, 1937), p. 264.

[115] Cf. C. Lattey, op. cit. p. 271; S. H. Hooke, op. cit. p. 12. Note further that the
first-born were killed in vicarious substitution for Egypt (Ex 12^{29-30}, cf. Num 3^{13}).

token, the righteous member could realistically confess the sin of the whole.

As in the case of the representative roles of priest and king, the intercessor is usually characterized by a degree of prominence. Thus, Moses offered availing intercession for Israel, because as the leader of the group, he could stand in its place (Ex 32³¹⁻⁵). Jeremiah 15¹ and Ezekiel 14¹⁴ also suggest that prominence on the part of intercessors might act as a palliative factor; the sin of Israel is so heinous, declare the prophets, that if Moses and Samuel, in the former case, and Noah, Daniel, and Job, in the latter, were to intercede for the nation, it would be of no avail or benefit.[116]

(e) The Realistic Representation of a Messenger. On a lower level the agency of messengers is thought of in terms of realistic representation. The sent ones are the extension of the personality of the sender. This is the reason the מַלְאָכִים of Jephthah say, 'What hast thou to do with *me*', when challenging the Ammonites to battle (Judg 11¹²). The messengers of Israel to Sihon, king of the Amorites, say: 'Let *me* pass through thy land . . .' (Num 21²²). The representatives of the nation address the priests and prophets in the place of Israel: 'Should I weep in the fifth month, separating *myself*, as I have done these so many years?' (Zech 7³). There is a less noticeable example in the dialogue of the envoy of Joseph with the eleven brothers when he came to recover the cup of his master. The brothers say: '. . . how then should we steal out of *thy* lord's house silver or gold? With whomsoever of *thy* servants it be found, both let him die, and we also will be *my* lord's bondmen' (Gen 44⁸⁻⁹). Within the scope of a few phrases the speaker sees Joseph's servant as a separate individual, then as an extension of his master. The latter role is adopted by the messenger in his answer: '. . . He with whom it is found shall be *my* servant' (44¹⁰).

(f) The Realistic Representation of the גּוֹאֵל. The understanding of the function of the גּוֹאֵל ('avenger', 'kinsman', 'redeemer') is based on an ancient Hebrew idea of representative solidarity. Properly, the consideration of the גּוֹאֵל should be related to the

---

[116] Cf. S. A. Cook, *The Old Testament: a Reinterpretation*, p. 117.

discussion of kinship, but the features of representation are so prominent that S. A. Cook points to the need for a study of the term in that light.[117] The 'avenger' is most often the son (e.g. Solomon, Amaziah) or the brother (Gideon, Joab); but he is always the nearest of kin.[118] It is the embodiment of the family that is implied in the 'redeemer'. He represents the interests of the family in requiring the payment for an offence against the family (e.g. in blood-revenge), or in the redemption of the family inheritance (cf. Lev 25²⁵⁻³⁴, Ruth 2²⁰, 3⁹, 4¹⁻⁸, ¹⁴). The precise character of the kin relationship is not necessarily important, but the function is significant in that the גֹּאֵל acts in the place of the family, as may be seen in the discussion of Boaz with Ruth: 'There is a kinsman, nearer than I.... If he will perform unto thee the part of a גֹּאֵל, well; let him do the kinsman's part: but if he will not . . . then will I do the part of a kinsman to thee' (Ruth 3¹²⁻¹³). The גֹּאֵל is the realistic representative of the kin-group; hence, the duty devolves upon him to vindicate and defend its rights.

The same conception is involved in the injunctions regarding Levirate marriage. The law enjoins that the husband's brother is to perform the 'duty' of raising up seed to preserve the name of the deceased (Deut 25⁵⁻¹⁰). The realistic character of the identity of a man with his dead brother is so close that the progeny arising from the new union is considered to belong to the deceased. It was the recognition of this factor which provoked Onan's sin, since he 'knew that the seed should not be his' (Gen 38⁷⁻⁹). As in the case of the גֹּאֵל, the leviratical duty devolves upon the nearest kin.[119]

Very similar in character to the ideas concerning Levirate marriage are those instances where the wife, in the event of her own sterility, proposes to give her maid to her husband. Thus, Rachel admonishes Jacob: 'Go in unto Bilhah my handmaid . . . that I may also be built by her' (Gen 30³, Heb.). When Dan is

---

[117] *Cambridge Ancient History*, pp. 440, 444.

[118] J. Pedersen, op. cit. I–II.390.

[119] When Ruth bears a son by Boaz, the women say to Naomi: '. . . he shall be a restorer of thy life unto thee' (cf. Ruth 4⁵ with Gen 38¹²⁻²⁶). These passages show that Levirate marriage might be contracted with men other than brothers. Note H. H. Rowley, *The Servant of the Lord and Other Essays on the Old Testament* (London, 1952), p. 167. The emphasis on this point in the early composition, Tobit (between 350 and 170 B C), is significant (cf. 6¹³).

born, Rachel thanks God for *her* son (30[6]; cf. 30[8]). Where there is a relationship of any kind in which solidarity plays an active part, it is possible for the Hebrew to see an identity between the one who acts and the one who is acted for. This is true because the group, as a psychic whole, is considered as a corporate personality. As long as the representative belongs to the group, he bears the personality type and may act *in the place* of any other member of the group.

(g) Realistic Representation in the Implication of the Community in Sin. More remotely related to the aspect of realistic representation is the conception of a contamination of the group through the sin of a part thereof. Thus far we have discussed instances which involved the conception of representation by appointment or prerogative. When, however, an individual or group involves the nation in sin, it is otherwise. Before Achan 'troubled' Israel, he was a non-entity among the myriads of the people (Josh 7[16-26]). The momentous character of his infringement meant, however, that he comprehended the congregation in his sin. It is for this reason that the judgement of God fell on the army of Israel and the Lord says explicitly: 'Israel hath sinned . . .' (7[11-12]). The same universal implication of the nation occurred in the case of the trespass of Korah as the plea of Moses implies: '. . . Shall one man sin, and wilt thou be wroth with all the congregation' (Num 16[22]). The indivisibility of the community made the action of one member in a realistic sense the action of the whole. For this reason one of two possible courses of action governed the judgement of a perpetrator of sin in Israel. He either must purify himself to remove the defilement of the whole community, or be 'cut off'.[120] D. Daube distinguishes the former as community responsibility, from the latter, which is personal.[121] 'Cutting off' from the community meant more than a relinquishing of citizenship in the nation. He ceased to be a Jew. Psalm 52[7] (Heb.; Eng. *A.V.*, 52[5]) 'declares that the soul that sins must be amputated from the complex organism which is the whole community'.[122]

---

[120] That is, excommunication, or as BDB (p. 504) take it, suffering the death penalty, as Leviticus 23[29-30] indicates.

[121] Op. cit. pp. 155-87. In the case that the sin was not expiated, it became communal responsibility.

[122] G. A. F. Knight, op. cit. p. 173. Cf. pp. 181-2.

D

In the communal responsibility described in Deuteronomy 21^{1-9}, there is no question regarding the prominence of the individual, since the culprit is unknown. The passage refers to the discovery of a murder in which the guilty party is not to be found. The city nearest the victim is responsible, and bears the guilt of the murderer, as long as he cannot be found. Says D. Daube: 'God might treat the whole community as answerable or tainted by the crime committed by the one, unknown murderer. "Lay not innocent blood unto thy people of Israel's charge" is the prayer to be recited by the elders.'[123] In the chiding of Abimelech it is not a particular man of Gerar who, by violating Rebekah, might have brought guilt on all the city, but 'one of the people' (Gen 26^{10}).[124]

(h) *Realistic Representation in Corporate Blessing.* On the opposite side from the implication of the community in sin through the sin of a member is the principle of corporate blessing, secured through the righteousness or innocence of a member. This is the basis for Abraham's plea that Sodom should not be destroyed, even if there should be as few as ten righteous members in that community. The merit of a righteous minority is supposedly sufficient to obviate the divine judgement on a majority (cf. Gen 18^{23-32}). It is the same point which is made in God's explanation for sparing Nineveh. It is absolutely just to forgive the wickedness of the majority because there are within the group 120,000 children as well as the cattle (Jonah 4^{11}). As in the case of the righteous ancestor, these two accounts imply: (1) the indivisible solidarity of the group, and (2) that a righteous or innocent minority of the group may act as the realistic representative of the community.

(i) *The Realistic Representation of the Sacrificial Victim.* The Hebrew conception of sacrifice involves the element of realistic substitution. Basic to the Old Testament conception of the sacrifice is the universal doctrine of the indivisibility of sin and its consequent *death* penalty. This is seen in such dissimilar instances

---

[123] Op. cit. p. 161.

[124] This discussion is not intended to suggest that the Old Testament omits the consideration of the responsibility of the group for a group action or decision. There is group sin as Numbers 15^{23-9} shows, in drawing a distinction between the ignorant sin of the congregation and the ignorant sin of the individual (cf. Lev 4^{13-21}).

as the transgression of Adam (Gen 3[3]), the harbouring of an 'evil imagination' (Gen 6[5-7]), or the murmuring of the Israelites in the wilderness (Num 21[7]), to name but three of many possibilities. For this reason provision was made in the divine economy for the transfer of the penalty to a sacrificial victim. In the transaction, the principle of corporate personality which identified the sinner and his offering was the rationale involved, something which is quite different from the idea of a mechanical transference of penalty.[125]

There is no compulsion to explain this identification merely on the basis of the psychic life of nature (i.e. *mana*) in which man shares. As in the case of the commemoration of the passover, or circumcision (in which the initiate or member was identified with the redemptive *event*), it is the event of the death of the victim in which the guilty party shares. This is the impression gained from an examination of the Passover ritual outlined in Exodus 12. The lamb was the vicarious substitute for the first-born of the nation,[126] which in turn realistically represented the nation. It is the vicarious substitution of the *experience* of death which must be recognized. What should have happened to the first-born is through the principle of a sacrificial commutation of the penalty brought upon the substitutionary victim.

There is beyond the conception of a shared experience, the necessity of possession. The animal must belong to the offerer, or be part of the household to adequately represent the psychic whole.[127] It is for this reason that David felt that he must purchase the sacrifice and the threshing-floor from Araunah (2 S 24[24]) lest there should be an inadequate relationship of vicarious solidarity between the sacrificial victim and the forgiven sinner. This principle governs the injunction against Israelites offering sacrifices secured from strangers; they are blemished and unacceptable (Lev 22[25]).

The role of the realistic representation of the offering for the guilty sinner is nowhere more clearly illustrated than in the ritual of the Day of Atonement. C. R. North comments:

[125] H. W. Robinson, 'Hebrew Psychology', p. 381. Cf. R. B. Townsend, *The Apocrypha and Pseudepigrapha of the Old Testament*, ed. R. H. Charles (Oxford, 1913), II.663.

[126] T. H. Gaster emphasizes the element of kinship ties which the ceremony established and which were outwardly manifested by the sign of blood, since the essence of kinship is blood; op. cit. p. 20.

[127] A. R. Johnson, *The One and the Many*, p. 8.

Here we have a clear example of the conception of guilt transferred from the human beings who have contracted it to an animal which is guiltless, and it is significant that the guilt so transferred was guilt incurred by the commission of real sins, not merely the sins of inadvertence which were all for which any sin-offering, even those on the Day of Atonement, could make expiation.[128]

When we examine the role of the Servant, portrayed in the Songs of the Servant (Isa 42$^{1-4}$, 49$^{1-6}$, 50$^{4-9}$, 52^{13}–53^{12}), we may note an integration of the ideas latent in the ritual of the scape-goat and the Israelite guilt offering.[129] Fundamental to both ritual elements was the conception of the solidarity of the group. The atonement of the Servant is not possible without the prior identification with the group, whether Israel, or the world. It is because the עֶבֶד יְהוָה is the realistic representative of Israel, that he may suffer vicariously and bear the sins of Israel (cf. 53$^{4-6, 10}$). 'The Servant so completely unites himself with the people that it is true to say that he is the people and the people is the Servant. We must recognize both, that he is throughout not the people, and yet nevertheless is the people.'[130] Thus, the Servant of the Lord is the culmination of the Hebrew conception of realistic representation in sacrifice. He stands as a substitute for Israel and for the whole world, yet not apart from the conception of this substitute as the embodiment of the nation and *corpus humanum* in whose place he bows to receive the judgement of God.

THE ASPECT OF OSCILLATION

The term 'oscillation' conveys a characteristic of the Hebrew thought process which enabled one to conceive of the individual

---

[128] *TWBB*, p. 213.

[129] There is an indication that the scape-goat ritual provides the frame of reference in which the self-offering of the Servant is cast. Of the scape-goat we read: 'And the goat shall bear upon him all their iniquities to the land of cutting off' (גְּזֵרָה, Lev 16^{22}).

Of the Suffering Servant, Isaiah 53^8 says, 'For he was cut off (נִגְזַר) from the land of the living', implying that the Servant fulfils in an expanded form the role of the goat which bore the sins of the nation on the Day of Atonement. Cf. E. G. King, *The Yalkut on Zechariah* (Cambridge, 1882), p. 105. On the other hand, that the death of the Servant is thought of in terms of sacrifice is evident from the use of the technical term אָשָׁם ('guilt offering') (53^{10}). Cf. H. H. Rowley, 'The Meaning of Sacrifice in the Old Testament', *BJRL*, XXXIII (September, 1950), p. 104.

[130] W. Vischer, *Jahrbuch der theologischen Schule Bethel*, ed. Th. Schlatter (Bethel bei Bielefeld, 1930), p. 102. 'It is the "paradox" of the *unio mystica capitis et corporis*'; ibid. p. 103. Noted from C. R. North, op. cit. p. 112. To the idea of the *unio mystica*, we must, with L. Köhler, op. cit. p. 172, take exception.

as the embodiment of the group, and the group as an individual. It is found in a fluidity of transition from the individual to the society and vice versa.[131] It must be accepted as a genuine characteristic of the Hebrew mind, manifesting itself in speech and writing, and requiring the conception of the corporate personality of the group for an adequate explanation.

Oscillation is not a rare feature in the transaction of business between two groups. A good example is found in the dialogue between the embassy of Israel and Sihon: 'Let *me* pass through thy land: *we* will not turn into the fields . . .' (Num 21[22]). Edom threatened the tribes of Israel that wished to pass through the southern part of Canaan thus, '*Thou* shalt not pass by *me*, lest *I* come out against *thee* with the sword'; but makes the portent of evil patent by coming out 'with much people' (Num 20[18, 20]). In this same passage Israel is spoken of in the plural (20[14-17]) but is addressed by Edom in the singular. Of the judgement of Achan, the text reads: 'And all Israel stoned *him* with stones, and burned them with fire, after they had stoned *them* with stones' (Josh 7[25]). Such examples of the transition from the individual to the collective and vice versa are relatively frequent (note e.g. Ex 34[15], Heb.; Deut 4 *passim*, 7[25], 8[19], 14[21], etc.).

The natural way in which the transition is made in Daniel 7[13-27] from the figure who is 'like unto a Son of Man' to the Saints of the Most High, is a most significant application of the principle of oscillation. It is not a member acting for the group, but an objective description made in individualistic terms. The prophet saw a figure resembling a man, which in reality was the Saints of the Most High (cf. Dan 7[13] with 7[18, 22]).[132] Thus, the Son of Man is a collective personality. He could be described equally well by the singular or plural. This figure is important in the New Testament, consequently it will receive further treatment later.

Equally objective to the sacred writer of the Songs of the Servant is the equipoise between the Servant as Israel, and as an individual in Isaiah's description of the עֶבֶד יְהֹוָה. Israel, 'the seed of Abraham', is the Servant in Isaiah 41[8-9]. It is difficult to determine whether the individualistic terms of Isaiah 42[1-4]

[131] H. W. Robinson, 'The Hebrew Conception', p. 53.
[132] J. Y. Campbell, 'The Origin and Meaning of the Term Son of Man', *JTS*, XLVIII (1947), p. 141.

apply to Israel or to the individual Servant. In Isaiah 44[1, 21]
the Servant is again identified with Israel, the nation (cf. also
45[4] and 48[20]). Isaiah 49[1-6] so telescopes the nation and the individual (or remnant) that it becomes enigmatic. A further com-
plication is introduced by the use of the first person: '. . . And
said unto me, Thou art my servant, O Israel, in whom I will
be glorified. Then I said, I have laboured in vain, I have spent
my strength. . . . And now, saith the Lord that formed me from
the womb to be his servant, to bring Jacob again to him, Though
Israel be not gathered yet shall I be glorious in the eyes of the
Lord, and my God shall be my strength.'[133]

Although the addressee is Israel (cf. 49[3]), it cannot be all of
the actual nation, for the mission of the Servant is to convert
Israel, and with that accomplishment to be a light to the Gentiles
(cf. 49[6]). It must either be an individual or a personified remnant,[134] which the writer embodies.[135] Isaiah 50[4-9] is most clearly
individual in its characterization of the Servant (note especially
50[6], where back, cheeks, hair, and face are mentioned).[136] The
transition from the plural 'you' (52[12]) to the singular third person
(52[13]–53[12]) again apparently requires an individual interpretation.[137]

The expansion and contraction of the terms which are used
to describe the Servant of the Lord in this section of Isaiah have
posed problems for the interpretation of this figure which are
still very much in dispute. Two recent writers have investigated
the problem and published the results for the English-speaking
world. C. R. North and H. H. Rowley substantially agree. We
may quote a summary of Rowley's conclusions:

It is probable that the Servant is in part the personification of the
mission of Israel, and in part the delineation of one who should embody
its mission with peculiar fullness so that he should play a notable part

---

[133] Isaiah 49[3-5]; cf. Psalm 136[22], Jeremiah 30[10], 46[27-8], for a similar designation of
the nation as the Servant of God.

[134] See C. R. North's examination of this question, op. cit. *passim.*

[135] Embodiment is to be understood in the sense already illuminated in the discussion of the realistic representation of the leader or prominent figure in the group.

[136] H. W. Robinson admits this, but understands the mission for God in a collective
sense. 'The Hebrew Conception', p. 59.

[137] H. W. Robinson takes this reference to refer to Israel as a whole (ibid), thus
concurring with the almost universal Jewish opinion on the meaning of the passage.
For an exhaustive examination of the Jewish interpretations see, A. Neubauer and
S. R. Driver, *The Fifty-third Chapter of Isaiah according to Jewish Interpreters,* 2 Vols
(Oxford, 1876).

in the achievement of the Golden Age. . . . Something of the fluidity of what has become known as 'corporate personality' is found here, so that the Servant is both the community and an individual who represents it. While the mission will be peculiarly fulfilled in one, it is nevertheless the mission to which all are called, and all should enter in some measure into it.[138]

In the oscillation between the nation and the individual, there is evidence to confirm the conclusion that the Songs employ the Hebrew conception of corporate personality to present the idea of the Servant as the Realistic Representative of Israel.

CONCLUSION

The foregoing presentation of the Hebrew conception of the corporate personality of the nation and its composite units is not exhaustive. The limitations of the space allowed would make that an impossible task. On the other hand, from the evidence presented, one clear fact emerges—the ancient Hebrew conception of solidarity held unity in higher esteem than its more modern sociological counterparts. This unity did not result from external imposition, but was fundamentally grounded in the psychological conditioning of the Israelite in the Old Testament period.

The evidence which can be garnered from almost every page of the Old Testament approves H. W. Robinson's choice of the descriptive term, 'corporate personality'. It is equivalent to W. R. Smith's employment of the metaphor of a tree to describe the ancient Semitic conception of the solidarity of the group. The race has a life of its own, of which individual lives are only parts. On the basis of the analogy between the group and a tree, the ancestor is the root, and the descendants are the branches.[139] The whole produces an organic unity transcending time and space and is properly described as a collective personality.

[138] 'The Meaning of Sacrifice in the Old Testament', pp. 108-9. Cf. also H. H. Rowley, *The Missionary Message of the Old Testament* (London, 1944), pp. 53-4. For more extensive studies by Rowley, see *Israel's Mission to the World* (London, 1939), and *The Servant of the Lord and Other Essays on the Old Testament*, pp. 1-57.
[139] *The Religion of the Semites*, p. 41.

CHAPTER II

EARLY JEWISH CONCEPTIONS OF THE SOLIDARITY OF THE HUMAN RACE

PROCEEDING with our objective of identifying and examining conceptions of human solidarity relevant to the understanding of Paul's doctrines of Anthropology and Soteriology, we must turn to early Jewish thought. Sources for the understanding of Jewish ideas in the period of the Second Temple are numerous and varied. These sources differ greatly in the extent to which they can be presumed to be accurate reflections of the Apostle's own training in the 'Jews' religion'. Because Paul's pre-Christian upbringing and education were in the hands of Rabbinic Pharisaism (Phil 3[5-7] and Acts 22[3]), the preserved speculation and tradition of the Rabbis must be given prior consideration.[1] Of very nearly comparable importance to the background of New Testament thought are the 'extraneous' compositions comprising the Apocrypha (with the possible exception of Ecclesiasticus) and Pseudepigrapha.[2] Although Paul makes little reference to this material in any direct allusion, Jewish Apocalyptic and the Epistles have much in common, forcing us to the conclusion that the ideas reflected in them had

---

[1] The late composition of the Talmud (c. A.D. fifth century) and other Rabbinic sources makes them suspect in the search for an accurate knowledge of Jewish thought in the middle of the first century. Other problems such as the 'large amount of tolerated difference of opinion' evidenced in the Haggada and Midrash (cf. C. H. Dodd, 'Jesus as Teacher and Prophet', *Mysterium Christi*, ed. G. K. A. Bell and D. A. Deissmann [London, 1931], p. 55) and 'organic thinking' add to the difficulty. Certainly it is a mistake to expect the Rabbis to yield a 'theology of Judaism' (see M. Kadushin, *Organic Thinking, passim*; F. Gavin, *The Jewish Antecedents of the Christian Sacraments* [London, 1928], p. 6). There is a certain amount of justification for citing opinions found in the Talmud and Midrash which are attributed to Rabbis which are later than the first century. Because much that the Jewish teachers say is characterized by impressionistic intention rather than logical dogma, it is possible to trace a 'mythopoeic motif' (cf. N. P. Williams, *The Ideas of the Fall and of Original Sin* (London, 1927), p. 75) which has a degree of unity and continuity over a considerable period of time. Thus, although a specific point of contact might be questionable, a broad concept recurring repeatedly cannot be successfully challenged.

[2] Cf. R. H. Pfeiffer, *History of New Testament Times* (New York, 1949), p. 60; W. O. E. Oesterley and G. H. Box, *Religion and Worship of the Synagogue* (London, 1907), p. 41; G. F. Moore, *Judaism* (Cambridge, Mass., 1927), I.127ff; II.281. H. St John Thackeray regards the Palestinian Apocryphal literature as more significant in Paul's background than Rabbinic influence; *The Relations of St Paul to Contemporary Jewish Thought* (London, 1900), p. 11.

wide currency in the first century. A third source, which may prove valuable to the understanding of early Christian backgrounds, is the recently discovered Dead Sea Scrolls and the Zadokite Documents produced by the Community of the New Covenant (evidently Essenes). Since they were dissenters from orthodox Pharisaic-Rabbinism, it is not likely that Paul had access to their writings or was greatly influenced by them. There are interesting parallels which may in time prove to be instructive. Of minor importance to the background of the Pauline Epistles are the writings of Philo of the Alexandrian syncretistic school of Hellenistic Judaism. There is no assured evidence to confirm the opinion that Paul had read or heard of Philo.[3] Of still less consequence for our purpose are the works of Josephus or the few surviving discussions of Christians with Jews (e.g. Justin Martyr's Dialogue with Trypho the Jew).

From these sources we shall attempt to ascertain distinctive Jewish conceptions of human solidarity. They will be discussed under the topics of (1) the Jewish self-consciousness of the solidarity of Israel, (2) the organic continuity of the nation, (3) implications drawn from the demands made upon Gentile proselytes, and (4) the transferability of merit and demerit. The second part of this chapter will deal with the early Jewish conceptions of the solidarity of the whole human race and its implications.

THE JEWISH SELF-CONSCIOUSNESS OF THE SOLIDARITY OF ISRAEL

THE UNITY OF ISRAEL IN DIRECT STATEMENTS AND ANALOGY

(1) *Direct Reference to the Unity of Israel.* To post-biblical Judaism, the unity of Israel was an unassailable proposition. Because this claim was presuppositional in character, there are few direct statements in early Jewish writings to confirm so self-evident a truth. The aphorism which Josephus quotes, θεὸς γὰρ εἷς καὶ τὸ 'Εβραίων γένος ἕν,[4] is actually didactic information for a non-Jewish audience. There is a claim referring to the unity of the nation in the 'Amida for Sabbath Vespers: 'Thou art one, Thy

---

[3] See W. D. Davies, *Paul and Rabbinic Judaism*, p. 52, and literature cited there.
[4] *Jewish Antiquities*, Bk. iv.201 (*LoClL*, IV.572).

Name is one, who is one in the world as Thy people Israel.'[5]
The emphasis on the oneness of the people of Israel in these
statements indicates the presuppositional character of this truth,
in that it is viewed in correspondence with the one dogma of
Judaism, namely, the unity of God.

The unity of the nation was founded on its divine election and
sealed by the irrefragable covenant which guaranteed that Israel
should be one as long as more than one Israelite remained. These
are familiar ideas in the Old Testament, but they had a new
urgency in the post-exilic period; they were produced by the
calamities which befell Israel. Thus, although individualism became more pronounced during the dispersion following the Exile
(through Hellenistic influence), a reaction against these disrupt-
ing influences tended to solidify the feeling of community among
all the Sons of Abraham.[6]

The absorbing fear of Judaism was that the nation should be
dissolved as a people, and the mission of Israel declaring the
truth of monotheism to the world come to an end. This fear was
counteracted by the eschatological hope of the complete restoration of the nation and the destruction of all paganism in the
Messianic Age. It was in this projected restoration that salvation
of individuals and the final unity of the dispersed People of God
was joined.[7] In the meantime, the goal of existence was found
for a Hebrew in not 'severing himself from the community', but
joining in the common effort to prepare the nation for the
Messiah's advent.

Many obstacles were encountered in the attempt to secure the
solidarity of Israel both in actual fact and in theoretical definition. Among these were the problems of corporate justice, as
opposed to the responsibility of the individual. There was in
addition an obvious tension between the future exaltation of
Israel and the present crushing burden of slavery to Gentile dogs.
There was the practical problem of association with the 'nations'
and the danger of mixed marriage. There was the question of
the inclusion of the Gentile convert into the community and his

[5] *The Authorized Jewish Daily Prayer Book*, ed. I. Singer (9th edn, London, 1912),
p. 175. Cf. A. E. Suffrin, 'God', *HERE* VI.295. Cf. also 4 Es 5^{28}; Suk. 55*b*;
S. Hanson, *The Unity of the Church in the New Testament* (Uppsala, 1946), p. 11.

[6] See W. D. Davies on the tension between universalism and nationalism, op. cit.
pp. 59ff. Cf. A. Cohen, *Everyman's Talmud* (London, 1932), pp. xv-xvi; N. Levison,
The Jewish Background of Christianity (Edinburgh, 1932), pp. 186-7.

[7] Cf. G. F. Moore, op. cit. II.312-22.

subsequent status. We shall encounter many more as we proceed. It is enough to note that all of these problems and conflicts
have their roots in the conception of the unity of Israel and a
desire to maintain a national identity.

(2) *The Jewish Teaching on the Unity of Israel by Metaphorical Analogy.*
The fact of Israel's unity is often expressed through the medium
of analogy. An almost innumerable series of metaphors and
similes represent Israel throughout the Talmud and Midrash.
Rabbi Simeon ben Yohai likens Israel to a body and soul: 'If
one of them sinned, they are all of them punished.'[8] The primary
emphasis of this Rabbi does not lie on a single life that pervades
Israel, but he is simply drawing an analogy between the indivisible body and soul and using it to express the Jewish conception of the solidarity of the nation. R. Hezekiah b. Hiyya evinces
the same intention in using the simile of a sheep to describe the
mysterious unity of Israel. Just as a lamb beaten on the head or
on one of its limbs feels it in all the parts of the body, likewise is
it with Israel. If one of them sins, all of them feel it.[9] According
to R. Jose, the Galilean, until the last Israelite had finished his
paschal sacrifice, the whole nation was in danger of obliteration.[10]
Throughout, in the exposition of the events of Israel's history
there is this emphasis on the dire implications of one Israelite
failing to fulfil his role as a sub-unit of the national whole.

The metaphorical employment of the figure of a tree was a
particularly choice manner of referring to Israel.[11] This metaphor was ideal for describing the unity and continuity of the
community. In one such parable, a point is made regarding the
inefficiency of inexperienced men who attempt to destroy Israel,
but fail because they only lop off the branches. But Balaam
('the wicked one'), being a man of experience, uncovered the
roots and purposed to sever them. That is why he said: 'Why
should I curse every single tribe? rather root out the whole.'

[8] Quoted by S. S. Schechter, *Some Aspects of Rabbinic Theology* (London, 1909),
p. 191, from *Mechilta de-Rabbi Simon b. Jochai*, ed. Hoffmann (Frankfurt-a-Main,
1905), p. 95.
[9] *Lev R*, 4[6], *Mekilta de-Rabbi Ishmael*, ed. and trans., J. Z. Lauterbach (Philadelphia,
1933-5), II.205-6. Cf. A. Marmorstein, *The Doctrine of Merits in Old Rabbinical Literature* (London, 1920), pp. 68, 187. For the use of pastoral imagery, see A. Feldman,
The Parables and Similes of the Rabbis (Cambridge, 1924), ch. xii.
[10] *Mek* I.94.
[11] For the prominence of the metaphorical use of trees, see A. Feldman, op. cit.
Chs. 3-5. Cf. Wis 4[4-5].

Setting to work he found them (i.e. Israel) too hard to uproot.[12]

The continuity of Israel is clear in R. Eleazar b. Pedath's explanation of Genesis 12[3]: 'And in thee shall all the families of the earth be blessed.' 'The Holy One, blessed be He, said unto Abraham, Two good shoots have I to engraft on thee, Ruth the Moabite and Naomi, the Ammonite.'[13] The willow tree spoke of the collective responsibility of Israel: 'As the willow has neither taste nor smell, so (are) the Israelites who have neither Torah nor good works. What is God to do with them? It is not possible to destroy them. God says: "Bind all together into one bundle, and the one will atone for the other."'[14]

A similar opinion was held regarding the bunch of hyssop employed to smear blood on the door-posts and lintels of Israel's houses in the Passover ceremony. The blood was a reminder of the three Patriarchs, but the lowly hyssop symbolized the People of Israel—lowly, yet bound together by the grace of God.[15]

Out of the numerous examples of a vine representing Israel, there is one which is significant in that it illustrates the conception of an organic unity which existed from the Patriarchs down through the entire history of the nation. The vine (which is Israel), 'while it is itself fresh and green' (i.e. alive), is 'supported by dry stakes' (i.e. the dead fathers and their accumulated merit).[16] It is possible to draw the inference which Sanday and Headlam do in describing the Jewish conception of the solidarity of Israel in terms of an organic body, the members of which were closely bound together.[17] The normally disruptive factor of death was transcended in the perception of the *unit*, Israel, which traversed all generations and included all the descendants of Jacob.

The emphasis placed on the Torah and its importance for the constitution of the unit Israel was the source of an insoluble tension between the concept of the unity of Israel and its moral integrity. This conflict may be seen in the interpretation of Song

[12] *Num R* 20[19]. In *Jubilees* 17[9], 21[22], to destroy a nation is to uproot it.
[13] *Teb* 63a. Cf. *Baba Kama* 38a. It is due to the merit of Ruth and Naomi, that Moab has been preserved.
[14] *Lev R*, 30[12]. Cf. F. Jackson and K. Lake, *The Beginnings of Christianity*, I (London, 1939), p. 57.
[15] Cf. T. H. Gaster, *Passover; Its History and Traditions*, p. 49.
[16] *Lev R*, 36[2]. For the Rabbinic use of the symbolism of the vine, see A. Feldman, op. cit. Ch. 4.
[17] *The Epistle to the Romans* (*ICC*), p. 331.

of Songs 2[13], 'The fig tree putteth forth her green figs', and its application to Israel. It was given a historical setting in the three days of darkness (in Egypt) during which, it was claimed, the wicked of Israel perished.[18] It is important to note that this type of midrash reflects a continuity with the exclusivism of the Old Testament, limiting the understanding of Israel to the righteous remnant, large or small. As long as Israel was recognized by the Rabbis as a moral unity, a theocratic nation, with the glory of God its sole purpose of existence, they were forced to accept the conclusion that the wicked of Israel were removed from the transcendent community. Although conflicting opinions were expressed, the idea is to be found of a 'true Israel', distinguished from an ethnic people. Thus, for example, R. Jehuda is claimed to have said: ' "Ye are sons of the Lord your God" (Deut 14[1]). If you behave as sons, you are called sons; if you do not behave as sons, you are not called sons.'[19] R. Hiyya explained Ecclesiastes 9[5] as a reference to the 'wicked who in their lifetime are called dead'.[20] Although this distinction between the people of God and Jewry is frequently encountered,[21] a contrary opinion is registered by the prominent R. Meir to the effect that whether they (Israel) carry on as children or not, they are always children.[22] The section ten of *Mishna Sanhedrin* states categorically that 'All Israel has a part in the world to come'.[23] There is no possible reconciliation of the opinions which we have considered regarding the wicked, and those who failed to observe the Torah apart from the conception of solidarity. The solution of a corporate merit which would atone for the sinners so that all Israel might be saved was a popular conclusion as we shall see. The very seriousness with which the problem of the inclusion or exclusion

[18] *Cant R* 2[13]. See W. D. Davies for other references, op. cit. p. 338, and p. 84.

[19] Cf. M. N. Bourke, *A Study of the Metaphor of the Olive Tree in Romans XI* (Washington, 1947), pp. 16-22.

[20] *Ber* 18b.

[21] Cf. *M. Pirke Aboth* 5[19], *Gen R* 53[12]; H. L. Strack and P. Billerbeck, *Kommentar zum Neuen Testament aus Talmud und Midrasch*, III (München, 1926), pp. 124-5. The idea is also found in 4 Ezra 7[75-87] and 2 Baruch 30[4]. Some Rabbis exclude whole segments of Israelites. For example R. Eleazar said: 'Those who die outside of Palestine will not live again. The Amme-ha-aretz will not live again. Whoever is slack about Torah will not live again' (*Ket* 111b). Cf. *RA*, op. cit. p. 600; G. Johnston, *The Doctrine of the Church in the New Testament* (Cambridge, 1943), p. 21.

[22] *Kid* 36a. Cf. *Hagigah* 27a where the wicked are typified by the golden Altar. Although the fire (i.e. Gehinnom) burned upon it for many years it could not affect it. R. 'Abba b. Zabda (A D 290) says: 'An Israelite, even though he has sinned, remains an Israelite' (*Sanh* 44a). Cf. *RA*, p. 240.

[23] *M. Sanh* 10[1].

of the wicked from Israel was discussed is a significant commentary on the self-consciousness of the unity of Israel.

In all of these metaphors and similes, the corporate unity of Israel was implied. Even in the collective figures of sheep, branches of a tree, or nuts (cf. *infra*, p. 68), the presupposition emerges that Israel is an integral unity.[24] The individuals of Israel are sub-units of the transcendent totality of the Chosen Race. As the writer of 4 *Ezra* puts it, 'Among all the multitudes of peoples, thou hast gotten thee one people' (5[27]). The nature and implications of this unity will become increasingly evident as we proceed.

INCORPORATION INTO ISRAEL

(1) *Introduction.* Our preceding discussion has attempted to present the presupposition of the dogma of Israel's ideal and real unity. Admittedly, the Old Testament had laid the foundation of the conception of the unity of the People of God,[25] but the seclusion of the nation prior to the Exile had provided little genuine challenge to the acceptance of the transcendent unity of Israel. Subsequent to the Captivity and the resulting dispersion, the unity of the disinherited people was no longer a self-evident fact. There arose an imminent danger that the Jews of the Diaspora, by intermingling with the heathen, should lose their Hebrew identity with its priceless heritage altogether.[26] This danger was present even in Palestine, as large sections of the books of Ezra and Nehemiah indicate, particularly in the prohibition of the intermarriage of Israelites with the local inhabitants (cf. Ezra 9–10 and Neh 13). No less serious is the problem of intermarriage in the Book of Jubilees. The writer paints the picture of utter horror, declaring that it is equivalent to fornication and merits the same penalty.

Thus far, we have already noticed evidence to suggest that the solidarity of Israel was based only partially on hereditary and civic foundations. Now it will become increasingly evident that spiritual factors must be given an equivalent status. Basic

---

[24] Cf. C. Guignebert, *The Jewish World in the Time of Jesus,* trans. S. H. Hooke (New York, 1939), p. 94. See S. Hanson, op. cit. p. 7.

[25] Cf. W. D. Davies, op. cit. pp. 77-83, and Ch. I, *supra.*

[26] Bousset lists five ways in which the integration of Jews of Palestine and those of the Diaspora was maintained, *Die Religion des Judentums in neutestamentlichen Zeitalter,* 3rd edn rev. and ed. by Gressmann (Tübingen, 1926), p. 71.

elements in the liturgy of Judaism will confirm this. Among these, the rites of initiation into the community, and practices designed to bolster the spiritual unity of the nation and define the gap between Israel and the Gentiles, are significant. They also reflect the Early Jewish conception of the covenantal bond which, it must be admitted in the final analysis, constituted Israel.

(2) *Circumcision and Incorporation.* Judaism postulated three basic requirements for the entrance of Gentiles into the Community: (i) מִילָה ('circumcision'), (ii) טְבִילָה ('baptism'), and (iii) הַלְעָאַת דָּמִים ('sacrifice').[27] The most important of the three was circumcision. For the 'homeborn' as for the proselyte, its performance was considered to secure undeniable entrance into the covenant.[28] This point is vividly illustrated by a curious example of Rabbinic reasoning: Because Israelites who are circumcised do not go down to Gehinnon, R. Berachiah said, 'That the *Minim* and the Wicked of Israel may not say, "We are circumcised, we shall not go down to Gehinnon", what does the Holy One, blessed be He, do? He sends an angel and effaces their circumcision, and they go down to Gehinnon. . . .'[29] According to the Midrash, the foreskin of Abraham prior to his circumcision alone was a blemish, without which he should be perfect.[30] The inference is unavoidable that circumcision was considered to be in effect a ticket of admission to the World to Come and that its benefits were irrevocable.[31]

There is some additional evidence in the New Testament. For Paul, circumcision of Gentiles meant that they had been made Jews. In his radical opposition to the Judaizers, this rite was never considered to be a religious technicality which one might accept or reject to soothe the whims of zealous legalists. It meant no less than reversion to Judaism and the abandonment of Christ

[27] E. Schürer, *The Jewish People in the Time of Jesus Christ*, trans. S. Taylor and P. Christi, Div. II, Vol. II, (Edinburgh, 1885), p. 319.
[28] Cf. *Sifre Num* par. 108. In the thanksgiving uttered in the grace said during the Passover, mention is made of the covenant which God has sealed 'in our flesh'. Cf. A. A. Green, *The Revised Hagada* (London, 1898), p. 61.
[29] *Ex R* 19⁴. Cf. R. T. Herford, *Christianity in Talmud and Midrash* (London, 1903), p. 191.
[30] *Gen R* 46⁵. See *Yoma* 86a on the gravity of non-circumcision.
[31] The houses of Hillel and Shammai agreed that in case of a male born circumcised, he was yet to be cut, that the blood of the covenant might flow (*Gen R* 16¹²). He who disguises his circumcision has broken the covenant (*Gen R* 16¹³). Cf. A. Büchler, *Studies in Sin and Atonement*, p. 98.

as the Mediator of salvation (Gal 3³, Acts 15¹⁻². ⁵). Circumcision, furthermore, served as a convenient term to distinguish Jews from Gentiles (cf. Gal 2⁷⁻⁹).

(3) *Baptism as a Rite of Initiation.* The second requirement of Gentile proselytes was the טְבִילָה ('proselyte bath'). Krauss claims that the origin of the practice was consequent to a recognized need of the Gentile to be cleansed from defilement (especially idolatry) and a conviction that the טְבִילָה had power to restore the initiate to the purity of a new-born man.[32] It is likely that in the latter part of the Talmudic period, baptism was merely an initiatory ceremony with no special theological significance.[33] This conclusion is supported by an equation drawn by the Rabbis: ' "And he shall be as one that is born in the land" (Ex 12⁴⁸). Even as the homeborn enters into the covenant in three ways, by circumcision, immersion, and sacrifice, so too, the proselyte enters into the covenant in three ways, by circumcision, immersion and sacrifice.'[34] Since the Jew was born clean and needed no ablution, there is an inference that baptism was not considered to carry that connotation for the proselyte.[35]

The baptism of the proselyte was formalized by the attendance of witnesses, and a period of instruction in which two learned men had to stand at his side and acquaint him with some of the minor and major commandments. 'After his immersion he is deemed an Israelite in all respects.'[36] To become acquainted with the whole of the written and oral Torah was too much to expect; therefore, when the novice acceded to the instruction of the few *mizwot* he was in reality accepting the whole of Judaism.[37]

There is an added significance to be noted in the 'proselyte

---

[32] In *JE*, II.500. Cf. O. Cullmann, *Baptism in the New Testament* (London, 1950), pp. 10-11.

[33] W. G. Braude, *Jewish Proselytizing in the First Centuries of the Common Era* (Providence, R.I., 1940), p. 74, note 1. The *Sib Or* IV.164 insist on Gentiles being baptized as an outward token of their conversion (E. Schürer, op. cit. p. 323).

[34] *Mechilta de-Rabbi Simon b. Jochai*, p. 30. Cf. *Ker* 9a; W. D. Davies, op. cit. p. 121; F. Gavin, op. cit. p. 51; G. F. Moore, *Judaism*, I.331.

[35] Cf. Jth 8¹⁸⁻²⁰ and the claim that Israelites are free from the bane of idolatry. Cf. W. D. Davies, op. cit. p. 30. E. Schürer interprets proselyte baptism as a ceremonial cleansing equivalent to the Levitical bath of purification (op. cit. p. 322).

[36] *Yeb* 47a-b. Cf. W. Braude, op. cit. p. 78. For assorted texts on the baptism of proselytes, see F. Gavin, op. cit. pp. 33-5.

[37] Cf. *Gen R* 70⁵, *Num R* 8⁹, *Hag* 14a, and Oesterley and Box, op. cit. pp. 124, 139. This confidence was not always justified as A. Büchler shows, op. cit. p. 94 and references cited there.

bath'. The טְבִילָה was, in a measure, the means by which the novice could experience the past events of Israel's history: in particular the Exodus, the crossing of the Red Sea, and the preparation for the Revelation at Sinai.[38] As Israel itself in symbolic manner put away all Gentile ways of life, leaving them on the western shore, or drowning them in the sea with the Egyptians, so the proselyte was enjoined to re-experience the same event sacramentally.[39] This symbolism was integrated with a new ethical motive, as W. L. Knox points out. 'A past event of history (or mythology), embodied in the ritual action, became an effective symbol for producing a change in the character of the believer.'[40] Nor did the Rabbis hesitate to point out that the proselytes were included in the covenant made at Sinai just as were the later generations of Israelites.[41]

The variety of baptism practised by John included another significance. His baptism was not confined to converts to Judaism but freely included all who wished through repentance to signify their anticipation of the coming Kingdom.[42] It was a symbol of moral cleansing, 'The baptism of repentance unto the remission of sins' (Mk 1[4]), rather than ceremonial or levitical cleansing.[43] It does compare favourably with proselyte baptism in that both were a means of incorporation into communities, whether Israel or the group awaiting the Messiah's advent (cf. Acts 19[1-5]).

(4) *Incorporation and Sacrifice.* The third requirement made of the alien upon admission to Judaism was the presentation of an offering of two doves for a sacrifice. This practice bound all proselytes as long as the existence of the Temple made it feasible. After the Destruction in AD 70 a small monetary substitute was

[38] Cf. H. L. Ginsberg, who notes that the preparation for Israel's reception of the Torah was circumcision, baptism (two days before the Revelation), and sacrifice (*Legends of the Jews* [Philadelphia, 1910-39], III.88).
[39] H. Sahlin, 'The New Exodus of Salvation According to St Paul', *The Root of the Vine*, ed. A. Fridrichsen (Edinburgh, 1953), pp. 88-91. Cf. W. L. Knox, *St Paul and the Church of the Gentiles* (Cambridge, 1939), pp. 87-8.
[40] Op. cit. p. 98.
[41] Note the comment on Deuteronomy 29[14] in *Shebuoth* 39a. Cf. W. Braude, op. cit. p. 30. In a more rationalistic outlook, R. Ashi admitted that the proselytes were actually absent but their stars stood in for them (*Shab* 145b-146a).
[42] C. A. A. Scott, *Christianity According to St Paul*, p. 39, note 1. Cf. O. Cullmann, op. cit. p. 9; H. Sahlin, op. cit. p. 88; Wm. Manson, 'Baptism in the Church', *SJT*, II (1949), p. 392; R. N. Flew, *Jesus and His Church* (2nd edn, London, 1943), p. 37.
[43] E. Schürer, op. cit. p. 324.

E

accepted by the treasury but was later abolished because of the danger of the fund's mismanagement.

Through sacrifice, the proselyte gave allegiance to the Presence of the One God and His chosen place of worship, the Temple. He had subsequently the right of participating in all the sacrificial rites and was included in the atonement of the Red Heifer with the rest of Israel.[44] Regarding the observance of the Passover, Braude significantly points out:

They were included in the first Passover which had been observed in Egypt. Thus we are told that together with the born Jews they were instructed to take a bunch of hyssop, strike the lintel with blood . . . and not go out until the morning. And then when the wrath of God had come upon all Egyptians, high and low, it had not touched the homes of the proselytes who presumably were of Egyptian origin. No wonder that when Pharaoh pleaded with Moses and Aaron that the children of Israel leave his sorely afflicted land, he begged that the proselytes go along too.[45]

Throughout the course of the pronouncements regarding the proselyte's status and its rationale, there is a recognition that the convert is incorporated into the united community of the covenant, which had no regard for temporal or racial distinctions.

(5) *The Status of the Proselyte.* The Rabbis for the most part show a benevolent attitude toward the Gentile proselyte. There are midrashim which compare the convert to a planted vine in contrast to the nations which were cast out. The proselytes become roots just like Israel.[46] They become, upon their incorporation into Israel, as a new-born babe.[47] He that persuades a Gentile to become a proselyte is equivalent to having created him.[48] It is not uncommon to encounter references to proselytes as the children of Abraham. A typical Rabbinic example of exegesis made biblical support comparatively easy to find. Thus, in a comment on Genesis 21[7] ('Who would have said unto Abraham that Sarah would have given suck to children?') one reads: 'The

[44] W. Braude, op. cit. pp. 84-5.

[45] Ibid. p. 88 and references.

[46] *Lev R* 1[2] with the explanation of Psalm 80[8]. Note J. Israelstam's comment in Vol. IV of the *Midrash Rabba* (Socino edn, London, 1939), p. 4 note 1. Cf. *Num R* 8[2]. See C. G. Montefiore in *RA*, p. 566.

[47] Just as Israel became at the reception of the Torah. Cf. W. Braude, op. cit. p. 88.

[48] *Gen R* 39[14].

Gentiles brought their children to Sarah that she might nurse them. . . . R. Levi said: Those who came in truth became proselytes, they became children with Israel; the others became great people in the world.'[49] When the proselyte brought his offering of the firstfruits, he was allowed to say along with the Israelite, 'I am come unto the land which the Lord swore unto our fathers to give us', on the grounds that God had told Abraham: 'The father of a multitude of nations have I made thee' (Gen 17[5]). 'He thus became the father of all the people that had taken shelter under the wings of the Shekinah. And it was after all unto Abraham that the promise had first been made that his "children" would inherit the land.'[50] This evidence contradicts Lietzmann's opinion that the proselyte was never given a status comparable to the natural Israelite.[51] J. Klausner is nearer the truth in his contention that 'Judaism in the days of the Second Temple, and after, made Gentile proselytes "sons of the covenant" in such a manner that they were absorbed into the *Jewish national community*'.[52]

It is of the utmost importance for the purpose of this study to note that the very idea underlying the practice of initiation is the presuppositional unity of Israel. It is the benevolent extension of privileges which accrue to the proselyte with which the Rabbis were concerned. These were not offered apart from the Gentile's becoming a true Israelite.[53] The universalism which this possibility suggests, in no way erases the line of demarcation separating Israel from the Nations.[54] It does make crossing the line a possibility.[55] This attitude makes the Rabbinic figure of the proselyte under the 'wings of the Shekinah'[56] particularly appropriate. The Presence was the particular divine gift to

---

[49] *Pes R* 180a, from *RA*, p. 574. Cf. *Num R* 8[3]; and F. Weber, *Jüdische Theologie* (Leipzig, 1897), p. 77. Although some of F. Weber's conclusions are suspect, his studies in Jewish thought are valuable guides to the location of Rabbinic statements.

[50] *Midrash Tannaim*, ed. Hoffmann (Berlin, 1908-9), p. 172, quoted in W. Braude, op. cit. p. 84. Cf. Strack and Billerbeck, op. cit. III.195-6.

[51] *The Beginnings of the Christian Church* (New York, 1949), p. 83.

[52] *From Jesus to Paul*, pp. 534-5.

[53] He must be included in the covenant. The school of Hillel says: 'He that separates himself from his uncircumcision is as one that separates himself from the grave' (*M Eduyoth* 5[2]).

[54] G. Guignebert comments wryly: 'It can be said with perfect truth that in Palestine, universalism was nothing more than an extension of particularism, implying the absorption of the Gentile world by the Chosen People' (op. cit. p. 157). Cf. G. Johnston, op. cit. p. 26.

[55] M. Kadushin, *The Rabbinic Mind*, p. 293.

[56] *Mek* II.186, *Lev R* 1[2].

Israel, signifying God's personal interest in Israel's welfare. The proselyte through his new status partook of this incomparably blessed relationship to the One God.

Besides this, a further implication of this figure was the characteristic of Kedushah (holiness). According to *Numbers Rabba* 8[2], the proselyte is described in terms of גרי הצדק. Even the children of proselytes are said to be born 'in Kedushah'.[57] Moreover, the pedigreed Israelite is not allowed to deride the descendant of a proselyte with the taunt, 'Remember the deeds of thy fathers',[58] for because of his new status, they no longer are his fathers. He is to be considered as a new-born child[59] of Abraham, whose deeds previous to conversion carry no more responsibility than the deeds of a child prior to birth.[60]

The realism used to describe the status of the proselyte as a 'Son of the Covenant' casts into relief the exclusion of the *Metuentes* (God-fearer) from Israel. This is not to say that a certain amount of goodwill was not extended to God-fearers, but they were considered to be on the outside, the fringe of Judaism (cf. Acts 10[2]).[61] Undoubtedly, the community of feeling with Gentiles who had adopted the broad ethical and religious ideals of Judaism was strong. It was produced by the contrast of friendship versus the animosity which characterized normal Jewish and Gentile relations.[62] But they were not included in the concept of 'Israel', the statement, 'He who renounces idol worship may be called a Jew',[63] notwithstanding. One who was not circumcised or immersed was not a proselyte,[64] and consequently not eligible for consideration as an initiate into the community.

[57] *M Yeb* 11[2], *Yeb* 87a-b and 47a. Cf. O. Cullmann, op. cit. p. 25; Strack-Billerbeck, op. cit. I.110-12.

[58] *M Baba Met* 4[10]. Cf. *Num R* 8[2]; W. Braude, op. cit. p. 14.

[59] *Yeb* 62a, 48b, *Ger* 2[6]. F. Gavin, op. cit. p. 51. Just how radically the proselyte was cut off from previous relationships, was a matter of serious Rabbinic discussion. Generally they insisted on a clean break to the extent that the Gentile mate was divorced and a new Jewish marriage was contracted. E. von Dobschütz, *Christian Life in the Primitive Church*, trans. G. Bremner (London, 1940), p. 31. Other passages insist on so complete a severance that even marriage to one's sister was tolerated without the charge of incest (*Yeb* 62a and 22a).

[60] Cf. Strack and Billerbeck, op. cit. II.421-2.

[61] W. Braude, op. cit. p. 138.

[62] On this point see S. Hanson, op. cit. p. 9. Cf. Bousset, op. cit. pp. 92-6.

[63] *Meg* 13a. The point is probably more homiletical than a designation of proselyte status. Note e.g. *M Neg* 3[1] and H. Danby, *The Mishnah* (Oxford, 1933), p. 356 note 9. The precise purpose of the revelation of the unclean animals to Peter in Joppa was to break down his prejudice against coming into contact with Cornelius, a God-fearer. Note Acts 10[28] and 11[2] for opinions regarding the God-fearer.

[64] *Ber* 47b.

To be accepted into the covenant implies subjection to the yoke of the commandments.[65] The God-fearer did not accept the yoke.

A different type of proselyte is encountered in the initiate to the community of the New Covenant. They are the fourth and last group in a series of categories including priests, Levites, Israelites, and proselytes. There is reason to agree with Rowley that the converts in question were Jewish rather than Gentile, due to the party's strict shunning of Gentile relationships.[66] They were persons who had not yet been admitted to full membership.[67] Their goal, however, was clear, namely, to become a part of the true Israel.[68] The Manual of Discipline prescribes a long period of initiation for the neophyte which was spoken of as incorporation into the covenant.[69] Elementary communism and a dedicated study of the Torah was the common lot of the community under the rule of the Inspector.[70] The eschatological character of the community of the Covenanters is seen in their imminent expectation of the 'coming prophet and the anointed ones of Aaron and Israel'.[71]

Although there are distinctions to be noted in the three major groups, (1) racial Jews, (2) Gentile proselytes, (3) and the neophyte in the Community of the New Covenant, there is one main point upon which they all agree. To be a true Israelite, one must be incorporated into the historic covenant of Israel. Thus the fundamental conception of the bond of the unity of Judaism, is the covenant. This unity transcends even the closest religious and kinship ties, which brings us to a point where we may consider the implications of this organic unity binding Israel together.

[65] Cf. A. Büchler, op. cit. p. 20.
[66] 'The Covenanters of Damascus and the Dead Sea Scrolls', BJRL, XXXV (1952-3), p. 127.
[67] The Dead Sea Manual of Discipline, trans. and notes by W. H. Brownlee (New Haven, Conn., 1951), p. 10 (col. 3 lines 20ff) notes only three divisions. See ibid. p. 11 note 21.
[68] See the DSD, col. 5 line 22, and W. H. Brownlee, op. cit. p. 22 note 52. Cf. R. H. Charles, APOT, II.785.
[69] Cf. ibid. col. 5 lines 8, 20; ed. 2 lines 20ff.
[70] Ibid. col. 6². Cf. further Cols. 5.3-7.7; A. Dupont-Sommer, The Dead Sea Scrolls, trans. M. Rowley (Oxford, 1952), p. 50. The neophyte was also baptized and given instruction (Cols. 3.6-9 and 5.13-14). Cf. G. E. Wright, The Biblical Doctrine of Man in Society pp. 89-90.
[71] Ibid. col. 9.11. Cf. W. H. Brownlee, op. cit. p. 50.

THE ORGANIC CONTINUITY OF ISRAEL

The post-biblical conceptions of the continuity of Israel show some striking similarities to those of the Old Testament. The idea of a single life which pervaded Israel from its national inception down through all time was not lost. The realism of the primitive Hebrew thought-world, in the days of the Second Temple, became incorporated into the liturgy of Judaism. Thus, in the most ancient Kaddish of Jewish liturgy, this petition occurs: 'May He establish His kingdom in your life-time and in your days, and in the *life-time* of all the house of Israel speedily and in a near time'[72] In a characteristic eulogy of Israel this statement is ascribed to God: 'And I have chosen the seed of Jacob from among all that I have seen and have written *him* down as my first-born son, and I have sanctified *him* unto myself for ever and ever, and I will teach *them* the Sabbath. . . .'[73] As the sanctification of the divine Name is eternal, it requires the unending continuity of Israel to sanctify it.

The conception of the organic continuity of the nation was founded upon two factors. (1) An unbroken line of life reached back from every Israelite to Abraham. The writer of 2 *Baruch* illustrates this idea: 'And truly I know that behold all we the twelve tribes are bound by one bond, inasmuch as we are born from one father' (78[4]).[74] The bond of heredity is the single life which all the descendants of Abraham share in common. (2) Along with heredity was the spiritual bond of the covenant into which every Israelite was incorporated through circumcision. The covenant provided as Bousset has said, a 'spiritual unity' of all Israel and can only adequately be described as a community whose organization crosses political and social boundaries.[75] It did more. It gave to each individual a realistic link with the past as well as the future on a spiritual level.

It will be illuminating to present the evidence of the Jewish conception of 'continuous contemporaneity' from liturgical formulae and festival ritual. Josephus assumes that the command

---

[72] Cf. W. O. E. Oesterley, *The Jewish Background of the Christian Liturgy* (Oxford, 1925), p. 73. Cf. *Pss of Sol* 13[9].

[73] *Jub* 2[20]. Incidentally, this is a good illustration of oscillation in post-biblical literature (109-105 B C).

[74] The *Book of Jubilees* traces the race back to Adam, thus enhancing the antiquity and prestige of Israel. Cf. G. Johnston, op. cit. p. 26.

[75] Op. cit. p. 71.

to recite the Shema twice daily originated with Moses. Consequently, he depicts Moses as enjoining: 'Let every one commemorate before God the benefits which he bestowed on them at *their* deliverance out of the land of Egypt. . . .'[76] The idea of all generations partaking in the Exodus is more explicit in a saying of R. Gamaliel:

In every generation a man must so regard himself as if he came forth himself out of Egypt, for it is written, 'And thou shalt tell thy son in that day saying, It is because of that which the Lord did for me when I came forth out of Egypt (Ex 13[8]).[77] Therefore are we bound to give thanks, to praise, to glorify, to honour, to exalt, to extol and to bless him who wrought all these wonders for our fathers, and *for us*. He brought us out from bondage to freedom, from sorrow to gladness, and from mourning to a Festive-day, and from darkness to a great light, and from servitude to redemption; so let us say before him the Hallelujah.[78]

R. Akiba in turn adds to the *Hallel* in a prayer of thanksgiving: '. . . Let us praise thee for our redemption and for the ransoming of our soul. Blessed are Thou, O Lord, for Thou hast redeemed Israel.'[79]

In the rules prescribed for the Passover observance contained in the *haggada shel pesah* the response to be given to the son's question concerning the meaning of the Passover ritual is as follows: 'We were slaves to thc Pharaoh in Egypt, and the Lord our God brought us forth from thence with a strong hand and outstretched arm.'[80] The implication of the inclusion of the later generations in the Exodus is poignantly recited in the condemnation of the wicked son who has asked: 'What mean you by this service?' (Ex 12[26]). 'When he thus says "you" he purposely excludes himself and so rejects one of the principles of Judaism. Therefore mayest thou retort upon him by quoting: "This is done because of that which the Lord did for *me* when *I* came forth from Egypt" (Ex. 13[8]).'[81]

[76] *Jewish Antiquities*, Bk. iv.212 (*LoClL*, IV.576).
[77] This whole sentence is omitted by the older sources. H. Danby, op. cit. p. 151 note 1.
[78] *M Pes* 10[5], cf. *haggada shel pesah* in *The Revised Hagada* (A. A. Green), p. 51; T. H. Gaster, op. cit. p. 63. M. Kadushin terms this a Rabbinic dogma (*The Rabbinic Mind*, p. 360).
[79] *M Pes* 10[6]. Cf. the 'Litany of Wonders': 'If He had cleft the Sea for *us*, nor let *us* pass dryshod, dayyenu! If He had let *us* pass dryshod, nor sunk *our* foes therein, dayyenu!', etc. (T. H. Gaster, op. cit. pp. 62-3).
[80] A. A. Green, op. cit. p. 27. Cf. 4 *Ezra* 8[22], 2 *Bar* 75[7-8].
[81] A. A. Green, op. cit. p. 31. Cf. T. H. Gaster, op. cit. p. 59.

The same conception of contemporaneity which was accorded the redemption from Egypt was also applied to the election of Israel. Thus the Abadah in its ancient and more or less original form includes this declaration: '. . . And us hast thou chosen from every people and tongue, and hast brought us near unto Thy great Name. . . .'[82] Actually, the election, the Exodus, and the reception of the Torah were interwoven so that the denial of the yoke of the Torah was declared to be the denial of all the others. Thus, he who denies the *mizwot* is deprecated as a denier of the Exodus from Egypt.[83] The basis of such a denunciation was the contemporaneity of Israel's acknowledgement of the Torah. For this reason, the Jewish teachers attempted to emphasize the literal sense in which Israel would die if she failed to observe the Torah[84] which as the denial of the Exodus meant also the dissolution of Israel.

The preceding discussion and quotations evince the conception of a vertical dimension in the unity of Israel. Through the enactment of circumcision and the partaking of the Passover feast, the Israelite of any given generation became realistically united with his ancestors and their actual experience became his own. The strength of the living bond uniting the members of the race with those yet to be born, became influential in the increasing hope for immortality. Davies is probably correct in attributing the unattractiveness of individual immortality to the Jewish sense of the oneness of the nation. As in the attitude toward the past, the aspirations for the future were modified strictly by the sense of a racial and spiritual solidarity.[85] Thus the writer of 4 *Ezra* says:

And I said, But lo, O Lord, thou art ready to meet (with blessing) those who survive in the end. But what shall our predecessors do, or we ourselves or our posterity? And he said unto me: I shall liken my judgement to a ring; just as there is no retardation of them that are last, even so there is no hastening of those that are first.[86]

[82] Cf. W. O. E. Oesterley, op. cit. p. 49.

[83] *Sifra on Lev* 11[45], ed. Weiss, p. 57b, in M. Kadushin, *The Rabbinic Mind*, p. 358.

[84] *Cant R* 2.2 par 6. Cf. *RA*, pp. 118 and 672 note 37. 'We who have received the Law and sinned must perish, together with our heart, which has taken it in; the Law, however, perishes not, but abides in its glory' (4 *Ez* 9[36]).

[85] Op. cit. p. 83. Cf. G. F. Moore, op. cit. II.367; A. Cohen, op. cit. p. 376. For the Old Testament conception, see A. B. Davidson, *The Theology of the Old Testament*, p. 244.

[86] 5[41-2]. G. H. Box comments: 'Just as in the case of a circle there is neither beginning nor end, so God's judgement will reach all generations at one and the same time' (*APOT*, op. cit. II.573; cf. 2 Bar 51[13]).

What in the Old Testament had been a primary emphasis on the immortality of the individual through racial continuity, became in the post-biblical literature an expectation of individual participation in the Kingdom community by means of the final resurrection. But the idea of salvation 'was indissolubly linked with the salvation of the people'.[87] Thus, the conception of the unity of Israel and her continuity culminated in the eschatological Day of the Lord, the revelation of the Messiah, the resurrection of the righteous,[88] and the inauguration of the eternal Kingdom.[89] This explains R. Joshua's comparison of Israel to a tree: 'Why is Israel likened to an olive-tree? To tell you that as the olive-tree loses not its leaves either in summer or winter, so Israel shall never be lost either in this world or in the world to come.'[90] R. Meir argued moreover: 'If to the oxen which were attached by the hand of man to the work of the tabernacle, God gave continued existence throughout all ages, how much more Israel who cleave to the Eternal. . . .'[91] Thus, the continuity of Israel was founded in the contemporaneity of her election and redemption historically, but reached into the future eschatologically. As the solidarity of Israel eliminated the demarcation between individuals, the covenant guaranteed the continuity of Israel and eliminated the demarcation of death between successive generations. The fullness of its implications was expected to be realized in the final resurrection.

THE IMPLICATIONS OF NATIONAL UNITY AND
CONTINUITY IN THE SOLIDARITY OF ISRAEL

(1) *The Accessibility of the Zachuth of the Fathers to all Israel.* The most frequently encountered implication of the solidarity of Israel because of its continuity is the notion that the merit[92] of the Fathers is shared by succeeding generations of Israel. The emphasis of

---

[87] G. F. Moore, op. cit. II.312-13.
[88] *Ber* 18b. Cf. *supra*, p. 58.
[89] See the *Test Judah*, ch. 25, *Test Zeb*, 10[2], *Test Ben* 10[7].
[90] *Men* 53b. Cf. Ecclus 14[18]: 'As the leaf that groweth on a luxuriant tree, one fadeth, and another sprouteth; So (are) the generations of flesh and blood, One dieth and another flourisheth.'
[91] *Cant R* 6[5].
[92] זכות is 'virtue', 'righteousness', 'good desert', as in *M Aboth* 2[2], but means 'acquittal' in a legal sense. In a theological sense, it may refer to something that has a protective or atoning value. It came to mean 'for the sake of'. See G. F. Moore, op. cit. III.164 and S. Schechter, op. cit. p. 171.

the Old Testament on the extension of God's love to Israel because of His love for the forefathers gained a full-blown expansion in the Rabbinic doctrine of the *Zachuth Aboth*.

As only merit of the highest perfection was of lasting benefit,[93] the singular holiness of Abraham was credited for Israel's partaking of many good things. This *zachuth* was personal and objective; that is, the Rabbis believed the merit of the Fathers to stem from their own personal righteousness.[94] Thus, it was for the sake of the patriarch Abraham that all the signal interventions (נסים) on Israel's behalf were wrought.[95] So great was the merit of Abraham that the redemption of Israel was accomplished on that account.[96] The parting of the Red Sea was ascribed by R. Shemaiah to the merit of the faith of Abraham.[97] More unusual is the pronouncement: 'Likewise did God create Adam for the merit of Abraham, as it is said, "Thou knowest my sitting in the garden of Eden; Mine uprising (i.e. my exile therefrom). Thou knowest for whose merit Thou hast taken counsel to create me, for the merit of his who comes from afar (i.e. Abraham), as it is said, "From a far country a man of his counsel".'[98] As the Rabbis encountered no difficulty in ascribing prescient knowledge to God, it was natural for them to proleptically account for an effect through a temporarily subsequent cause. Finally, when in the Messianic Age, Israel is privileged to sing a new song, it will be in consequence to Abraham's trust in God (cf. Gen 15[6]).[99]

Of the meritorious actions of the Patriarchs, the most notable in all regards was the offering of Isaac. As a result of this exemplary obedience, Abraham found himself in a position to bargain with God over the welfare of his progeny: 'I subdued my feelings and carried out thy command. So may it be acceptable before Thee, O Lord God, that when the descendants of my son Isaac are afflicted by trouble and there is nobody to speak in their defence, do Thou defend them.'[100] The Rabbinic literature makes a great deal of the voluntary character of the offering on Isaac's

---

[93] Cf. S. Schechter, op. cit. p. 182.
[94] A. Marmorstein, op. cit. p. 65.
[95] Cf. G. F. Moore, op. cit. I.538-9.
[96] *Mek* I.219-20.
[97] See A. Marmorstein, op. cit. p. 47.
[98] *Gen R* 15[4]. Cf. A. Marmorstein, op. cit. p. 135; *RA*, p. 38. There are opinions declared by the Rabbis to the effect that the world was created because of Abraham (*Gen R* 1[7], 12[2, 9]).
[99] *Ex R* 23[5].
[100] *Gen R* 56[10], *Lev R* 29[9]. Cf. A. Cohen, op. cit. p. 123; see *Jubilees* 18[15-16].

part. Instead of a child or youth, Isaac is considered to have been a man in the fullness of his strength, whom the aged father could not have bound against his will.[101] So unique was the self-surrender of Isaac that 'the binding' became elevated to a liturgical position.[102] The Midrash goes to the length of claiming that the binding of Isaac atones for the sins of Israel.[103] Thus Isaac was added to the roster, and given a comparable position with Abraham in supplying *zachuth* for the children of Israel. Jacob as the single patriarch who was exclusively the father of the nation of Israel completed the number of the 'Fathers'.

The high esteem accorded the *zachuth* of the Fathers was probably due to the intercessory prayer of Moses (cf. Ex 32[13]). It was explained that when Israel sinned in the desert (by worshipping the golden calf) Moses entreated God for forgiveness with many prayers and supplications but was unheeded. Even the forty days and the forty nights were of no avail until he said, 'Remember Abraham, Isaac, and Jacob thy servants', and his prayer was heard at once.[104] It is little wonder that the writer of the Testament of Levi was constrained to conclude: '. . . But for the sake of Abraham and Isaac and Jacob your fathers, not one of my posterity should be left on earth.'[105] There was scarcely any limit to which the merit of the Fathers might not extend. Solomon, before he sinned, earned his own *zachuth*, but subsequently was dependent upon the merit of his ancestors. Even the world was created for the sake of the Patriarchs.[106] The very continuance of the Chosen Nation is due to the goodwill earned by the patriarchs. Therefore, the Midrash blandly states: 'Israel lives and endures, because it supports itself on the Fathers.'[107]

Another Rabbi, recognizing the evil of his contemporaries, commented on Song of Songs 1[5]: 'I am black, but comely,' thus, 'The congregation of Israel speaks: I am black through mine own works, but comely on account of the deeds of my ancestors.'[108]

[101] Cf. G. F. Moore, op. cit. I.539.

[102] Cf. H. Loewe's remarks in *RA*, p. ci.

[103] *Cant R* 1[14] par. 1. Cf. *Ex R* 44[5]. See H. J. Schoeps, 'The Sacrifice of Isaac in Paul's Theology', trans. R. H. Pfeiffer, *JBL*, LXV (1946), pp. 385-6 *passim*.

[104] *Shab* 42a. Cf. *Ex R* 44[1]; S. Schechter, op. cit. p. 174; W. D. Davies, op. cit. p. 271.

[105] 15[4].

[106] *Bar* 21[24]. Less exclusive are *Ass. of Mos.* 1[11-12], 4 *Ez* 6[55, 59], 7[11], 2 *Bar* 14[19], 15[7], 21[24], which credit this event to the merit of Israel. Cf. R. H. Charles, *APOT*, I.415.

[107] *Ex R* 44[1].

[108] *Ex R* 23[10]. Cf. Strack and Billerbeck, op. cit. I.118.

Although the emphasis which the Rabbis placed upon individual responsibility was too great to give wide support to the idea that future salvation was assured all Israelites independently of their own righteousness,[109] apparently it was a common lay opinion that access to the merit of Abraham was sufficient for sharing in the World to Come. These benefits were seen in a hereditary light primarily. What the Jewish teachers were hesitant to state, John the Baptist openly ascribes to his audience, namely, the opinion that repentance was unnecessary for a son of Abraham.[110] In the Rabbinic literature, the redemption of Israel is more often posited on the basis of the merits of the fathers in conjunction with other *piacula*.[111]

Less frequently, appeal was made to the good desert of the tribal ancestors or Israel's great leaders of the past. That there was *zachuth* available from Judah that the tribe might become worthy of the honour of bearing the sceptre was a deduction drawn by R. Tarfon.[112] The *Mekilta* tells of an opinion regarding the dividing of the Red Sea in consequence of the merit of Joseph.[113] R. Nehemiah (AD 140-65) contended that the redemption from Egypt was the result of the accumulated merit of Moses and Aaron.[114] With more regard for the Bible, another Jewish teacher saw the deliverance of Jerusalem from Sennacherib as a direct consequence of the merit of David.[115]

R. Eliezer b. Jacob was more impressed with the possibility of a diffused merit coming from contemporaries. 'There is no generation which has not got a just man like Abraham, like Jacob, like Moses, and like Samuel'[116] was his opinion. Another statement of the Midrash claims that the world exists for the merit of the righteous and there is no generation lacking such men.[117] The conception of a 'contemporary *zachuth*'[118] lent itself to hortatory

---

[109] Cf. A. Cohen, op. cit. p. 123. Cf. *M Pes* 10¹; John 8³³, ὅτι ἐλεύθεροι γενήσθε. Cf. John 8³⁹.

[110] Cf. Luke 3⁸. Cf. W. D. Davies, op. cit. pp. 269-70.

[111] Cf. H. Loewe, *RA*, pp. 229-30; Strack and Billerbeck, op. cit. I.116-21. Thus, Moore states: 'Salvation is assured every Israelite on the basis of the election of the nation by the free grace of God—not of merit but love of God which began with the fathers' (op. cit. II.94-5. Cf. S. Schechter, op. cit. p. 174).

[112] *Mek* I.236.

[113] *Mek* I.220.

[114] *Ex R* 15³⁻⁴.

[115] *Ber* 10b. Cf. 2 Kings 19³⁴.

[116] *Gen R* 56⁹. Cf. *Num R* 3¹; W. D. Davies, op. cit. pp. 270-1.

[117] *Gen R* 74². Cf. A. Marmorstein, op. cit. p. 57; H. Loewe, *RA*, op. cit. p. 231.

[118] Cf. S. Schechter, op. cit. pp. 190-5.

exploitation more readily than the notion of merit acquired from the past. It is probable that the author is appealing to patriotic and altruistic instincts when he declares: 'If there is one righteous man among you, you will all be sustained by his merit, and not only you alone, but also the whole world. . . .'[119]

Other Rabbis, seeing an inconsistency in the justice of the corporate application of merit controvert the majority opinion. Such was R. Hanina b. Gamaliel who said: 'Merit and guilt are never interchanged, except in the case of Reuben and David.'[120] In any case, the Early Jewish conception of a transferable *zachuth* is quite different from the Roman Catholic doctrine of the virtuous action cancelling culpability. The Rabbis maintain that the merit of the ancestors or contemporaries is only the ground upon which God acts with favour toward Israel collectively, without any idea of a measurable amount of merit which may be tapped individually when the occasion arises.[121] The Doctrine of Merit is clearly founded upon the solidarity of the community.[122]

(2) *The Expiatory Value of the Suffering of Righteous Martyrs.* Out of the same thought-background and possibly under the influence of the theme of the Songs of the Servant, comes the conception of the atoning value of the deaths of Israel's martyrs.[123] Specific support for this view was deduced from 2 Samuel 21[14]: 'They buried the bones of Saul and Jonathan . . . and after that God was entreated for the land.'[124] But more basically, the idea of justice was involved. Thus, Baruch is chagrined at the apparent injustice of God who is allowing Zion to go into captivity in spite of those within her walls who '. . . always feared Thee, and have not left Thy ways'.[125] As Abraham had argued over the destruction of Sodom, Baruch continues: 'And if others did evil (within Jerusalem), it was due to Zion, that on account of the works of those who wrought good works she should be forgiven, and should not be overwhelmed on account of the works of those who wrought unrighteousness.'[126] But one more step was needed to arrive at

---

[119] Cf. ibid. p. 191 and refs. See also *M Sanh* 8[5] and H. L. Ginsberg, op. cit. V.67.
[120] *Sifra Deut* par. 347.
[121] Cf. G. F. Moore, op. cit. I.543; F. Jackson and K. Lake, op. cit. I.70.
[122] Cf. W. D. Davies, op. cit. p. 206.
[123] Cf. H. Loewe, *RA*, p. ci.
[124] Cf. G. F. Moore, op. cit. III.164-5.
[125] 2 *Bar* 14[5-6, 8].
[126] Ibid. 14[7].

the conclusions drawn in the histories of the Maccabees. The prayer of one of the seven brothers martyred by Antiochus is very significant:

I, like my brothers, give up body and soul for our fathers' laws calling on God to show favour to our nation soon . . . and to let the Almighty's wrath, justly fallen on the whole of our nation, end in me and my brothers.[127]

An identical conception is reflected in the prayer recorded in 4 *Maccabees*:

Be gracious to Thy people, being satisfied with our penalty on their behalf. Make my blood their purification and take my life as the substitute for theirs. Because of them the enemy hath no more power over our people, and the tyrant was punished, and the fatherland purified, inasmuch as they have become a substitute (for the life forfeited by) the sin of the people; and through the blood of these pious men and their propitiatory death, the divine Providence rescued Israel that before was afflicted.[128]

The underlying conception in these prayers and comments is the idea of the accessibility of the benefits of vicarious substitution within the confines of the nation.[129] Because of the unity of Israel and the unquestionable justice of God, the unmerited suffering of the righteous martyrs provides atonement and propitiation for the unrighteous within the group. This is more than a wider application of the Doctrine of Merits; it is the elevation of the conception of the vicarious substitutionary atonement from a commonplace in the Jewish sacrificial system, coupled with divine justice rigidly defined, to conclude in a doctrine of expiation through human suffering or death.

There is an identical principle involved in the controverted and problematic Jewish conceptions of a Suffering Messiah.[130] Such a statement as the *Testament of Benjamin* claims to preserve from the mouth of Jacob in dialogue with Joseph bears this out:

[127] 2 *Macc* 7[37-8]. Cf. also 7[32], 'We are suffering this on our own account . . .' doubtless refers to Israel as a whole.

[128] 6[28-9], 17[21-2]. Cf. comparable parallels in the Rabbis, e.g. *Lev R* 20[12] and *Mo'ed Katon* 28a. On the conception of the expiatory value of death see *M Yoma* 8[8-9], *M Sanh* 6[2]; A. Cohen, op. cit. p. 114; R. B. Townshend, *APOT*, II.663-4.

[129] Cf. H. W. Robinson, *The Cross of the Servant* (London, 1926), p. 61. Robinson sees in this passage an example of the martyrs' acceptance of Israel's corporate personality (ibid. pp. 59ff). Note further the discussions of G. F. Moore, op. cit. III.166, and F. Weber, *SASPT*, pp. 267-294.

[130] See W. D. Davies's appraisal, op. cit. pp. 276-84.

'In thee shall be fulfilled the prophecy of heaven [concerning the Lamb of God and Saviour of the world], that a blameless one shall be delivered up for lawless men, and a sinless (one) shall die for ungodly men [in the blood of the covenant, for the salvation of the Gentiles and of Israel and shall destroy Beliar and his servants].'[131] The context leaves no doubt that the 'lawless' men are Joseph's own brothers.[132] Thus, this passage still maintains that the transference of the penalty will remain within the group of Israel. It is not an instance of a pious man voluntarily accepting the sin of others by becoming one with them in experience on moral lines rather than on the basis of physical association, or racial-covenantal lines. This last step remains to be taken by the New Testament.

In the later eschatological speculation, the expectation of a Messiah who would come and through his suffering produce atonement, becomes more prominent.[133] One example is found in the *Pesikta Rabati*:

Great will be the suffering which the Messiah of the tribe of Ephraim has to undergo for seven years at the hand of the nations, who lay iron beams upon him to crush him so that his cries reach heaven; but he willingly submits for the sake of his people, not only those living, but also the dead, for all those who died since Adam; and God places the four beasts of the heavenly throne-chariot at his disposal to bring about the great work of resurrection and regeneration against all the celestial antagonists.[134]

Although there is no conclusive proof, a strong suspicion has been raised to the effect that the speculation regarding the suffering[135] of the Messiah received some of its impetus from Christian doctrine. C. C. Torrey vigorously denies this position.[136] Certainly

[131] 38. The brackets denote what R. H. Charles considers to be obvious Christian interpolations. Cf. *The Testaments of the Twelve Patriarchs* (London, 1917), p. vi.
[132] Compare the reference to the rest of Israel as the domain of Belial, in the *DSD, passim*.
[133] Cf. M. J. Lagrange, *Le Messianisme chez les Juifs* (Paris, 1909), pp. 236-7. For citations from the Rabbis, see *RA*, pp. 584-6. See G. H. Dix, 'The Messiah ben Joseph', *JTS*, XXVII (1926), for the origins of the conception of the suffering Messiah. Besides the line of proof offered by E. G. King in his appendix to the *Yalkut on Zechariah*, there is an indication to be found in Genesis 49 and the *Testament of Benjamin*. G. H. Dix, op. cit. pp. 130-1.
[134] 36, in K. Kohler, 'Eschatology', *JE*, V.215.
[135] Cf. Zech 12¹⁰ (cf. *Suk* 52a), Isa 53 (see Justin's *Dialogue with Trypho*, chs. 68, 89-90; *Sanh* 98b refers to the Messiah as the 'Leper' (*hiwwara*, cf. Isa 53⁴); Ps 22⁸⁻¹⁶ (cf. *Pes R* 37). See W. D. Davies, op. cit. pp. 280-4. For the confusion between the Messiahs of Joseph and Judah, see K. Kohler, *JE*, V.215.
[136] 'The Messiah Son of Ephraim', *JBL*, LXVI (1947), p. 257.

the idea was latent in the Old Testament. Moreover, the cases of the Maccabean martyrs may have stimulated the idea of an all-inclusive vicarious atonement by so prominent a figure as the Messiah b. Ephraim. It is of more than general interest to note that the suffering of the Ephraimite Messiah produces atonement also for the dead, and that going back as far as Adam. This merit did not, of course, avail the wicked, but there is reason to think that the resurrection was expected to include all of the righteous, extending even beyond the national confines of Israel. Although the evidence is inconclusive, there is the suggestion of a solidarity which binds all the righteous of all time together.[137]

The Jewish conceptions of the corporate sharing in an ancestor's merit or the atoning value of the death of righteous martyrs was born in the matrix of the self-consciousness of the mysterious unity of Israel. The awareness of this solidarity coupled with an unswerving confidence in the justice and mercy of God led to these fundamental elements of Jewish thought.

(3) *The Corporate Implication of Israel in the Sin or Demerit of a Member.* A corollary to the conception of corporate merit was the conception of the united group sharing in the guilt, defilement, or penalty, deserved by a member or segment of Israel. Because suffering in the Jewish mind was invariably integrated with chastisement,[138] no alternative to the explanation that the righteous shared the demerit of the wicked occurred to the Jewish thinkers, since in fact the innocent do suffer. Beyond the evidence deduced from Israel's historical experience, the Scriptures themselves spoke directly of the judgement of God upon sons for the iniquity of the fathers. Thus, sin became the direct counterpart of the *zachuth* of the ancestors, prompting Marmorstein to speak of a treasure of good or bad deeds, the fruits of which differed according to the character of the action.[139]

The Rabbinic subscription to the inviolable justice of God was difficult to square with the suffering of the righteous.[140] Some

---

[137] Primary reference was made to Israel, but E. Schürer traces the universalizing tendancy of the Messianism of this period which included all mankind in its scope; op. cit. pp. 130-1. Cf. 4 *Ez* 7[29, 32].

[138] 'There is no suffering without iniquity' is the categorical Jewish conviction. Cf. *Shab* 55a-b, *Sanh* 90a.

[139] Op. cit. p. 7.

[140] M. Kadushin claims that one of the four fundamental concepts of the Rabbis was the justice of God. Cf. *Organic Thinking, passim.*

adopted the position that although Moses had said, 'Visiting the iniquities of the fathers upon the children', Ezekiel came and annulled it, saying: 'The soul that sinneth, it shall die.'[141] But this solution solved nothing, since in fact the innocent suffered with the sinners. This led to the explanation that one's lot at present was not dependent upon one's righteousness or wickedness; the World to Come would settle accounts.[142] But these explanations did not become universal, for they assumed an independent individualism which ran counter to the ingrained conception of the solidarity of Israel.

The starting-point of the more traditional doctrine of the corporate responsibility of each individual was the maxim: 'All Israel are a surety, one for another.'[143] This precept was developed in its ethical connotation to emphasize the importance of the interaction of human influence. The interpretation of Leviticus 26[37], 'and they shall stumble one upon another', was thus given: 'One (will stumble) through the sin of the other, which teaches that all are held responsible for one another. There the reference is to such as had the power to restrain (their fellow men from evil) but did not.'[144] The Rabbinic reticence in admitting that Achan's children suffered death along with their father was conditioned by the problem of the justice of God, but they were quick to add that the children's presence at the execution was essential because of its deterring effect on evil actions.[145]

The corporate responsibility of the Israelites stemmed from the giving of the Torah:

Ye stand this day, all of you, before the Lord, all the men of Israel (Deut 29[10]). All of you are pledges one for the other: if there be but one righteous man among you, you exist all of you through his merit, and not you alone, but the whole world, as it says: 'And the righteous is the foundation of the world (Prov 10[25]). If one man sins, the whole generation suffers, as was the case with Achan (Josh 22[20]). How much more will the good done by an individual benefit his environment.'[146]

141 *Mak* 24a. Cf. *Num R* 19[33].
142 Cf. A. Marmorstein, op. cit. p. 34. Cf. S. Levy, *Original Virtue and other Short Studies* (London, 1907), p. 51.
143 Cf. *Num R* 10[5]; S. Schechter, op. cit. p. 191.
144 *Sanh* 27b. Cf. *Kid* 40a, where the sin that bears fruit is that which spreads, causing others to sin also (*RA*, p. 288.)
145 Cf. *Sanh* 44a; S. Schechter, op. cit. p. 191. G. F. Moore, op. cit. I.471.
146 *Tanh B, Nizzabim* 25a in *RA*, p. 221. Cf. A. Marmorstein, op. cit. p. 71.

This citation indicates a departure from the notion of a mere interaction of influence within a group. It is rather a recognition that all Israel will share in the penalty of the sin of one of its members. This is better illustrated in the comments of R. Simeon b. Yohai (AD 140-65) on Numbers 16$^{20-50}$. A number of men sitting in a boat observed one of their companions take an auger and begin to bore a hole beneath his own seat. Upon being required to account for his purpose, he answered: 'What business is it of yours?' But they retorted: 'It is our business, because the water will come in and swamp the boat with us in it.'[147] The same point is made in the Midrash on Song of Songs 6^{11}, employing the figure of nuts. 'How is it with the nuts? you take one out of a heap and all begin to roll and get into commotion. Even so it is with Israel, when one of them is beaten, all feel the blow.'[148] The liability of each member of the community for the actions of all its members was a two-pronged proposition. On the one hand, it required that no deterrent influence might exist; and on the other, it claimed that the judgement of heaven visited the divine wrath upon the wicked and righteous alike within the confines of the group. R. Hezekiah b. Hiyya claimed that the sinning of even one Israelite endangered the whole of Israel.[149]

As in the application of the principle of *zachuth aboth*, corporate justice freely crossed the generation barriers,[150] visiting the sins of the fathers upon the children and causing the penalty of the children's iniquities to be required of their parents. According to the Rabbis, the baneful touch of the guilt which Israel incurred through the worship of the Golden Calf fell on all human succession. In brief: 'There is no generation in which there is not an ounce from the sin of the Golden Calf.'[151] The idea of the children being implicated in the guilt of their forebears is not infrequently encountered in the New Testament. Jesus' disciples inquire: 'Who did sin, this man, or his parents, that he was born blind?' (John 9^2). When Pilate seeks to absolve himself from the guilt of condemning an innocent man, the mob shouts: 'His blood (i.e. guilt) be on us, and upon our children'

---

[147] See G. F. Moore, op. cit. I.471. Cf. *Lev R* 4^6.
[148] *Cant R* 6^{11} par. 1. See also A. Feldman, op. cit. p. 179.
[149] Cf. A. Marmorstein, op. cit. p. 68.
[150] Cf. e.g. 1 *Bar* 1$^{19-20}$, 2$^{1-10}$; *Gen R* 41^{11}.
[151] *Jer T Taanith* 68c in A. Cohen, op. cit. p. 102. *Sanh* 102a limits the effects to twenty-four generations.

(Matt 27[25]). Jesus endorses corporate justice in his denunciation of the scribes and Pharisees, declaring that, 'All the righteous blood shed upon the earth, from the blood of righteous Abel unto the blood of Zacharias son of Barachias . . .' would surely be required of their generation (cf. Matt 23[35-6]).

The discussion thus far shows an affinity to the later Christian doctrine of Original Sin. But there are noteworthy distinctions as we shall see. The pernicious implications of sinful members existing within the Sacred Society resulted in effects which could not be properly limited to the precise offender.

A derived idea from the conception of a corporate contraction of guilt within the group was the uncoerced assumption of sin by innocent or righteous individuals. The example of Moses was archetypal, a source of Rabbinic marvel. Seeing that there was no continuance for Israel, 'He united his life with their life, and he broke the Tables, and he said to God, "They have sinned, and I have sinned. If thou wilt pardon them, pardon me too; but if thou wilt not pardon them, then pardon not me; blot me out of thy book" ' (Ex 32[32]).[152] By such selfless surrender of his own deserved reward of righteousness,[153] Moses set the immortal pattern for successive generations of Israelites in general and the righteous in particular. The challenge to communal responsibility was accepted by Judaism as Israel's liturgical expression amply illustrates.

A classic example of the Jewish awareness of corporate guilt occurs in the sixth benediction of the *Shemoneh 'Esreh*. Oesterley translates from the Babylonian recension:

> Forgive us, our Father, for we have sinned;
> Pardon us, our Father, for we have transgressed,
> For Thou are the God of goodness, Thou dost forgive. . . .[154]

The effective spread of the conception of communal responsibility may have been due in part to the most impressive ritual in ancient Judaism. On the Day of Atonement the high-priest became a stand-in for all of the congregation of Israel. The Mishna describes his role as follows:

---

[152] *Ex R* 46a; cf. 35[4], *Sot* 14a.

[153] Note the promise that God would make of Moses a great nation (Ex 32[10]).

[154] *The Jewish Background of the Christian Liturgy*, p. 63. Note also the Prayer of Azariah, vvs. 5-9, 14.

And the priest stood at the east, with his face westwards, and pressed his two hands on it (i.e. the goat), and made confession; and thus did he speak, O God (lit. Name), I have done iniquity, I have transgressed, I have sinned (הטאתי עויתי פשעתי), before Thee, I and my house. . . . And they responded after him, Blessed be the Name of the glory of His Kingdom for ever and ever.[155]

It is apparent that the assumption of the corporate guilt of the nation by the High-priest is considerably more explicit than the directions require for the observation of the Day of Atonement in Leviticus 16.

The *Selichoth* (i.e. prayers for forgiveness) were both an early and significant element in Jewish liturgy. They were based in their original form on such texts as 2 Samuel 24:14 and Daniel 9[9] and incorporated into the Temple ritual.[156] In these as well as in the forms of confession adopted by the Synagogue worship, an indomitable witness is borne to the strong conception of communal responsibility in Israel. The modern *Authorized Jewish Daily Prayer Book* reflects ancient confessional prayers which date back to the turn of the era, which also emphasize the theme of the corporate implication of all Israel in the sin of individual Israelites.

It is not surprising that the stress placed upon the corporate involvement of the nation in the sin of a part[157] had two opposing effects on the individual awareness of personal guilt. (1) Levison is impressed with the willingness of the Jew to take his stand on the fact of lineal descent from Abraham, and rise or fall with the nation.[158] Thus, it became decreasingly important that individual sin offerings be made, since the national slate which included those sins was wiped clean by the high-priest on the Day of Atonement. (2) On the other hand, it must be recorded to Israel's credit that the reality of corporate implication in sin was genuinely recognized. 'When the community is in distress, a man must not say, I will go home and eat and drink, peace be unto thee, O my Soul; but a man must share with the com-

[155] *Yoma* 3[8].

[156] Cf. W. O. E. Oesterley, *The Jewish Background of the Christian Liturgy*, p. 76.

[157] We have failed to discuss, for lack of space, the Jewish conception of a *community sin*, in distinction from the individual. For the former idea, see *Rosh Ha-shanah* 17b, *Ab Zar* 4b-5a, *M Hor* 1[5]. Cf. J. D. Eisenstein, 'Sin', *JE*, XI.377.

[158] Op. cit. p. 73; cf. A. Marmorstein, op. cit. p. 4, but note the modifications made by MacGregor and Purdy, *Jew and Greek: Tutors unto Christ* (New York, 1936), p. 77.

munity and its distress, like Moses, and then he is worthy to see its consolation.'[159]

Maybe the most striking example of the application of the principle of the corporate involvement of all Israel in the sin of one member is encountered in the denunciation of the practice of mixed marriage. The incorporation of an unclean Gentile into the Holy Community is viewed with horror in the *Book of Jubilees*:

And Israel will not be free from this uncleanness if it has a wife of the daughters of the Gentiles, or has given any of its daughters to a man who is of any of the Gentiles. . . . Then shall the whole nation together be judged for all the uncleanness and profanation of this man (who takes a Gentile wife).[160]

This passage serves well to conclude a discussion on the solidarity of Israel. In the first instance, the mixed marriage is viewed as a violation of the holiness of the united community. In other words, the unity of the group is a unity of kind which is destroyed through any unsanctified element being inserted into it. In the second instance, the solidarity of the group is of such a realistic nature, that the sin of the one was the sin of the many. As we go on to discuss the Jewish views regarding the implications of Adam's transgression, this latter element will be again brought into play.

JEWISH IDEAS REGARDING THE SOLIDARITY OF MANKIND

THE UNITY OF THE HUMAN RACE THROUGH CREATION

From the Jewish doctrines of the unity of Israel we turn now to the stated opinions regarding the unity of the human race. As we noted in our examination of the evidence for solidarity in the Old Testament, the solidarity of mankind falls out of the awareness of the group as it expands to include the world, becoming more or less the property of theological speculation. Both the historical assurance that all men were the descendants of one

---

[159] *Taan* 11a. Cf. F. Jackson and K. Lake, op. cit. I.57-8.
[160] 30[14-15]. Cf. 33[11]; *T Levi* 9[10]; *Pirkê de R Eliezer*, trans. G. Friedlander (London, 1916), p. 304.

man, and the eschatological hope, implemented the Rabbinic and Apocalyptic discussions on the unity of the race.

(1) *The Creation of Man and Its Implications.* That Adam was the human father and origin of the race was unquestioned Jewish doctrine. The unimpeachable declaration of the Scriptures assured as much, but the Rabbis found that this teaching could be used profitably in hortatory exposition. It was used primarily to promote an awareness of the universal collective responsibility of each individual. A quotation from G. F. Moore based on Rabbinic sources will illustrate this:

All men notwithstanding their different appearance were stamped by God with one seal, the seal of Adam. Therefore every man is bound to say: 'On account of me the world was created.' That is, is to feel himself individually responsible as though the whole human race depended on his conduct.[161]

Thus, man has been accorded a special dignity through his creation. This is the particular burden of R. Akiba (A D 120-40), 'Beloved is man for he was created in the image of God; but it was by a special love that it was made known to him that he was created in the image of God. . . .'[162] This type of statement indicates that Judaism upheld the principle of the unity and mutual responsibility of mankind on the basis of its own ethical monotheism.[163] The consequent value of the individual in community motivates a noteworthy statement from the annals of Early Judaism:

Why was only a single specimen of man created first? To teach us that he who destroys a single soul destroys a whole world, and that he who saves a single soul saves a whole world; furthermore, in order that no race or class may claim a nobler ancestry saying, 'Our father was born first'; and finally to give testimony to the greatness of the Lord, who caused the wonderful diversity of mankind to emanate from one type. And why was Adam created last of all beings? To teach him

[161] Op. cit. I.445. Cf. *Kid* 40b, 39b.
[162] *M Aboth* 3[18]. The Rabbis found the essential principle of the Torah in Genesis 5[1], which treats of the descent of all mankind from Adam and hence provides the basis for the doctrine of the universal brotherhood of mankind. Cf. R. Gordis, 'Adam', *The Universal Jewish Encyclopedia* (New York, 1939), I.78.
[163] K. Kohler, *Jewish Theology* (New York, 1918), p. 314; S. Hanson, op. cit. p. 7.

humility; for if he be overbearing, let him remember that the little fly preceded him in the order of creation.[164]

These quotations were supposed to impress Gentile and Israelite alike with the rationale behind the second of the two great commandments (Lev 19[18]).

Beyond this, an orthodox belief in the origin of the race and the universe served not only to enhance the majesty of the one God, but also to reflect the wonder of Israel's divine election. For this reason, it is not surprising that the New Year Festival came to stress the creative acts of Jehovah. Through an effective use of the Psalms and their stress on the omnipotence of God in Creation, a conscious union was sought between the exaltation of God and its corollary, namely, the assured exaltation of His peculiar treasure [165]

The Rabbinic interest in the creation of Adam was not primarily motivated by such a rationale. On the contrary, the chagrin over the successive calamities sustained by the nation forced upon Judaism an intensified awareness of sin.[166] As a result, a stimulation to examine the source of evil in the world, and a desire to explain its propagation, held sway. Not by chance, the search for the origin of evil in the world led to one of two possibilities. (1) A theory which gained support among the Apocalyptic writers was the story of the Watchers in Genesis 6[1-4]. (2) The source favoured by the Rabbis and which later gained more or less universal support was the Fall of Adam, pointing to Genesis (Ch. 3) as the explanation for the origin of evil in the world. Hand in hand with this inquisitive attitude toward sin came the eschatological speculation regarding the restoration of the primeval utopia in the Messianic Age.[167] This led to the development of a rather elaborate doctrine of the creation of the first man.

Apparently under the influence of Iranian mythology, the Jewish speculation treated the formation of Adam in a panegyrical fashion. R. Eliezer b. Azariah (A D 100) propounded

---

[164] Tosefta *Sanh* 8[4-9]. K. Kohler maintains this is the correct reading in opposition to *M Sanh* 4[5]. See further, A. Cohen, op. cit. p. 72 note 1, and H. Danby, op. cit. p. 388 and note 4. The quotation is taken from *JE*, I.174.

[165] See W. O. E. Oesterley, 'Early Hebrew Festival Rituals', *Myth and Ritual*, p. 128.

[166] Cf. W. D. Davies, op. cit. p. 38. Much of the Apocrypha and Pseudepigrapha supports this conclusion.

[167] See E. Schürer, op. cit. pp. 130-1; W. D. Davies, op. cit. p. 39; Strack and Billerbeck, op. cit. IV.888; C. H. Kraeling, *Anthropos and Son of Man* (New York, 1947), p. 161. Cf. e.g. *4 Ez* 7[29, 32]; *2 Bar* 3[7]; *T Levi* 18.

the view that the original creation of man was a living mass which extended the length and breadth of the earth and reached from earth to heaven.[168] In a similar manner the Sibylline Oracles speak of God 'who fashioned four-lettered Adam, the first man fashioned, who completes in his name morn and dusk, antarctic and arctic. He too both established the fashion of the form of mortal men.'[169] While this mental diversion may not have in every case reflected serious theology,[170] the glory of the First Adam was apparently considered to be common knowledge. Thus, the *Midrash Rabba* says that the angels mistook Adam for a divine being;[171] 2 *Enoch* (30[11]) refers to him as a 'second angel'. Probably the most extravagant opinion of the glory of Adam is found in the Books of Adam and Eve where the Fall of Satan is explained by the latter's refusing to worship Adam.[172]

There is more than an exaggerated opinion of Adam's original glory implied in these divergent statements. There is an unmistakable further connotation of the universal unity of the race. The descriptions of the actual creation confirm this point. 'It has been taught', R. Meir (AD 150) used to say, 'the dust of the first man was gathered from all parts of the earth', for it is written, 'Thine eyes did see mine unformed substance' (Ps 139[16]), and further it is written: 'The eyes of the Lord run to and fro through the whole earth' (Zech 4[10]).[173] In the same section of the Talmud, a diversity in the honour or value of distinct races is not allowed to offset the fundamental unity of mankind. 'R. Oshaiah said in Rab's name: "Adam's trunk came from Babylon, his head from *Eretz Israel*, his limbs from other lands, and his private parts according to R. Aha, from Akra di Agma." '[174]

In another citation, there is a possible allusion to the assorted colours of different races as suggested by Friedlander:[175]

[168] Cf. *Gen R* 8[1], *Sanh* 38b, which ascribes the pronouncement to R. Judah in Rab's name. See Strack and Billerbeck, op. cit. III.325, IV.946; H. L. Ginsberg, op. cit. I.59, V.79.
[169] 324-7. The date is roughly the second half of the first century AD (cf. *APOT*, II.371-4. Cf. 2 *Enoch* 30[13]: 'And I appointed him a name from the four component parts, from East, West, South and North.' A stood for Ἀνατολή, D stood for Δύσις, A stood for Ἄρητος and M stood for Μεσημβρία (W. D. Davies, op. cit. p. 55).
[170] W. D. Davies, op. cit. p. 53.
[171] *Gen R* 8[10].
[172] Cf. chs. xii-xvii. See also H. L. Ginsberg, op. cit. I.62-4.
[173] *Sanh* 38a, *Gen R* 8[1]. Cf. Strack and Billerbeck, op. cit. III.479.
[174] *Sanh* 38a-b. Cf. W. D. Davies, op. cit. p. 54; F. Weber, *SASPT*, p. 203.
[175] *Pirkê de R. Eliezer*, p. 77 note 2. Ginsberg thinks the colours refer to no more than the distinct elements of man's body (op. cit. V.72).

The Holy One, blessed be He, spake to the Torah: 'Let us make man in our image, after our likeness' (Gen 1[26]) . . . He (God) began to collect the dust of the first man from the four corners of the world; red, black, white and pale green (which) refers to the body.'[176]

At a later date, the feature of bisexuality was added to the description of the original creation of man who was androgynous.[177] The full intention of the writers who proposed so fantastic and mythological a reconstruction of the original creation of man, cannot be examined in this brief presentation. It is enough to maintain that the fundamental purpose of the Jewish teachers was the promotion of the conception of the unity of the whole race.

The statements given thus far indicate symbolic unity of the race through the original creation. Still more pertinent are those fanciful descriptions of the race as it was incorporated in Adam. *Exodus Rabba* mentions the first man being adorned with the descendants which were yet to be born from him. They are pictured as individuals attached to his hair, nose, ears, and so on, over the whole of his body.[178] Other passages speak of God's causing all the generations of men, both righteous and wicked, to pass before Adam, saying to him: 'See wherefore thou hast brought death upon the righteous.'[179] R. Johanan b. Zakkai (A D 10-80) and R. Akiba interpreted the passage, 'They did eat, and the eyes of both of them were opened', as Adam and Eve seeing the dire consequences of their sin upon all coming generations.[180] More to the point is another opinion ascribed to R. Johanan, namely, that all souls until the end of the world were created in the six days of creation and consequently lodged in the

---

[176] *Pirkê de R. Eliezer*, pp. 76-7. From the *Jer Targum* on Gen 2[7] comes the idea that the dust was collected from the holy place (as the centre of the earth) (cf. *Pirkê de R. Eliezer*, pp. 76-7), and the four parts of the world, mingling it with the water of all the seas and made him (Adam) red, black and white. See K. Kohler, in *JE*, I.174.

[177] *Gen R* 8[1]. Cf. G. F. Moore, op. cit. I.453; Strack and Billerbeck, op. cit. I.802; H. L. Ginsberg, op. cit. I.66, V.88 note 42.

[178] *Ex R* 40[3]. Cf. Strack and Billerbeck, op. cit. II.174.

[179] *Tanh Ber* par. 29 in G. F. Moore, op. cit. I.476. Cf. *Gen R* 8[8], *Abodah Zar* 5a; Strack and Billerbeck, op. cit. II.173; H. L. Ginsberg, op. cit. I.61, V.75. Note *Hag* 12b for the widely held view that the spirits and souls await corporeality in the seventh heaven (*Araboth*) (cf. A. Cohen, op. cit. p. 83). Cf. Wis 8[19]. According to *Ab Zar* 5a the Messiah awaits the exhausting of all the souls destined to inhabit bodies for his advent (cf. *Yeb* 62a).

[180] *Gen R* 19[10]. Cf. K. Kohler, op. cit. p. 222.

Garden of Eden.[181] Some opinions refer to the souls of all men as a part of Adam's soul, but were destined to inhabit bodies in subsequent generations.[182]

All of the divergent intentions behind the Adam-speculation cannot be seen in this brief citation of some of the reconstructions of the creation. W. D. Davies suggests that two dominant interests colour most of these passages: (1) an emphasis on the unity of the race, and (2) the universal responsibility of love.[183] While these sum up the general purpose of those propounding these theories, they reflect a conception of solidarity which coupled with views on the universality of sin confirm the contention that early Judaism held a very strong conception of the unity binding all men into one totality.

(2) *The Implications of Eschatological Speculation.* Our previous discussion of the eschatological speculation of the Rabbis regarding Israel's unity apply here also. Beyond that, it is important to note that Adam as the head and master of the race is the microcosm[184] of the Kingdom of God. In this role he invites the whole of the creation to clothe God with majesty and might that it might find favour in His eyes.[185] The reason that man can fulfil this duty is founded in his endowment with free will epitomized in the two inclinations. Through sin's incursion into the creation, the recognition of the divine Kingship of God was corrupted in darkness which reigned twenty generations between Adam and Abraham.[186] With the institution of the covenant, Israel became the locus of the Kingdom, awaiting the purging of humanity and the restoration of the universal domain of God.[187] The earnest desire for the accomplishment of this Hope is found in the Amidah-prayer for the New Year Service (*Rosh-ha-shanah*):

[181] Cf. F. Weber, *SASPT*, pp. 217-18. H. L. Ginsberg claims that this doctrine is of Christian origin (cf. Rom 5[14], 1 Cor 15[22]) (op. cit. V.75, note 19). If that is the case it is questionable why the Kabbalah later expanded the doctrine unless it did so under Hellenistic and Stoic influence.

[182] Cf. *Gen R passim*. Cf. H. L. Ginsberg, op. cit. I.56. Cf. *M Sanh* 4[5], where the witness in capital cases is responsible for the blood, not only of the victim, but also of the blood of his posterity (which should have been born of him) to the end of the world. Such was the case with Cain who slew his brother, for it is written: 'The bloods of thy brother cry' (*Gen* 4[10]). The plural refers to his blood and that of his posterity.

[183] Cf. W. D. Davies, op. cit. p. 53.

[184] Cf. H. L. Ginsberg, op. cit. I.49, V.64-5.

[185] *Gen R* 9[4].

[186] Cf. *M Aboth* 5[1].

[187] See S. Hanson's excellent discussion, op. cit. pp. 20-3.

Now therefore, O Lord God, impose Thine awe upon all Thy works and Thy dread upon all that Thou hast created, that all works may fear Thee and all creatures prostrate themselves before Thee; that they may all form a single band to do Thy will with a perfect heart, even as we know, O Lord our God, that dominion is Thine, strength is in Thine hand. . . .[188]

The restoration of the disunited race of men to the original unity is the culmination of the Jewish conception of history itself. We may note an example of this in the *Testament of Levi:*

And he (the Messiah) shall open the gates of paradise,
And he shall remove the threatening sword against Adam,
And he shall give to the saints to eat of the tree of life,
And the spirit of holiness shall be upon them,
And Beliar shall be bound by him,
And he shall give power to his children to tread upon evil spirits.[189]

The Messiah was expected to be the one re-enacting the life of Adam in reverse.[190] As he did so, the whole of the creation would be implicated in the restoration of the primeval unity. Throughout the corruption of the race and its restoration the principle of solidarity is an inviolable law of history itself.

THE SOLIDARITY OF THE HUMAN RACE IN SIN

Introduction. The second paramount factor in Jewish theological speculation which confirmed the solidarity of the race was the recognition of the universality of sin. It is the counterpart to the admission that all men are brothers because of the common fatherhood of Adam. We have already shown how strong Israel's sense of corporate implication in sin had become in this period. But moral defilement was by no means confined to Israel. Indeed, the Gentiles were by definition 'sinners',[191] 'unclean', heathen, invariably worse than Israel.[192] But the holiness of the Elect

---

[188] *Authorized Jewish Daily Prayer Book*, p. 239. Note also the petitions for the universal restoration in the Alenu prayer (ibid. pp. 76-7).

[189] 18[10-12]. Cf. C. H. Kraeling, op. cit. p. 161; Bousset, op. cit. p. 260.

[190] Cf. *supra*, p. 65 and *infra*, pp. 150-73.

[191] So, Paul: 'We who are Jews by nature and not of ἐθνῶν ἁμαρτωλοί' (Gal 2[15]). Cf. H. G. Marsh, *The Origin and Significance of New Testament Baptism* (Manchester, 1941), p. 7 note 2.

[192] This idea is especially prominent in 2 *Baruch*, in which the author repeatedly must question the justice of God in allowing the Gentiles to prosper at the expense of Israel's calamity. When the Sib. Oracles characterize Israel as the 'guiltless race of men' (4[136]), this contrast is in perspective.

Race was ascribed to it only in the interest of emphasizing the contrast. The truth of the universality of sin became increasingly impressed on the Jewish mind through the conviction that an inseparable connexion existed between punishment and sin.[193] The heavy hand of divine chastisement on Israel left no alternative to the Hebrew mind other than the admission that it was the national desert. But whence came this moral pollution, the inveterate tendency to evil? If a solution to this problem might be found, and the nature of sin defined, the application to Israel's problem might effect a cure which would in turn inaugurate the New Age.

(1) *The Search for the Origin of Sin in the World.* The attempt on the part of Jewish thinkers to locate the source of evil and the cause for its universality must engage our attention first. One more or less assured premise held by early Judaism was the conviction that death and the deteriorating effect of sin were not the original lot of mankind.[194] A citation from the *Book of Enoch* might be considered normative: 'For men were created exactly like the angels, to the intent that they should continue pure and righteous, and death which destroys everything, could not have taken hold of them; but through this their knowledge, they are perishing.'[195] The writer of the *Wisdom of Solomon* concurs with this opinion: 'God created man for immortality and made him the image of his own peculiar nature; but by the envy of the devil death entered into the world and they who are of his party make experience of it.'[196] In these passages a generic conception of mankind corresponds to the unity of men in Adam; consequently, the glory of the original man is given to all men.

If we may draw a distinction between the more official doctrine of the Rabbis and the popular theology of the Apocalyptic writers, we will note two features. (1) Both agree on the original majesty and phenomenal attributes of Adam at formation. (2)

---

[193] The universality of death confirmed the inclusive character of sin (cf. *Shab* 55a). Tobit explicitly affirms this conviction, e.g. in 3[1-6], 14[4-7]. Cf. F. R. Tennant, *SDFOS*, p. 121.

[194] N. P. Williams, op. cit. p. 57.

[195] 69[11]. The knowledge referred to is that imparted by the fallen angels.

[196] 2[23-4]. Cf. 1[13]; G. F. Moore, op. cit. I.475. That there would be no death without sin, is the natural inference from the story of the Fall in Genesis. Cf. 2 *Enoch* 30[16].

The Rabbis held a modified view of the Fall,[197] clinging to the doctrine of the *yetzer hara*,[198] because it neither denied the freedom of the human will nor affected the value of repentance.[199] The popular theology held with less loathing a view that Adam's progeny had in fact inherited certain effects and consequences of the first transgression.

(a) *The Theory of the Watchers*. One widely held view regarding the origin and dissemination of sin had nothing to do with Adam. Rather, the corruption of all flesh including 'men, cattle, beasts, and birds' (cf. 1 *Enoch* 7[5-6]), came as a result of the intermarriage of rebellious angels and the daughters of men.[200] The *locus classicus* of this hypothesis is found in 1 *Enoch* 6–16. In full detail the angels are named with their leader 'Semjaza'. For their lawless deeds they are bound and confined to the abyss of fire. Their bastard sons are destroyed because they had wronged mankind.[201] The *Testament of Reuben* curiously lays the blame on the daughters of men who by cunning allurement tempted them.[202] A close evaluation of the evidence preserved in our sources does not support the conclusion that the Watchers were actually the cause either for the origin of evil in the earth or an explanation for the universality of sin. These passages do not give to them the representative place of Adam: their sin implicates only their own generation.[203] If there is any causal relationship between their evil and that of mankind, it must be sought in the sphere of influence or imitation.

197 N. P. Williams, op. cit. p. 59. R. Meir claimed that Adam's proportions were reduced by his sinning from the extent of all space to 100 yards. *Gen R* 12[6] claims that Adam, through sin, lost glory, immortality (lit. 'life'), his height, the fruit of the earth, the fruit of trees, and the luminaries. Every generation has shared his deprivation except two. Cf. Strack and Billerbeck, op. cit. IV.946-7; H. L. Ginsberg, op. cit. V.126. Note further ibid. V.102 note 87 and I.79, 82.

198 I.e. the 'evil inclination' (Gen. 6[5]). Cf. *infra*, pp. 85-7.

199 Cf. J. Abelson, *The Immanence of God in Rabbinical Literature* (London, 1912), p. 311; and, on repentance, J. Klausner, op. cit. p. 519.

200 Cf. *Jub* 52-3 and 7[21]. Compare with this view the parallel assertion that, 'Unclean demons began to lead the children of the sons of Noah astray, and to make to err and destroy them', which in turn confirmed the presence of sin in the world again (*Jub* 10[1]). See F. R. Tennant, op. cit. p. 193.

201 10[15]. Cf. *T Naphtali* 3[3], where the desolation of the whole earth is attributed to the Watchers. According to *Jub* 7[21], they were the efficient cause for the flood and made the beginning of uncleanness. This theory was also held by the Zadokite Party (cf. *Fragments*, 3[4]-4[1]), but the Fall of the Watchers was due to their surrender to their 'evil imagination'.

202 56-7. The original good intention of the Watchers is affirmed in *Jub* 4[15].

203 This must be modified by recognizing that the offspring of the giants (disembodied spirits) cause a great deal of trouble and evil among men. Cf. 1 *Enoch* 15[8-12].

(*b*) *The Theory of the Seduction of Eve.* Another crude strain of thought may be traced through Jewish sources in which sinful pollution of the race finds its source in the seduction of Eve by the Serpent.[204] 'On this account, he (Satan) conceived designs against Adam; in such a manner he entered and deceived Eve. But he did not touch Adam.'[205] This hypothesis was used to explain the initiation of the principle of death. Therefore, Adam chides Eve: 'What hast thou done? A great plague hast thou brought upon us, transgression and sin for all our generations.'[206]

It is more than likely that the Rabbinic expansion of the notion of the seduction of Eve into a Jewish counterpart of Original Sin was founded on the Apocalyptic theory. While Ecclesiasticus goes on record declaring: 'From a woman did sin originate and because of her we all must die',[207] the Talmud refers to a poison or filth which in consequence of its injection into Eve, continued in her descendants through the process of procreation.[208] Although this is not a doctrine of Original Sin in the later Christian sense,[209] the affinities are self-evident. The normative character of Eve's action in introducing the principle of sin (uncleanness) and death to succeeding generations was not seen in isolation, but drew heavily on the feature of solidarity. Despite the opinion that the normative role of Eve determined the lot of all women, it did not fully explain the universality of sin in itself.

(*c*) *The Theory of the Determinative Role of Adam.* After all is said and done, the primal hypothesis adopted by Early Judaism to

---

[204] Cf. F. R. Tennant, op. cit. pp. 156, 168; N. P. Williams, op. cit. p. 57. 2 *Enoch* asserts that death came to Adam by Eve (30¹⁷), and the widowed mother of the seven martyred brothers says: 'Nor did the false, beguiling Serpent sully the purity of my maidenhood' (4 *Macc* 18⁸). See F. Weber, *SASPT*, p. 212, for Rabbinic traces of this theory.

[205] 2 *Enoch* 31⁶. Cf. Bousset, op. cit. pp. 408-9.

[206] *The Books of Adam and Eve*, 44²; cf. 35². For Rabbinic parallels see, *Gen R* 18⁶, *Ex R* 28², *Sanh* 59b, *Sot* 9b, *Yeb* 103b, and *Ab Zar* 22b. Contrast *Gen R* 19¹². In the Targums, note *Eccles* 7²⁹ (God made man upright), 'But the serpent and the woman led him astray, and caused death to be inflicted upon him and upon all the inhabitants of the earth.' Cf. also on *Ruth* 4²².

[207] 25²⁴; cf. 14¹⁷⁶: ἡ γὰρ διαθήκη ἀπ' αἰώνος θανάτῳ ἀποθανεῖσθε. Note *Apoc of Moses* 14², 321-2, where Eve cries: 'I have sinned before Thee and all sin hath begun through my doing in the creation.' Cf. Strack and Billerbeck, op. cit. III.226.

[208] *Yeb* 103b. See also *Ab Zar* 22b, *Shab* 146a. Since this baneful influence was removed from Israel through the Torah, the Gentiles continue to be 'like a man with an unclean issue', i.e. unclean in the highest degree. Cf. *Ab Zar* 36b, *Nid* 34b; F. Gavin, op. cit. p. 30.

[209] Cf. Strack and Billerbeck, op. cit. III.71; F. R. Tennant, op. cit. p. 176; Oesterley and Box, op. cit. p. 240; W. D. Davies, op. cit. p. 34.

account for the origin of evil blamed Adam for human misery in general[210] and death in particular.[211] A collation of pertinent texts from the early Jewish period indicates a preponderance of evidence supporting the view that beyond the implications of his own punishment, Adam also brought death upon the whole race. Thus, in the very early extra-canonical *Book of Wisdom*, death is man's inheritance from Adam.[212] The difficulty is that although 2[23-4] (quoted *supra*) is probably a reference to the Fall, the death is apparently moral.[213] With the Rabbis, there is no doubting the point that death and Adam's judgement are allied. G. F. Moore affirms:

> That Adam's sin involved all his posterity, the righteous as well as the wicked, in death, is the consistent teaching of the Rabbis. . . . The ancient conceptions of solidarity made this theory unquestioned that the sins of the fathers are visited upon the children. It was the doctrine of experience as well as of Scripture.[214]

In support of this contention one of the many possible citations may be noted. From the *Sifra on Leviticus*, R. Jose (A D 150) said:

> If you wish to know of the reward of the righteous in the world to come, consider the case of Adam. One single negative command was given him. This he violated, and see how many deaths have been decreed for him and for all his generations unto the end of time.[215]

For contemporary and pre-Christian declarations to the same effect, ample support may be gathered from the Apocalyptic literature. From the *Secrets of Enoch* we may note a typical citation:

> And I saw all forefathers from all time with Adam and Eve, and I sighed and broke into tears and said of the ruin of their dishonour: 'Woe is me for my infirmity and for that of my forefathers' and thought in my heart and said: 'Blessed is the man who has not been born or who has been born and shall not sin before the Lord's face, that he come not into this place, nor bring the yoke of this place.'[216]

---

[210] Cf. Strack and Billerbeck, op. cit. I.19-20, III.246.

[211] F. Prat, *The Theology of St Paul*, I.440.

[212] Cf. 7[1].

[213] Note 3[1]: 'But the souls of the righteous are in the hand of God.' Cf. F. R. Tennant, op. cit. p. 124.

[214] Op. cit. I.476. Cf. F. Weber, *SASPT*, p. 238; J. Klausner, op. cit. p. 517.

[215] 27a in *RA*, p. 205; cf. p. 543; *Gen R* 16[6], *Erubim* 18b.

[216] 41.1f. See further, e.g. 2 Bar. 17[3], 23[4], 19[8], and possibly 54[15] and 56[6], which ascribe premature death to the corporate judgement of Adam's transgression.

This passage, as well as the Rabbinic *Haggada*, assumes that Adam has caused death to rule in the world of men, but maintains strenuously that if an individual should keep himself from sin, he should in turn be preserved from death.[217] Enoch and Elijah, archetypal figures from the Old Testament, were cited in favour of this contention in conjunction with seven others.[218] That some righteous men, who despite unblameworthy lives, died, caused a problematic contradiction. Thus, in the case of Moses, whose death was not the judgement of his own sin, Rabbinic lore attributes these words to God:

I announced death to thee with the word, 'Behold,' saying, 'Behold, thy days approach that thou must die', because I wanted to point out to thee that thou diest only because thou art a descendant of Adam upon whose sons I had pronounced death with the word, 'Behold,' saying to the angels, 'Behold, the man is become as one of us. . . .'[219]

Similar examples of righteousness were such an exception, that the Rabbis did not feel obliged to solve the contradiction between universal death and an individual dying in spite of his innocence. The dictum, 'There is no death without sin',[220] in the vast majority of instances, raised no questions at all. Thus the problem of the justice of Adam's judgement falling on his descendants was resolved in the appeal to personal desert and individual responsibility.[221] For this reason, the justice of God was not impugned as the angel implied in his solution of Ezra's difficulty: 'Ask no more about the multitude of those who perish, for they themselves having freedom given them, spurned the Most High, and despised his law and abandoned his ways.'[222]

Some passages, in the Apocalyptic literature especially, attribute broader consequences to the original transgression of Adam. These form a sort of peroration of human misery. Thus the racial effects of Adam's sin are listed in 2 *Baruch*: (1) untimely death,

---

[217] Cf. *Gen R* 8[11].

[218] Cf. Strack and Billerbeck, op. cit. III.227-8, I.754.

[219] H. L. Ginsberg, op. cit. III.423. Cf. *Gen R* 9[8], *Shab* 55b.

[220] *Shab* 55a. Cf. S. Schechter, op. cit. p. 247; 'Sin', in *Bible Key Words* (*TWNT*), trans. J. R. Coates (New York, 1951), p. 45.

[221] Cf. N. P. Williams, op. cit. p. 74 and references cited there.

[222] 4 *Ez* 8[55-6]. Cf. 2 *Bar* 54[19]: 'Adam is not the cause, save of his own soul, but each one of us has been the Adam of his own soul.' See G. F. Moore, op. cit. I.455, 475; F. R. Tennant, *SDFOS*, pp. 218, 220.

(2) grief, (3) anguish, (4) pain and trouble, (5) disease, (6) a demanding Sheol, (7) the begetting of children, (8) passion, (9) humiliation of humanity, (10) the languishing of goodness.[223] The whole gamut of human ills is the fruit of the original judgement on Adam's sin. The involvement of the whole race in the judgement of Adam is precisely the same explanation which was used to solve the problem of God's judgement of the whole of Israel for the transgression of a part. In other words, it is the reapplication of the principle of corporate justice within the group. In the case of mankind, the group is larger, but the unity does not differ in kind from the solidarity of Israel as one of its constituent parts.

The further question of the relationship of universal sin to the original transgression is more complex. Various solutions were tendered on this subject. The *Letter of Aristeas*, preserving the alleged answers of the seventy Jewish wise men to the questions of Ptolemy, emphasizes the interaction of influence and the natural inclination. Thus, one answers: 'Everyone has a natural tendency toward the pursuit of pleasure';[224] another says: 'Men catch their depravities and become miserable through association with bad men.'[225] A teaching emphasized in the *Sibylline Oracles* (Books I and II) is that the weakness of the flesh, making the avoidance of sin so difficult, is a racial characteristic. Both *Enoch* (*Secrets*) and 2 *Baruch* suggest affinities to the doctrine of Original Sin.[226]

It is the pseudepigraphic writer(s)[227] of 4 *Ezra* who comes nearest to the Christian view of sin. In the words of Oesterley and Box:

Hitherto every sin was regarded as an isolated act, unconnected with anything in human nature inherently, a thing which could be avoided if man so willed, but being committed could easily be obliterated. In

[223] 56⁶. Cf. *Jub* 3²⁸⁻⁹ and the *Books of Adam and Eve*, 34², which refer to seventy blows which were appointed Adam in all parts of his body, but included also his race.
[224] Para. 108; cf. 277-8. Such is also Philo's interpretation of the Serpent of Genesis 3 (cf. F. R. Tennant, *SDFOS*, p. 136).
[225] Para. 130.
[226] Cf. 2 *Enoch* 41¹⁻², quoted above, in which Tennant sees a definite implication of the doctrine of depravity through the sin of Adam, *SDFOS*, p. 210. Compare also 3 *Macc* 3²², *Wis* 12¹⁰. According to R. Mackintosh, 2 *Baruch* is the unique location of a doctrine of original sin which has not been influenced by Christian thought; *Christianity and Sin* (London, 1913), p. 53. This opinion is contested accurately (especially if the book is taken as a unity) by H. St J. Thackeray, op. cit. p. 35, and F. R. Tennant, *SDFOS*, p. 216: cf. p. 229.
[227] See G. H. Box's discussion of the authorship in *APOT*, II.552-3.

this book, however, it is taught that the whole human race is involved in sin, and that the reason for the universal prevalence of sin is to be sought in the innate badness of the human heart. . . . So steeped is the world in sin that it seems to the writer of the book that the only remedy lies in a new age; a fresh start must be made, and a new Era will dawn, then all sorrow will be turned into joy, for sin will be rooted out.[228]

In 3[7-8], the heavy judgement on Adam for one transgression (his own death and that of his generations), is contrasted with the punishment his progeny should expect for walking after their own way. In Chapter 7 solidarity comes still more to the fore. The writer cries in anguish:

O Adam, what hast thou done! For though it was thou that sinned, the fall was not thine alone, but ours also who are thy descendants! For what does it profit us that the eternal age is promised to us, whereas we have done the works that bring death![229]

In 7[68], the solidarity in sin is still more explicit declared in view of the expressed doctrine that all who are born are defiled with iniquities and full of sin.[230] The core of the doctrine of sin in 4 *Ezra* is found in chapters three and four:

For the first Adam, clothing himself with the evil heart, transgressed and was overcome; and likewise also, all who are born of him. Thus the infinity became inveterate; the Law indeed was in the heart of the people, but (in conjunction) with the evil germ; so what was good departed and the evil remained.[231]

In the following chapter we read:

A grain of evil seed was sown in the heart of Adam from the beginning, and how large a quantity of the fruit of sin hath it borne and will it bear until the threshing floor appear.[232]

---

[228] Oesterley and Box, op. cit. pp. 238-9. Cf. 4 *Ezra* 7[17-25].
[229] 7[118-19]. See F. R. Tennant, *SDFOS*, p. 229.
[230] Curiously, this description apparently includes Israel.
[231] 3[21-2]. See N. P. Williams, op. cit. p. 79.
[232] 4[30-1]. C. R. Smith comments appropriately on this passage: '2nd (4th) *Ezra* 4[28-32] points out that "a grain of evil seed was sown in the heart of Adam from the beginning", and all sin is the harvest of this one sin which is as the recurrent sowing of seed and reaping of harvest since the unity of all men with Adam is assumed (cf. 3[7])'; *The Bible Doctrine of Sin* (London, 1953), p. 107. G. F. Moore rules out the inference of an 'infection of sin' in this passage on the basis of statements elsewhere in the book; op. cit. I.477. Cf. e.g. 7[127-30] and 8[56]; W. D. Davies, op. cit. p. 33.

Sin is thus a living power which controls the world of men at its deepest level.[233] It is organic, growing in the human tree from generation to generation, as the seed reproduces in kind its parent type. This view of sin is based on the conception of heredity which has made of all men a single unity through birth; it is comparable to the ethnic unity of Israel.

(2) *The Normative Rabbinic Solution of the Problem of the Universality of Sin.* The *cor malignum* which the writer of 4 *Ezra* considers to be the inheritance every man has received from Adam[234] corresponds roughly to the Rabbinic *yetzer hara*.[235] The norm of Rabbinic speculation, however, must be distinguished from the doctrine of the pseudepigraph. The *yetzer hara* was the evil motive or sinful inclination which is inherent in the race. But the *yetzers* (*hara* and *hatob*) were provided Adam at his creation,[236] and are not passed from father to son through procreation, being given to man at birth.[237] Various views are tendered by recent writers on the subject of the influence of the transgression of Adam on the *yetzer hara*. Some would maintain that the Rabbis thought of the sin of Adam as enslaving the evil inclination in human nature.[238] F. C. Porter maintains that the Rabbis did not even think of the original transgression as strengthening the *yetzer*.[239]

There is less difference of opinion regarding the seat of the *yetzer*, that is, in the heart or the inner self.[240] It is at the worst a powerful dynamic incentive to sin. Although it may be successfully resisted, when the individual surrenders to its demands, he finds the power of evil to grow upon him as a current.[241] One

[233] 'Sin' in *Bible Key Words* (*TWNT*), pp. 43-4.

[234] Cf. 3[20, 22, 26], 4[4].

[235] F. R. Tennant, *SDFOS*, op. cit. p. 265.

[236] *Ber* 61a, *Sanh* 91b. Cf. R. Mackintosh, op. cit. p. 54; F. Weber, *SASPT*, p. 204. Note also 4 *Ezra* 4[30], Ecclus 15[14].

[237] Cf. N. P. Williams, op. cit. p. 69; W. D. Davies, op. cit. p. 25; S. Schechter, op. cit. p. 253.

[238] Cf. e.g. F. V. Filson, *St Paul's Conception of Recompense* (Leipzig, 1931) pp. 11-12; F. Prat, op. cit. I.440; H. L. Ginsberg claims that the evil inclination was one of the evils decreed upon Adam; op. cit. I.79.

[239] 'The *Yeçer Hara*', in *Biblical and Semitic Studies, Yale Bicentennial Publications* (New York, 1901).

[240] N. P. Williams, op. cit. p. 65; Bousset, op. cit. pp. 404-5. Since the evil impulse is original in the creation of the individual, it is not evil in itself. R. Samuel b. Nahman affirms that it is an essential part of human nature, declared to be good, by God (*Gen R* 9[7]). Cf. *Sanh* 107b; G. F. Moore, op. cit. I.482-8; W. D. Davies, op. cit. p. 22 note 3; S. Schechter, op. cit. pp. 264-92.

[241] S. Schechter, op. cit. p. 249.

Rabbinic opinion cited in the Talmud held that 'Satan, the evil *yetzer*, and the Angel of Death' were one.[242] Nothing conclusive can be maintained from such a statement. It is enough to see a close relationship between the *yetzer* and Satan as the source of temptation, which in turn produces death (identified with the Angel of Death) for those who succumb to its demands.

The antidote for the evil inclination is the Law.[243] For this reason, there is a constant interchange between the *yetzer hatob* (the good inclination) and the Torah in the Rabbinic writings.[244] The battle for the control of the individual is waged in the heart.[245] The personification of the *yetzer hara* as a totality is used as a figure by R. Judah to predict the freedom of the individual from temptation in the Age to Come. 'In the world to come, God will bring the Evil Impulse and slay it in the presence of the righteous and the wicked.'[246]

Despite the impossibility of affirming any dogmatic opinions regarding the Rabbinic view of the incursion of sin and its subsequent control of the actions of man, a few general conclusions may be listed. There is apparently a fundamental difference between the Rabbinic views and those of the Apocalyptic writers. In the latter, a more intense view of the universal sinfulness of the whole race dominates the scene. There is a great reliance on the conception of the inter-relationship of men within an organic whole so that beginning with Adam, there is a solidarity of sin which envelopes mankind of all generations. The transgression of Adam is posited as the fuse of this corporate involvement in evil.[247] The Rabbis, on the other hand, held to a considerably more modified view of the inter-relationship of sin and the unity of the race. They propounded a more individualistic responsibility for the universality of sin in the race. While the opportunity or incentive to sin approaches man from without, the *yetzer* responds to produce the actual temptation.[248] Man's weakness, particularly without the Torah, makes him

---

[242] *B Bathra* 16a. Cf. Ecclus 21[27].

[243] *B Bathra* 16a, *Kid* 30b. Cf. F. R. Tennant, *SDFOS*, p. 116; Bousset, op. cit. p. 405. Others would say repentance; cf. G. F. Moore, op. cit. I.489; W. D. Davies, op. cit. pp. 24-5.

[244] The same interchange is found in 4 *Ezra*. Cf. 3[19], 9[30f], 7[21], 8[6], 3[19].

[245] Cf. *T Asher* 5[8]. Cf. Strack and Billerbeck, op. cit. IV.466-7.

[246] *Suk* 55a.

[247] 4 *Ezra* 3[7].

[248] Cf. G. F. Moore, op. cit. I.481. The impulses are not evil; the temptation is subjective (ibid. p. 482).

hopelessly susceptible to sin, which explains why there have been so few down through history who have been morally perfect. As F. C. Porter has pointed out: The Jews never regarded as adequate the idea that the *yetzer* became evil solely through man's sin. It must rather have explained his sin.[249] Thus, in conclusion, it becomes evident that the solution of the paradox between Adam's implicating the race in his condemnation and the universality of sin as the result of individual choice, was really never discovered.[250]

CONCLUSION

The content of the early Jewish literature reveals that in spite of a conscious relating of ideas to the Old Testament and ancient historical tradition, there are distinctive modifications in thought and belief.[251] Rabbinic sources reveal a more organic mental frame of reference. Many new emphases replaced the old. The nature and implications of the Jewish modifications cannot be exhaustively discussed, but a few of the more important points may be cited.

The fundamental conception of the nation as a corporate personality in the Old Testament is altered in the period of early Judaism.[252] The opinions on corporate justice[253] and the interpretation of the Pesach celebration remained, to a large extent, unmodified. At the same time, the unity of Israel became increasingly an idealistic and theological dogma, in contrast to the more primitive solidarity in the social consciousness of the nation in the Old Testament period. At the same time, the contact with the outside world in general and the Greek culture in particular, introduced a new awareness of the individual which made the ancient conception of the organic unity of the group less acceptable.[254] The representative roles of the king and priest were realized only sporadically at best, only to be lost altogether as time progressed. With no strong religious hierarchy to impose a unified interpretation on the distinctive code of Israelite life,

---

[249] Op. cit. p. 118. So also H. W. Robinson, *The Christian Doctrine of Man*, p. 120.
[250] Cf. W. D. Davies, op. cit. pp. 33-4.
[251] H. St J. Thackeray, op. cit. p. 3. Cf. MacGregor and Purdy, op. cit. pp. 70-1, 76; Oesterley and Robinson, *Hebrew Religion*, p. 292.
[252] Note *Mek* II.200, and the interpretation of the principle of oscillation. Cf. Oesterley and Robinson, op. cit. p. 263.
[253] M. Kadushin, *Organic Thinking*, p. 268. Cf. e.g. *Gen R* 53[18].
[254] See F. V. Filson, op. cit. p. 5.

the Torah became a decisive force within the nation, breeding sects and parties as a result. Since sin came to be conceived as the transgression of the Law, responsibility became dissociated from the community to a large extent and attached to the individual.[255]

On the other side of the ledger, we have seen that there were circumstantial factors which emphatically established the unity of Israel as a theological actuality. Anti-semitism in its more original expression was practised by Antiochus of Syria as well as Hellenistic Egyptian conquerors. This intolerance was interpreted by Jews as a frontal attack on their religious loyalty. Coupled with these outward factors, came the absorbing conviction of Jewish thinkers that the unit Israel was the last bulwark of the true knowledge of God. The Rabbis sought to imbue an urgency into the Covenant People to fulfil its mission. Consequently the Torah (the only true guide to the worship and knowledge of God) and Israel (the locus of God's reign on earth), became fundamental conceptions in the Jewish mind.[256] Thus, the unity of God, His singular purpose in choosing Israel, and His identification with the nation became integral elements in the solidarity of Israel. The People of God were characterized as a 'religious commonwealth', at once State and Church where no secular notion could exist and the love of God was integrated with the love of an Israelite.

Eschatological speculation, although forbidden by the Rabbis, was effectively stimulated by the syncretism of the period. Correlative to the problems of cosmology and the existential situation, arose the quest for the origins of sin, misery, and universal death.[257] The problem of meaningfulness in human existence led to the postulation of the exogenous conclusion to history itself. Thus, eschatology came into its own with its integration in the theological milieu of Jewish religious philosophy. This raised new questions regarding Israel's duty in securing the eschaton. A fresh

---

[255] See 'Sin' in *Bible Key Words* (*TWNT*), pp. 40-1.

[256] The organic complex of thought which enabled the Jew to live in a spiritual unity of thought and action within the unit Israel, has been examined by M. Kadushin. He concludes that the group mind of the Jewish people was no disembodied ghost. Unity of thought and action was possible because the inevitable and unique configuration of values possessed by every individual was but an original configuration of the organic complex of concepts common to all. *Organic Thinking*, p. 211. Cf. *The Rabbinic Mind*, p. 77.

[257] This quest was not allowed to destroy individual responsibility. See S. Levy, op. cit. p. 55.

emphasis on the solidarity of the race in lieu of the original creation became the counterpart of the new unity to be actualized in the re-creation of the Messianic Age. In the meantime, the Rabbis in contrast to their natural inclination, urged an increased altruism as the preparation for the new order.

PART II

CHAPTER III

THE PAULINE CONCEPTION OF THE SOLIDARITY OF THE HUMAN RACE IN ITS RELATIONSHIP TO THE OLD TESTAMENT AND EARLY JUDAISM

INTRODUCTION

THE study of the Old Testament and Jewish thought in the general period of the Second Temple has been conducted for the purpose of disclosing the sources of the conceptions of solidarity which are reflected in the Epistles of Paul. Our present task is to present the Pauline ideas of unity and their relationship to these source materials.

At the outset we must justify this portion of our investigation by considering the implications of the conversion experience of the Apostle. But for that event, the rest of our study would not only be unnecessary, but impossible. Saul of Tarsus might have been another of the illustrious Rabbis of his day.[1] As a matter of fact, because of his experience on the Damascus Road, a reorientation of thought transpired. (1) Many ideas were completely reversed; these are exemplified in the controversies with Judaizers and elsewhere. (2) Other ideas were incorporated into his system of thought unchanged. (3) Still another category of conceptions was subjected to the principle of 'stimulus diffusion'. This term refers to an old idea given a new orientation or content; the old and the new agree in form only.[2] Of these three classifications, the latter two alone concern us.

Before we proceed to the central objective in Part Two, it will be necessary to explain the omission of various Hellenistic systems of thought which have been proposed as the background of Paul's conception of human solidarity by an influential segment of scholarship. We will discuss briefly the most plausible Hellenistic sources and objections to them.

---

[1] Cf. H. F. Rall, *According to Paul* (New York, 1947), p. 3 note 2; A. C. Headlam, *St Paul and Christianity* (London, 1913), pp. 14, 18-21.
[2] Cf. C. C. McCown, *Munera Studiosa*, ed. M. H. Shepherd and S. H. Johnson (Cambridge, Mass., 1946), in T. S. Kepler, *Contemporary Thinking about Paul* (New York, 1950), p. 121.

(1) *Stoicism*. Because there was a Stoic 'school' in Tarsus,[3] a presumption is lodged that Paul must have been influenced by this philosophy. But the objections overrule the evidence. In the Stoic system, man was a part of nature, or more accurately a member.[4] Man was declared to be mortal by reason of his body, which decayed, but immortal by reason of his οὐσιώδης ἄνθρωπος ('essential humanity').[5] The fundamental unity of the cosmos constituted a living being, an organic unity.[6] The life which animates the cosmic organism is the true reason (λόγος ὀρθός),[7] or alternatively τὸ τοῦ κόσμου πνεῦμα ('the spirit of the world').[8] Reason is the essence of the divine. Since it is the common possession of all men, humanity is the incarnation of God, a portion of the universal pantheism;[9] in Epictetus' memorable phrase the soul is 'a fragment of God'.[10] It is this feature of the Greek system which most radically contrasts with the fundamental Hebraic distinction between God and Man. The Stoic conception of the immanence of the divine would have been utterly revolting to a Jew.

As a Jewish theist, Paul maintains the impassable gulf between the Creator, who in self-consciousness is free to will into existence that which is, and man, the creature, as the object of the divine creative will.[11] The bond of Paul's human solidarity is not divine immanence or a metaphysical unity. It is only through a mediated κοινωνία ('fellowship'), that the one God may be imparted to mankind.[12] The basic division between God and man in Paul's view, justifies our search for the source-background of his thought in his Hebraic heritage, rather than in Stoicism,[13] Platonism,[14] or other less important Greek philosophical systems.

[3] Cf. T. A. Lacey, *The One Body and the One Spirit* (London, 1925), p. 233; T. R. Glover, *Paul of Tarsus* (London, 1925), p. 5.

[4] C. H. Dodd, *Man in God's Design* (Newcastle, 1952), p. 11; T. A. Lacey, op. cit. p. 233.

[5] C. H. Dodd, op. cit. p. 13.

[6] S. Hanson, *The Unity of the Church in the New Testament*, p. 52.

[7] Ibid. Cf. W. Morgan, *The Religion and Theology of Paul* (Edinburgh, 1917), pp. 134-5.

[8] T. A. Lacey, op. cit. p. 233. Cf. W. Morgan, op. cit. p. 28.

[9] Cf. C. H. Dodd, *The Meaning of Paul for Today* (London, 1920), p. 139.

[10] Cf. H. R. Willoughby, *Pagan Regeneration* (Chicago, 1929), p. 294.

[11] Cf. L. S. Thornton, *The Incarnate Lord* (London, 1928), pp. 111-12; T. A. Lacey, op. cit. pp. 62-3; C. H. Dodd, *Man in God's Design*, op. cit. pp. 14-15. See C. S. Lewis, *Surprised by Joy* (London, 1955), p. 21.

[12] Cf. Wm. Robinson, *The Biblical Doctrine of the Church* (St Louis, 1948), pp. 15-34.

[13] Cf. J. B. Lightfoot, 'St Paul and Seneca', *St Paul's Epistle to the Philippians* (London, 1868), pp. 291-333.

[14] A. C. Headlam, op. cit. p. 125. For the Platonic conception of man, see C. N. Cochrane, *Christianity and Classical Culture* (Oxford, 1940), p. 79.

In these, abstract thought is paramount in contrast to the empirical conclusions of the Jewish mind.[15] For this reason great caution must be exercised in the interpretation of words and ideas in the Epistles which might be assumed to bear their normal Hellenistic association.

(2) *Gnosticism*. Other scholars have sought to trace Pauline dependence on Gnostic mythology, particularly in his doctrine of the organic unity of the race.[16] But this position raises numerous problems in its attempt to correlate the Gnostic view of sin and redemption with Pauline theology. For the former system evil is not primarily a moral phenomenon but purely natural; it becomes identical with the imperfect, the relative, and the finite.[17] The dualism presupposed by such an understanding of evil, is far closer to Philo's thought (in which the realm of settled being and the world of becoming had by nature tendencies frequently at variance with the good of the totality)[18] than it is to Paulinism.[19] Docetism and dualism of a Hellenistic variety (the evil matter captivating a good spirit) is not only unknown in the Epistles, but it is actively controverted by Paul.[20] The dualism of Pauline theology is exclusively moral, not metaphysical.[21] We shall have occasion to return to this contention in the last chapter where a fuller discussion of the differences of the conception of solidarity in Paul from Gnostic mythology will be presented.

(3) *The Mystery Religions*. A third source for the Pauline doctrines of redemption and anthropology has been sought in the Hellenistic Mystery Religions. The importance of these Cults in the Roman Empire of the first century in conjunction with the similarity

---

[15] Cf. C. H. Dodd, *Man in God's Design*, p. 17.
[16] Notably R. Bultmann; cf. *Theology of the New Testament*, trans. K. Grobel, Vol. I (London, 1952), 174, 250; and 'New Testament and Mythology', in *Kerugma and Myth*, ed. H. W. Bartsch, trans. R. H. Fuller (London, 1953), p. 15; L. G. Rylands, *The Beginnings of Gnostic Christianity* (London, 1940), pp. 210-11.
[17] Cf. H. L. Mansel, *The Gnostic Heresies of the First and Second Centuries* (London, 1875), p. 13.
[18] Cf. E. R. Goodenough, *By Light, Light* (New Haven, 1935), p. 394.
[19] Cf. J. M. Creed, 'The Heavenly Man', *JTS*, Vol. XXVI (1925), p. 133; E. R. Goodenough, op. cit. p. 394. See W. D. Davies's excellent discussion of the whole issue of dualism in the teaching of Paul, *Paul and Rabbinic Judaism*, pp. 17ff.
[20] Cf. B. Weiss, *Biblical Theology of the New Testament*, trans. D. Eaton, Vol. I (Edinburgh, 1882), 339-40.
[21] J. S. Stewart, *A Man in Christ* (London, 1938), p. 104. Cf. J. A. T. Robinson, *The Body*, pp. 24-6; R. Bultmann, 'New Testament and Mythology', p. 17.

of the Pauline terminology, has given the case considerable plausibility in the minds of notable sponsors such as R. Reitzenstein,[22] W. Bousset,[23] K. Lake,[24] among a number. The similarities have been well summarized by H. A. A. Kennedy:

> Like the Mystery religions, he proclaimed a great 'redemption'. Like them he could point to a 'knowledge' of God which meant not intellectual apprehension but practical fellowship. Like them he could think of a transformation into the Divine likeness which was the very goal of being. . . . But his presuppositions were different. Redemption from *sin* was primary with him, not redemption from *fate*.[25]

There are other reasons for denying any essential relationship between Christianity according to Paul and the Mysteries. W. D. Davies has suggested some of the most fundamental divergencies.[26] (1) The Mysteries were individualistic while Christianity is social —incorporation into a Community, the Body of Christ.[27] (2) The Hellenistic religious experience depended on mythological creations and speculative reconstruction; Christianity was founded on recent historical events and persons. Its founding was witnessed by individuals then alive. (3) There is no mystical absorption in Christianity such as the Mysteries promulgated. (4) There is no counterpart to faith (in the Pauline sense) in the Mystery religions. (5) The whole atmosphere of Christianity is radically different from that of the Mysteries.

As in other areas of thought and experience, the clue to a proper understanding of the relationship between Paul and alien religious ideas is found in 'stimulus diffusion'. In the Apostle's search for a meaningful terminology, he was obliged to adopt terms with which his audience was acquainted; but, he gave new meanings to them in the new context of Christianity.[28] In Paul, mysticism is always subordinate to monotheism.[29] The human plight is not immersion in an irresponsible εἱμαρμένη, but a moral solidarity in sin. Redemption is not mystical absorption into an

[22] Cf. e.g. *Die Hellenistischen Mysterienreligionen* (3 Aufl., Leipzig, Berlin, 1927); *Poimandres* (Leipzig, 1904).

[23] Cf. e.g. *Kurios Christos* (2nd edn., Göttingen, 1921).

[24] Cf. e.g. *The Earlier Epistles of St Paul*, p. 215.

[25] *The Theology of the Epistles* (London, 1919), p. 25.

[26] Op. cit. pp. 89-100. W. L. Knox agrees in general with this conclusion in *St Paul and the Church of Jerusalem* (Cambridge, 1925), p. 147; so also A. Schweitzer, *The Mysticism of Paul the Apostle*, trans. W. Montgomery (London, 1931), *passim*.

[27] C. A. A. Scott, *Christianity According to St Paul*, p. 22.

[28] Cf. ibid. pp. 127-33; C. Chavasse, *The Bride of Christ*, p. 19.

[29] See E. Best, *One Body in Christ* (London, 1955), *passim*.

esoteric and consequently irresponsible Mystery; justification is cast in ethical terms of holiness and absolute moral purity (cf. Eph 5^{27}, 4^{17}–5^{16}).[30]

The procedure to be followed in this chapter is the presentation of the basis of Paul's view of human solidarity and the implications which are derived from it in the Epistles. Of primary importance in the first section are both the unity of God and the origin of mankind from one ancestor. The second part of the chapter will examine the representative character of Adam and the corporate personality of the race in Adam. The implications of the corporate judgement of Adam and racial involvement in the Old Aeon will be treated in that context as a preparation for the discussion of the last chapter and the conception of the solidarity of the redeemed and re-created humanity.

THE FOUNDATIONS OF THE SOLIDARITY OF THE RACE

Creation by the One God

The unity of all mankind is a presupposition transferred without challenge from Judaism and the Old Testament into the theology of the Epistles of Paul. The conception is of such a fundamental nature that one searches almost in vain for explicit declarations of the proposition. While there is no argument for what W. Wrede calls 'an undefinable coherence between the race and the individual',[31] the assumed unity of the race is the only possible explanation in Paul's mind for the universality of sin and all the determining factors in human existence apart from the obvious inter-relationship of cause and effect (e.g. environmental or personal influence, etc.). This presupposition was not held by Paul in isolation or superimposed by him upon the contemporary scene, but it was a solidarity which he perceived to be rooted in the original creation of man.

(1) *The Implications of the Unity of God.* The threshold of Paul's doctrine of the unity of mankind, is the unity of God or his Jewish monotheism.[32] Without recourse to the pantheism of current pagan cults and philosophy, the Apostle's doctrine adheres

---

[30] Contrast W. L. Knox, *St Paul and the Church of the Gentiles*, p. 107.
[31] *Paul*, trans. E. Lummis (London, 1907), p. 82.
[32] On the unity of God, see S. Hanson, *The Unity of the Church in the New Testament*, p. 57. The explicit phrase εἷς θεός is found in Rom 3^{30}, 1 Cor $8^{4, 6}$, Gal 9^{20}, 1 Tim 2^5. It is the direct antithesis to the pantheon 'who are called gods' (1 Cor 8^5).

to the unity of the Creator as the cause and ground for the unity of the race. It was impossible for him to conceive of men as the atomistic offspring or creations of sundry deities. Individual men are the branches of a human tree growing in its historical dimension from a single seed. It was God who had created and planted that seed which makes of men an organic unity.

The most explicit reference to human unity in its derivation from the Creator, is made in the Mars Hill address. Paul declares that humanity as a whole is the offspring (γένος) of God (Acts 17[28-9])[33] implying a common unity akin to the Jewish conception of the corporate sonship of Israel. Although it is impossible to determine any direct relationship between the two ideas, the underlying conception is the same. Both predicate a corporate divine sonship[34] to a group without denying the creation of that group in history (cf. Col 1[16-17] with Deut 32[6, 18]).[35] The intention of Paul in using this terminology was two-fold. On the one hand, it implies the unity of the race; on the other, a common responsibility incurred through the total family relationship to the Creator. In a less defined form, this same idea is found in Ephesians 3[15]. Referring to God as the Father in the preceding verse, Paul continues: 'From whom every family in heaven and on earth is named. . . .' The term Father in the same context, and the Hebraic connotation of the term, 'name', suggests the idea of a family possessed by God and its consequent responsibility. The reference to the Fatherhood of God is not clear in another passage in Ephesians (4[6]: '. . . One God and Father of us all, who is above all and through and in all') as to its scope. Whether it is restricted to the Church or not, however, all of these passages seek to establish the unity of the corporate son or

---

[33] This passage is a quotation from Aratus, a Stoic of Cilicia. Cf. T. A. Lacey, op. cit. p. 233. This manner of speaking is an apt illustration of the principle of 'stimulus diffusion'. There is no more of a confusion of the human and the divine in this passage than elsewhere. God is the Creator (Acts 17[26]), not 'Infuser'. This point applies with equal force to the alleged Stoic formula found in Rom 11[36], ὅτι ἐξ αὐτοῦ καὶ δι᾽ αὐτοῦ καὶ εἰς αὐτὸν τὰ πάντα (so also with variations, 1 Cor 8[6]. Cf. Eph 4[6], Col 1[16]). E. Norden has established the currency of this formula in the early centuries of the era. See Agnostos Theos (Leipzig, Berlin, 1913), pp. 240-50, 374. Cf. E. C. Rust, Nature and Man in Biblical Thought, pp. 207, 212; T. W. Manson, The Teaching of Jesus (Cambridge, 1931), p. 91; A. Schweitzer, Paul and His Interpreters, trans. W. Montgomery (London, 1912), pp. 96, 239.

[34] L. S. Thornton, The Common Life in the Body of Christ (2nd edn, London, 1944), p. 115 note 1.

[35] Cf. E. Brunner, Man in Revolt, trans. O. Wyon (London, 1939), pp. 108-13; G. S. Duncan, Jesus, Son of Man (London, 1947), p. 44.

family while they declare the united responsibility of the race to God.

It is in this relationship of man to God that Paul's conception of righteousness finds its basic application. Neither sin nor perfection can be judged by a human standard. 'There is not one righteous among men' (cf. Acts 17[30], Rom 3[19, 23], 5[12])[36] makes reference to the corporate and individual failure of man to fulfil the requirements of the divine standard.[37]

The basis for Paul's doctrine of responsibility is man's creation by one holy and personal God. The nature of human responsibility is dual; there is the duty towards God and a concomitant duty toward fellow men. The two areas of responsibility interpenetrate each other in such a way that they are not always distinguishable. Paul felt no obligation to argue for this point on the basis of man created in the *Imago Dei*. In the existence of the law and man's rationality, the dual responsibility of the race is self-evident. Mankind is universally faced with the requirement of maintaining a moral standard which is his through creation by God.[38] The revelation of this standard to man was made in two distinct ways, involving corresponding dimensions of human solidarity.

(1) The Special Revelation given to Israel.—Paul teaches that it is the former Jewish law which embodies the revealed will of God for His creatures (Rom 2[18]). It provided the gauge by which man must be judged (Rom 2[12], Gal 3[10]).[39] The Jews, however, despite their boasting the privileged role as bearers of God's standard (Rom 3[2]) and doers of His will (Rom 2[17]), had fallen far short of its requirements. In brief, they had done the same things for which they had condemned Gentile sinners outside the law (Rom 2[1, 18-29]). The conclusion of the argument is the corporate guilt of Israel and its consequent condemnation before God (Rom 3[9]).

(2) The Natural Revelation given to Mankind.—The objection might have been raised that the law could only determine

---

[36] For the attestation of an identical view in the Old Testament, see Quell, 'Sin', *Bible Key Words (TWNT)*, pp. 17-21.
[37] Cf. E. H. Wahlstrom, *The New Life in Christ* (Philadelphia, 1950), pp. xi, 7.
[38] Cf. 1 Cor 11[14]: '. . . ἡ φύσις αὐτὴ διδάσκει. . . .' See R. Bultmann, *Theology of the New Testament*, p. 250.
[39] For the Jewish conception of sin, see 'Sin', *Bible Key Words (TWNT)*, p. 39. Cf. R. Bultmann, *Jesus and the Word*, trans. L. P. Smith, E. Huntress (London, 1935), pp. 66-72.

the responsibility of those to whom it was accessible. This problem was recognized by Paul. In his estimation, it provided the primary distinction between the Jew and the Gentile. Yet the Gentile was not without law of some kind. This conclusion was confirmed in the Apostle's mind by the fact that non-Jews in some cases fulfilled the basic principles of the law. It was written on the heart, witnessed to by the συνείδησις ('conscience'), and provided the basis for the comparative judging of one man by another (Rom 2¹⁴⁻¹⁵).[40]

Roughly equivalent to the conscience is the νοῦς. This term is used to designate that element in man which knows the good and apparently would accomplish it, were it accorded the sufficient power (cf. Rom 7²²⁻³, ²⁵).[41] But both conscience and mind may be defiled, cancelling any good which they might otherwise instigate (see Tit 1¹⁵; cf. 3¹¹). It is quite possible that this innate element opposed to τὸ φρόνημα τῆς σαρκός represents the Rabbinic yetzer hatob.[42] But the mind, unaided, is strictly limited in its ability to understand and respond to the wisdom of God.[43] But even as the Jews have fallen short of their duty in observing the revealed law, the Gentiles have violated the innate law written on the heart. 'The fearful vices which beset the Gentile world are due to the rejection of τὴν φυσικὴν χρῆσιν for τὴν παρὰ φύσιν χρῆσιν' (Rom 1²⁶).[44] This natural law, apprehensible to the 'mind', is undoubtedly equivalent to the Jewish Rabbinical preceptive code known as the Noachian commandments. This name denotes their universality through humanity's common descent from Noah.[45] These precepts, given to Adam under similar circumstances to the revelation of the Torah to Israel, were indelibly inscribed in the hearts of all Adam's descendants. It is described by Paul as the revelation to all men from the foundation of the world, the 'truth held in unrighteousness' (Rom 1¹⁸⁻³²). It further

[40] Cf. F. Prat, *The Theology of St Paul*, II.50. The idea of a conscience in man originated in Stoicism, but was evidently adopted by Judaism and given a convenantal basis.

[41] Cf. B. Weiss, op. cit. I.348.

[42] The difference and similarities between the Pauline νοῦς, συνείδησις and the *vetzer hatob* suggest another instance of 'stimulus diffusion'.

[43] Cf. F. Prat, op. cit. II.50-1. This is a point of contrast between Paul and the Hellenistic conception of the νοῦς.

[44] W. D. Davies, op. cit. p. 116.

[45] Cf. ibid. p. 114. See *Sanh* 56a-b. Cf. K. Lake, op. cit. pp. 55-8. Note that these commandments are reflected in the precepts given to Gentile converts and endorsed by Paul in Acts 15²⁸⁻³⁰.

serves as the basis of man's inexcusability (Rom 1[20]) and universal guilt apart from the question of the possession of the Mosaic Torah (a more external and expanded form of the innate law—Rom 2[12]).[46]

It is of supreme importance to recognize at this juncture that any conception of an inherent or universal law can be predicated only on the basis of the solidarity of the race. If a Stoic or Hellenistic conception of the cosmic spirit is rejected on the grounds of Paul's doctrine of creation as the source of the common unity of the race, we are left with no alternative to the Hebraic postulation of the unity of the race through creation and heredity. The corollary of this conviction in both Judaism and Paul's mind is the corporate responsibility of the race to God in a vertical dimension and to one another on a horizontal level.

Although Paul postulated the conception of a racial solidarity, it does not imply that a common unity amongst men could be found in his day. The universal kinship of mankind should have found its expression in a universal *koinonia*; but, with the severance of the covenantal bond of unity with God (Rom 1[18-32]) came an inevitable dissolution of the external bond of love which should have united all men.[47] The incursion of sin (i.e. failure in responsibility to God) brought strife and factions into the human scene. For this reason Paul condemned the Christians of Corinth for walking as (κατά) men in their tolerance of schismatic splinters within the Church (1 Cor 3[3]; cf. verse 4: ὀυκ ἀνθρωποί ἐστε). As Israel had broken the special covenant (cf. Jer 11[10], 22[9], the Gentiles have broken the 'natural' covenant, especially in idolatry and immorality (cf. Rom 1[23-4] with Isa 24[5]).

(2) *The Implication of Common Descent from One Man.* The clearest declaration of the means by which the solidarity of the race is secured is not found in the Epistles but in Paul's sermon on the Areopagus (Acts 17[22-31]). It was apparently a fundamental feature of his earliest message to a Gentile audience to emphasize the unity of the race because of its descent from the first man to be created. In any case, we are not left to speculation in Paul's message to the Athenians. In this sermon Paul establishes the

[46] Note that there is a universal recognition of the good implied in Romans 12[17]: '. . . Provide things honest in the sight of all men.' Cf. W. D. Davies, op. cit. p. 327. It is the basis of the argument in Romans 13[1-7].

[47] Cf. E Brunner, op. cit. p. 141.

organic unity of the race and a concomitant responsibility of each individual on the basis of the universal human descent from one ancestor.[48] In the record preserved by Luke he says: 'And (God) has made of one (man)[49] every race ($\pi\hat{\alpha}\nu$ $\check{\epsilon}\theta os$) of men to live on all the face of the earth, having determined allotted periods and the boundaries of their habitation, that they should seek God . . .' (Acts 17[26-7]). The implication of the postulate is no less than the universal kinship of all men. It is the logical expansion and conclusion of the Old Testament conception of the family, in which either the kin-group immediately, or a whole nation, was designated a מִשְׁפָּחָה on the basis of common descent. The exclusivism which prevented Judaism from capitalizing on the postulation of a universal brotherhood of mankind was contradicted in the teaching of Jesus to which Paul became heir (cf. e.g. Jn 10[16], Matt 5[22, 23-4, 47], 7[3-5], 18[15, 21, 35]). Paul further relates the proposition of a common kinship to descent from one man. This provides the first element in the involved teaching of the Epistles which conceives of Adam as the ancestor and head of the race. Mankind is consequently a corporate unit. It is a totality of an identical character to that of Israel in the Old Testament and early Jewish thought. As Abraham was ascribed the determining role of an ancestor of the nation bearing his name, Adam's character and decisions have implicated his race.[50] This means that the human race composes a corporate personality in Paul's theology and that Adam as its ancestral head and realistic representative is its determinative figure.

The importance of the Apostle's adoption of the conception of the corporate personality of the kin-group without qualification from the Old Testament is readily seen. Far from being the application of a principle which was endorsed by human psychological and social exigencies, Paul establishes the basis of this solidarity in the eternal counsels of God. Herein is the justification of divine election and predestination. As long as Esau is

[48] Cf. N. Söderblom, *The Mystery of the Cross*, trans. A. G. Hebert (London, 1933), p. 29; T. W. Manson, op. cit. pp. 332-3.

[49] The word $\alpha\H{\iota}\mu\alpha\tau os$ must be omitted as S. Hanson has well contended and confirmed by the best texts—op. cit. p. 103. That $\check{\epsilon}\nu os$ signifies 'one man' is supported by the parallel drawn with Christ in this passage (17[31]) and elsewhere (cf. Rom 5[18]). Cf. M. Burrows, *An Outline of Biblical Theology*, p. 322.

[50] W. Wrede (op. cit. p. 81) relates Paul's view of Adam to the ancient conception of what happens first in history is repeated in succeeding series or cycles. F. V. Filson, (*St Paul's Conception of Recompense*, p. 11) sees a reflection of the Rabbinic doctrine of merit and demerit. Both are correct in part only.

Edom and *vice versa*, there is no injustice in the indistinguishable hatred of the one or animosity toward the other (Rom 9[11-13]; cf. Mal 1[3-4]). The expanded application of the principle of corporate personality by Paul has long since been proposed by H. W. Robinson,[51] and adopted by C. H. Dodd,[52] A. Nygren,[53] and most fully by E. Best,[54] to explain the problematic Pauline mysticism. As we proceed, it will become increasingly apparent that the whole of Paul's anthropology and soteriology is built on Hebraic conceptions of the solidarity of the race.

Within the scope of Paul's general conception of Adam and the corporate personality of the race are two distinctions which, upon their recognition, aid in the understanding of his thought. The first is the role of Adam as the ancestor of the race, involving his historicity as the first man to be created (cf. Acts 17[26], 1 Cor 15[45, 47-50]).[55] The second is Adam as the realistic representative of the race, cast in the role of a collective personality (cf. Rom 5[12-21], 1 Cor 15[21-2]). The race is identified with Adam and Adam with the race in such a manner that the experience and consequent judgement of both are mutual.[56] The collective totality (*the many*) has both a horizontal and vertical extension, so that all men are 'in Adam' (*the one*, 1 Cor 15[22]) at any given point in history as well as throughout all history. These two distinctions are not to be treated as though they were mutually exclusive but have been adopted primarily for convenience.

THE FATHERHOOD OF ADAM AND THE TERRESTRIAL CHARACTER OF HIS PROGENY

On the basis of our presupposition that Paul accepted the historicity of Adam, it will be necessary to examine briefly the account of the creation of man in the Old Testament. The Genesis narrative establishes the formation of Adam from the dust (עָפָר) of the earth (Gen 2[7]), creation in the image and likeness of God

---

[51] Cf. *The Christian Doctrine of Man*, p. 121; 'Hebrew Psychology', *The People and the Book*, p. 378; *The Cross of the Servant*, p. 34.

[52] Cf. *The Epistle of Paul to the Romans* (London, 1932), pp. 79-80, 86.

[53] Cf. *Commentary on Romans*, trans. C. C. Rasmussen (Philadelphia, 1949), p. 213.

[54] Op. cit. *passim*.

[55] Historicity is not only of primary importance out of deference to the scriptural account, but it is fundamental to a nondualistic explanation of evil. Cf. C. N. Cochrane, op. cit. p. 240.

[56] This distinction corresponds in general to G. B. Stevens's phrase 'mystical realism', *The Pauline Theology* (London, 1892), pp. 32-40.

(1^{27}, 5^1), his animation by living breath (2^7), his naming in conjunction with Eve as אָדָם ('man') (Gen 5^2), his unique position
in the creation as lord (1^{26}; cf. $2^{15,\ 19\text{-}20}$), his unique role as the
progenitor of the race (1^{28}; cf. 3^{20}). By noting the nature of Adam
through creation and the nature of humanity as it is, Paul concluded that the latter is a derivation from the former. For this
reason, the three basic characteristics of natural humanity have
been determined by the solidarity of all mankind with Adam who
was the original human creation. But the implications of human
generic relationship to Adam must be distinguished from Adam's
realistic representative role. Generically, the historical Adam
has determined the human possession of a perishable, 'soulish',
and fleshly body.

(1) *The Perishable Body.* The first implication which we shall
consider is the corruptibility of the human body. In the words of
Paul:

The first man was from the earth ($\gamma\hat{\eta}s$; cf. עָפָר, Gen 2^7), a man of
dust ($\chi o\ddot{\iota}\kappa\acute{o}s$). . . . As was the (man) of dust, so are those who are
of dust (οἱ χοϊκοί). . . . Just as we have borne the image ($\epsilon\grave{\iota}\kappa\acute{o}\nu a$) of
the man of dust, we shall also bear the image of the man of heaven. I
tell you this, brethren: flesh and blood cannot inherit the kingdom of
God, nor does the perishable inherit the imperishable (1 Cor $15^{47\text{-}50}$;
cf. Rom 1^{23}).

In this passage, the Apostle compares the body of the first man
with that of all men. He recognizes the incontrovertible fact that
human flesh is subject to the laws of natural decay. Thus, the
mortality of the flesh is one of its essential characteristics (1 Cor
$15^{44,\ 50}$; cf. 2 Cor $4^{11,\ 16}$, 5^1, Rom 6^{12}). Man is a part of the
changeable physical order.[57] His finitude is equivalent to the
Old Testament description of man as grass (cf. e.g. Isa $40^{6\text{-}7}$,
Ps 103^{15}). This was common knowledge to both Paul and the
troubled Corinthian Christians. It is the Apostle's vehement
argument that there is a logical necessity for the resurrection
because of the perishable nature of man's body which cannot
exist in the New Order; rather, the body must be re-created after
the pattern of Christ's glorious body (1 Cor 15^{49}; cf. 2 Cor 5^1).

[57] Cf. A. Robertson and A. Plummer, *The First Epistle of St Paul to the Corinthians,*
ICC (Edinburgh, 1911), pp. 370, 373.

It is more than incidental to Paul's case that there is no definite allusion to the relationship of mankind to Adam through natural descent; if there had been, it would have destroyed the parallel between Adam and Christ and their respective communities. It is apparent in the context that the medium of the actualization of the old creation is the natural process of birth,[58] while the New Humanity is created through a supernatural process of inclusion into Christ (2 Cor 5[17]).

(2) *The Psychic Body.* In a further refinement of his point Paul describes the natural body as ψυχικόν ('soulish'). 'If there is a "soulish" body, there is also a spiritual body. So also it is written, the first man, Adam became a living soul' (1 Cor 14[44-5]).[59] This is an extension of the comparison between humanity and Adam. Not only is the human body corporeal, but the life principle which animates it derives its finite character from the original נֶפֶשׁ חַיָּה of Adam. All men partake of this creative life principle which stands over against the new life principle of the New Creation (τὸ πνευματικόν), which is not temporal but eternal (1 Cor 15[45-6]). Again, the explanation for the common possession of a 'soulish' body, is the natural process of procreation. 'As the same flesh and blood, so also, so to speak, the same soul essence is propagated through the human race.'[60]

(3) *The Body of Flesh.* The third basic element in Paul's anthropology is mankind as σάρξ. A considerable amount of confusion has centred around conjectures introduced to explain the Apostle's broad and enigmatic use of this term.[61] Burton suggests seven distinctive uses of the term from the reference to the merely physical nature of man's body, all the way to an 'element that makes for sin'.[62] For our purposes, a simpler classification suggested by Wahlstrom is quite adequate: (1) the ordinary sense of the material flesh (cf. e.g. Gal 4[13], 1 Cor 15[39]); (2) σάρξ used as

[58] That is, the organic principle of biological reproduction which requires that that which is born be of the same kind as the parent (cf. Gen 1[11-12, 21, 24], Matt 7[16-18], Gal 6[7-8]).
[59] The contrast between Paul and Philo is readily seen at this juncture. The latter sets σάρξ and ψυχή in sharp antithesis. Cf. H. A. A. Kennedy, op. cit. p. 34 note 3.
[60] B. Weiss, op. cit. p. 338 note 8.
[61] These conjectures follow two general lines: (1) those who interpret the 'flesh' as the point of sin's attack, and (2) those who find a basic dualism in Paul's use of the term. In this view, flesh is, like the Hellenistic conception of matter, evil in itself.
[62] See his discursus in *The Epistle to the Galatians*, ICC (New York, 1920), pp. 492-5.

the symbol of human existence.[63] It is vital for our study to further sub-divide the second category into human nature apart from any connotation of sin, and σάρξ as a symbol of man's involvement in the Old Aeon.[64] In this sub-division, we may note a very distinct echo from the Old Testament conception of בָּשָׂר.[65] On the one hand, it defined the kin-group constituted of one flesh through generic descent. On the other, בָּשָׂר was used to describe a relationship which could be acquired, such as one might secure through the union of marriage (cf. Gen 2²⁴ with Eph 5²⁹) which was essentially spiritual in its character. When 'flesh' denoted an acquired relationship, it was often given an ethical connotation. Thus, it was 'flesh' which corrupted itself (i.e. morally, cf. Gen 6¹²) in all the earth.

Corresponding to the distinctions in the Old Testament, σάρξ is used by Paul to refer to a purely racial or physical symbol (cf. Col 2⁵ [note 1 Cor 5³], Gal 4¹⁴ [note 1 Cor 6¹³]); however, in the context of the Old Age, the 'flesh' has a very definite ethical connotation, a characteristic achieved through acquisition.[66] We shall discuss this latter usage under the implications of the corporate judgement of Adam.

Conclusion. We have sought in this section to present the implications which natural descent had for the human race as the progeny of Adam. The three terms, body, soul, and flesh, are variously used by the Apostle to describe the creaturely finitude of mankind. We have also contended that the universality of these characteristics is an evidence of the Old Testament conception of the family, in which the succeeding generations share in the בָּשָׂר of the ancestor. There is more. As in the Old Testament, flesh is a totality denomination which is descriptive of the solidarity of the group; so in Paul, '. . . σάρξ stands for man, in the solidarity of creation in his distance from God'.[67] Such an idea of a universal totality comes primarily from the Old Testament period of Hebrew thought.

---

[63] Op. cit. p. 9.

[64] See pp. 121-3 *infra.* Cf. P. C. Boylan, *St Paul's Epistle to the Romans* (Dublin, 1934), p. 83; F. Prat, op. cit. II.402-3.

[65] See J. A. T. Robinson's whole discussion in *The Body,* pp. 11-16.

[66] The usage of σάρξ, in the Epistles, is distributed in a proportion of 56 cases of the former, and 35 of the latter. H. W. Robinson, *The Christian Doctrine of Man,* p. 114; W. D. Davies, op. cit. p. 19.

[67] J. A. T. Robinson, op. cit. p. 31.

There may be some intimations of a Rabbinic doctrine of the creation of the race in Adam. As the summary of Davies shows, there was a type of mythological unity of the race mediated through its origin:

That doctrine implied that the very constitution of the physical body of Adam and the method of its formation was symbolic of the real oneness of mankind. In that one body of Adam, east and west, north and south were brought together, male and female, as we have seen. The 'body' of Adam included all mankind.[68]

The Jewish doctrine of human reproduction maintained that the physical and natural body was the heritage from the parents. The soul was infused directly by God. If we are restricted in this particular section to treating the naturally inherited characteristics of the race, it would be correct to see a coincidence between the Old Testament and Judaism as the background. On the other hand, Paul's emphasis on the universal kinship of all men, savours more of the ancient conception of the race as the extension of the flesh or the soul of the ancestor.

ADAM'S REALISTIC REPRESENTATION OF THE RACE

The Corporate Transgression

Our detailed study of the conception of corporate personality in the Old Testament indicated that realistic representation of a group might devolve on the head of that group. It might in one case be the father, in others, a master, priest, or king. Paul did not choose to emphasize the hereditary relationship in his doctrine of mankind's corporate involvement in sin and death.[69] His sole purpose in mentioning the relationship of Adam to his progeny is to draw a direct antithetical parallel between Adam, including his community, and Christ, including the New Humanity.[70] If we heed Barth's warning to interpret Adam as merely the type of the real thing, that is, the Christ-collectivity,[71] we are

---

[68] W. D. Davies, op. cit. p. 57.

[69] E. Brunner objects strenuously to Augustine's first argument for Original Sin, i.e. a hereditary bias stemming from Adam. Brunner maintains that to accept this view is to ground something personal in a natural fact. Op. cit. pp. 121-2; cf. *The Christian Doctrine of Creation and Redemption* (*Dogmatics* II), trans. O. Wyon (London, 1952), p. 82.

[70] Cf. P. Wernle, *The Beginnings of Christianity*, trans. G. A. Bieneman (London, 1903), I.230.

[71] *Christus und Adam nach Röm 5* (Zurich, 1952), p. 11. Cf. idem, *The Epistle to the Romans*, trans. E. Hoskyns (London, 1933), pp. 170-1.

forced to allow that realistic representation is the primary element in Paul's Adam-typology.

Paul's discussion of Adam's representative role in the introduction of sin is confined in large to two passages: (1) Romans 5$^{12-21}$ is central. (2) In a more contracted form, the same theme occurs in 1 Corinthians 15$^{21-2}$: 'Wherefore since by (διά) (one) man is death, also through (one) man is the resurrection of the dead. For as in Adam all die, so also in Christ shall all be made to live.'

The theme of these passages is the relationship of the one to the many. One man (in this case, Adam) sinned. Because of his realistic representation of the race, his original transgression was not isolated, but corporately involved the whole of the race.[72] It is Adam's position as the archetypal head of the race, which he embodies as a corporate personality, that makes his rebellion against God the revolt of his group. Under such a conception (particularly as it is found in the Old Testament) it was quite possible for Paul to see the individual and the group as identical. This identity is evident in such a phrase as, e.g. 'in Adam' (cf. 1 Cor 15^{22}), which is the direct converse of the phrase, 'in Christ'.

But does Paul actually intend that his readers should understand that in Adam's disobedience all men in some mystical manner participated? This question has both perplexed and divided interpreters down through the history of Pauline exegesis.[73] If we examine this passage in the light of the principle of corporate personality a two-fold answer is probably justified.

(1) Yes, we must in the first analysis admit that Adam's sin was corporate or shared by all men.[74] The use of the aorist, ἥμαρτον, is an indication in this direction.[75] In the words of A. Nygren: 'If we are to keep the translation, "because all have

---

[72] Cf. S. Hanson, op. cit. p. 68; A. Nygren, op. cit. p. 213.

[73] See discussions by F. Prat, op. cit. I.218; Sanday and Headlam, *Romans* (ICC), p. 134; and S. Hanson, for more recent views, op. cit. pp. 66-8.

[74] Cf. F. R. Tennant, *SDFOS*, p. 261; A. B. Bruce, *St Paul's Conception of Christianity* (New York, 1907), p. 130; H. Weinel, *Biblische Theologie des Neuen Testaments* (Tübingen, 1911), p. 245; W. Beyschlag, *New Testament Theology*, trans. N. Buchanan (Edinburgh, 1896), II.60; W. D. Davies, op. cit. p. 32; G. B. Stevens, *The Theology of the New Testament* (Edinburgh, 1899), pp. 357-8. Contrast the opinion of Sanday and Headlam, op. cit. p. 134; K. Barth, *Romans*, p. 172; H. C. Sheldon, *New Testament Theology* (New York, 1911), p. 212; C. Weizsäcker, *The Apostolic Age of the Christian Church*, trans. J. Millar (London, 1894), I.149-50; E. Best, op. cit. p. 34.

[75] Contrast H. C. Sheldon, op. cit. p. 211, who sees an escape from this view in the possible use of the aorist with a perfect sense.

sinned", we shall have to understand it as Augustine did, "all men have sinned in Adam".'[76] A confirmation of this conclusion is found in Romans 5[19], where a direct antithesis is drawn between the disobedience of Adam and the obedience of Christ: In 2 Corinthians 5[14] this act is explicitly defined as the corporate death of Christ: 'For the love of Christ constrains us, this judging, that one died for all; then indeed all died' ($\dot{\alpha}\pi\dot{\epsilon}\theta\alpha\nu\sigma\nu$). On the basis of the realistic representation of the heads of the two respective types of humanity, Paul affirms that the two corresponding groups have actually participated in the archetypal acts of human history. Only on such a basis, can any adequate parallel be drawn between the original transgression of Adam and the obedience of the Second Adam.

(2) The second aspect of Paul's answer rests on the empirical fact of the universal human endorsement of Adam's representative act. The aspect of oscillation in the Hebrew conception of corporate personality comes into view as the focus turns to examine mankind. It is noteworthy that Paul does not even begin his theology of Romans with a reference to the corporate transgression of Adam; on the contrary, it is his conclusion.[77] In the interest of establishing the universal involvement of the human race in sin, no mention is made of Adam at all. It is the unfolding of the sordid human story, the increasing corruption within the group and individual relationships through following one's free choice.[78] Nor was Paul's introduction of Adam as the source of sin intended in any sense to detract from man's responsibility for sin. It is of the very essence of Paul's argument to maintain the complete inexcusability of man. This individual option is particularly evident in Romans 7. There Paul depicts every man as 'the Adam of his own soul' since the powerful influence of sin comes to overcome and deceive him, yet not apart from the self-determinate will of the individual.[79]

For Paul, our division of the answer to the original question

[76] Op. cit. pp. 214-15.
[77] Cf. H. F. Rall, op. cit. pp. 36-7. H. Weinel contrasts the metaphysical (Rom 5) with the empirical (Rom 1-2). Op. cit. p. 370.
[78] Cf. A. S. Peake, *The Quintessence of Paulinism* (Manchester, 1916), pp. 27, 30; F. R. Tennant, *The Concept of Sin* (Cambridge, 1912), pp. 40-2; J. Weiss, *The History of Primitive Christianity*, ed. in E. trans., F. C. Grant (London, 1937), p. 607.
[79] Some scholars point to $\dot{\epsilon}\phi$' $\dot{\tilde{\omega}}$ $\pi\dot{\alpha}\nu\tau\epsilon\varsigma$ $\ddot{\eta}\mu\alpha\rho\tau\sigma\nu$ (Rom 5[12]) as an example of this idea (cf. W. D. Davies, op. cit. p. 32), but it is not well substantiated. The same idea is found in 2 Thess. 2[9-12], where men are deceived by the 'lawless man' but at the same time love unrighteousness and hate the truth. Cf. J. Weiss, p. 435.

into two opposing aspects, would savour of a scholastic distinction. As long as the one is the many, and the many are the one, no distinction is necessary between the sin of the representative and that of his group.[80] In itself, the whole issue was less problematic than the corporate treatment of the sin of Achan or David would have been; there is a vindication of God's treatment of Adam's sin as a racial act in the universal human adoption of his way. In the particular conception of solidarity which Paul applies to the whole race, the archetypal action of the representative is indistinguishable from the innumerable acts of members within the human totality.[81] But this is not true only because of the solidarity of mankind. As we have already discovered in the Old Testament and Judaism, sin was itself unconfined to the individual. It was organic, contagious, invariably involving the group in guilt.[82] Like dye when poured into a body of water discolours the whole, so the original pollution has spread from the fountain-head to sully the entire human stream. In this manner, Adam's Fall and the universal guilt and propensity to sin are inseparably bound together.[83] Both the unity of the race and the impossibility of maintaining sin's immurement produce the confirmation of Paul's doctrine.

THE CORPORATE JUDGEMENT

A further confirmation of the doctrine of the corporate sin of the race was deduced by Paul from the corporate judgement of the race. Holding an unmitigated conception of the justice of God, there assuredly could be no punishment where there was neither guilt nor sin. On the basis of the fact that sin can be imputed only on the ground of a transgression of law (Rom 5^{13}; cf. 4^{15}) and the second consideration that there was no law existent between Adam and Moses, the universal punishment of the race with death implies the corporate sin of the race in Adam (Rom

---

[80] A similar failure to notice any paradox in an inherent bias to sin, and individual responsibility was noted in 4 Ezra (cf. H. A. A. Kennedy, op. cit. p. 40; P. Feine, *Theologie des Neuen Testaments* (Leipzig, 1910), p. 272) and 2 Baruch. Even the Rabbis at times reflect this conception. But Paul's teaching on sin is unique in its predication of a corporate sin of the race in Adam. This is nowhere to be found in our Jewish sources.

[81] Cf. W. P. Dickson, *St Paul's Use of the Terms Flesh and Spirit* (Glasgow, 1883), p. 318; E. Burton, op. cit. pp. 422-3.

[82] Cf. E. Brunner, *The Christian Doctrine of Creation and Redemption*, p. 96; C. H. Dodd, *Romans*, p. 80.

[83] Cf. 'Sin', *Bible Key Words* (*TWNT*), p. 78.

5[13-14]).[84] Since there could be no sin as individual transgression between the original injunction laid upon Adam and the revelation of the Torah, it is Paul's conclusive argument that the race sinned in Adam. Despite the absence of sin as individual transgression, death reigned over all; it was the application of corporate justice at the provocation of a corporate transgression.[85]

In the whole of this discussion we are forced to see the Jewish heritage of Paul. In both the Old Testament and the post-canonical Jewish writings, the conception of a divine corporate justice is frequently encountered. As the group might be punished with or for the sin of a member who represents the group realistically, the whole race is involved in the judgement of Adam's archetypal act. It is the expansion of the idea of demerit from its normal restriction to Israel, and a re-application to the human totality. One is further impressed by the organic nature of Paul's thinking. Inseparably related to the proposition of a corporate sin is the individual's free choice of evil. The corporate judgement of God, applied on the basis of the solidarity or corporate personality of the race, is vindicated by the individual's willingly entangling himself in guilt. For these reasons, it is quite unrealistic to maintain stubbornly that Paul is dependent upon specific Jewish documents such as 4 *Ezra* or 2 *Baruch*, or even the opinions of certain Rabbis. The principles were right at hand. That which is unique in the Apostle's thought, apparently, are contrasting deductions arising out of his soteriological doctrine of Christ's realistic representation of the New Humanity.[86]

THE SOLIDARITY OF HUMANITY IN THE OLD AEON

Introduction

We have already attempted to establish the contention that Paul applied the Hebraic ideas of kinship and corporate personality to the entire race of men. This, however, does not exhaust the Apostle's conception of the solidarity of the race. Other passages, as well as those which have been examined, posit the mysterious

---

[84] Cf. P. Wernle, op. cit. p. 229; W. Beyschlag, op. cit. II.59; F. R. Tennant, *SDFOS*, op. cit. p. 257. Paul affirms the less apparent universality of sin from the undeniable inevitability of death in these verses (cf. F. C. Baur, *Paul: His Life and Works*, trans. A. Menzies, Vol. 11 [London, 1875], p. 185; A. B. Bruce, op. cit. p. 129).

[85] This point may be further attested by the death of infants.

[86] Note, e.g. Romans 8[10]: 'And if Christ be in you, the body is dead because of sin' (i.e. of Adam; cf. L. S. Thornton, *The Common Life*, p. 143); 'but the Spirit is life because of righteousness' (i.e. of Christ).

conception of an Old Aeon or Age (αἰών). The connotation of the term involves both the solidarity of the creation and a corresponding continuity of humanity under subjection to powerful forces which control all material existence. O. Cullmann has made a noteworthy contribution to a biblical understanding of the Aeon in his book *Christ and Time*. He correctly shows that in the Hebraic conception of man, humanity is not isolated in the Creation. On the contrary, man holds a representative position over all that God has made.[87] In the New Testament man's exalted role of lordship in the Creation lies behind the solidarity which is inferred to exist between man and nature (cf. Rom 8[19-23]. See Gen 3[17-19] and Jewish views, pp. 73-6 *supra*). For this reason, the curse of corporate humanity in Adam implicates the rest of creation.[88]

In man's miserable failure to effect the destiny which was designed for him by God, he is actually allying himself with the nefarious forces of the Old Age in open rebellion against the universal authority of God. United together, it has become the formation of an enemy stronghold within God's universal state. If we were to ask how this all came about, the accusing finger again points to Adam, who was responsible for bringing the race into this alien alliance. As the Apostle does not in stated terms ascribe this initiatory role to Adam, this point is clear only as it can be derived from the Adam-Christ parallel.

In this parallel, certain facts may be deduced. In the relationship of the redeemed to Christ (who is the Figure under discussion, Adam's antitype), there is no question of a hereditary connexion. Rather, it is the One taking the place of the many, including them in Himself (note the reiteration of this idea in Rom 5[8-21], 1 Cor 15[19-28, 45-49]). The Community is related to Christ through faith and personal choice in such a manner that He, as their Representative, does in and for them what they could not do for themselves (cf. Rom 5[8]). An identically inclusive role is played by Adam, who as the first man is the universal archetype of all men, a sort of comprehensive personality.[89] As Christ implicated the New Humanity in the New Age, Adam has involved his race in the Old.

---

[87] Cf. Gen. 1[28], Ps 8[5-8] for the lordship of Adam and humanity.

[88] O. Cullmann, *Christ and Time*, trans. F. V. Filson (London, 1951), pp. 101, 115-18. Cf. S. A. Cook, *The Cambridge Ancient History*, III.443.

[89] Cf. J. Weiss, op. cit. p. 434; S. Hanson, op. cit. p. 68.

The Nature of the Old Aeon

The root of the aeon-concept lies buried in the ancient astrological observation of time-cycle patterns. The variation in the seasons due to the miscalculation of the length of a year and the omission of any compensatory leap year, provided the basis for a calculation of the World Year. This period of 1460 years became known as an aeon or age. How it came about that Judaism assumed only two aeons (the postulation of seven is more common) is not easily explained.[90] It is probable that the aeon-conception was modified by the doctrine of the Fall, the antithesis of Satan and God, and the eschatological expectation of the restoration of Israel. M. Dibelius has established that in the aeon-concept, there was an integration of the astral and the spirit-world. Since a star-spirit rules the world during any stated epoch, there is an apparent alliance between the aeon-theory and the belief in a world-ruler.[91]

In the Epistles of Paul the terminology used to denote the Old Aeon is both varied and confusing. For our purposes it will be sufficient to confine our discussion to αἰών and κόσμος. The term αἰῶνος τοῦτος 'this age' (cf. Rom 12², 1 Cor 1²⁰, 2⁶˙⁸, 3¹⁸, 2 Cor 4⁴, Gal 1⁴) or τοῦ αἰῶνος τοῦ ἐνεστῶτος (Eph 1²¹), or ὁ νῦν αἰών (1 Tim 6¹⁷, 2 Tim 4¹⁰, Tit 2¹²), is a total concept which refers to both time and sphere.[92] At the same time, the term κόσμος may denote the total relationship between the creation and the age (cf. 1 Cor 3¹⁹, 7³¹).[93] J. Weiss says succinctly: 'The fundamental conception that this present world will be replaced by a new world, a "new creation" (2 Cor 5¹⁷, Gal 6¹⁵), while the former itself "passes away" (1 Cor 7³¹), is the basic apocalyptic pattern of Paul's thinking.'[94]

[90] Cf. J. Weiss, op. cit. p. 603 note 15; E. D. Burton, op. cit. pp. 427-31. The latter claims that Paul provides the earliest evidence of the acceptance of this idea among Christians.

[91] *Die Geisterwelt im Glauben des Paulus* (Göttingen, 1909), pp. 193-4.

[92] Cf. E. C. E. Owen, 'αἰών and αἰώνιος', *JTS*, Vol. XXXVII (1936), pp. 266-8, where he lists a parallel usage in the LXX; e.g. 'a generation, race of men' (Sap 14⁶), 'this world' (Ps 89 (90)⁸, Ecc 3¹¹, Ecclus 38³⁴, in the sense of the sensible, material, sinful world). There is more than one example of the use of αἰών in the plural (cf. 1 Cor 10¹¹, τὰ τέλη τῶν αἰώνων; 2⁷, Gal 1⁵, Col 1²⁶, Eph 3⁹, 2 Tim 1⁹, Tit 1²); but this usage has a less technical meaning, i.e. successive periods of time, ages.

[93] Cf. Eph 2²: κατὰ τὸν αἰῶνα τοῦ κόσμου τούτου. The phrase represents a single Hebrew phrase often encountered in the Rabbis. Cf. J. Armitage Robinson, *St Paul's Epistle to the Ephesians* (London, 1903), p. 48.

[94] Op. cit. p. 604.

The κόσμος and the αἰών have a very definite relationship to spiritual beings. Paul refers to being made a spectacle (θέατρον) in the cosmos as becoming the gazing-stock of both men and angels (1 Cor 4⁹). The formulae ἐπουρανίων καὶ ἐπιγείων καὶ καταθονίων (Phil 2¹⁰), and τὰ πάντα ἐν τοῖς οὐρανοῖς καὶ ἐπὶ τῆς γῆς, τὰ ὁρατὰ καὶ ἀόρατα (Col 1¹⁶; cf. 1²⁰), show the same corresponding inclusion of the spirit-world and the material creation under the term κτίσις (κτίζω) (cf. Col 1¹⁵ with 1¹⁶) which in turn is similar in its connotations to κόσμος.⁹⁵

In Paul's use of the problematic phrase στοιχεῖα τοῦ κόσμου there may be the idea of the inter-relation of metaphysical, spiritual, and material elements.⁹⁶ Apparently, this phrase carries a connotation of spirits and demons which are in active opposition to the original intention of the Creation (cf. Gal 4³·⁹, Col 2⁸·²⁰). There is in this phrase the suggestion of the spirits which control the heavenly bodies of the universe and determine the succession of seasons and days.⁹⁷ In Galatians 4⁸⁻⁹, Paul evidently relates the στοιχεῖα to the heathen deities (which according to 1 Cor 10¹⁹⁻²⁰ have a real existence as demons), in that he refers to Christians having formerly been subjected to them. In the opinion of E. Y. Hinks, there is nothing in the Pauline theology which conflicts with his expressed opinion that the elemental forces of the world were spirits.⁹⁸

In still other passages one encounters apparent reference to the spirit-rulers who govern the cosmos. In 1 Corinthians 2⁶·⁸ Paul asserts that the wisdom of God was unknown to the ἀρχόντων τοῦ αἰῶνος τούτου, which is now generally conceded to mean angelic or spiritual powers.⁹⁹ Cullmann maintains that the

---

⁹⁵ Ibid. p. 596. The terms κτίσις and κόσμος by no means always imply a connexion with evil (cf. e.g. Col 1¹⁵). There were, of course, the good angels for both Judaism and Paul, which, although part of the universal creation, were free from the corruption of sin (cf. 1 Cor 15⁵², 1 Thess 4¹⁶, Gal 3¹⁹, 1 Cor 13¹).

⁹⁶ Cf. E. C. Rust, op. cit. pp. 235-6. The connexion of the στοιχεῖα with the aeon may be no more than terminological. Burton claims that apparently there is no evidence that στοιχεῖον meant 'spirit', 'angels', or 'demon' earlier than the *Test Sal*, which is probably late (cf. E. Y. Hinks, 'The Meaning of the phrase τὰ στοιχεῖα τοῦ κόσμου in Gal 4³ and Col 2⁸', *JBL*, XV.191). Burton continues his contention that Paul does not accept the demonic connotation but refers merely to imperfect teaching (cf. op. cit. pp. 514-15, so also J. B. Lightfoot, *The Epistles of St Paul to the Colossians and Philemon* [London, 1886], pp. 180-1; F. Prat, op. cit. II.422-3).

⁹⁷ Cf. E. Y. Hinks, op. cit. p. 190.

⁹⁸ Op. cit. p. 190.

⁹⁹ J. Weiss, op. cit. p. 494; A. S. Peake, op. cit. pp. 28-9. Contrast Robertson and Plummer, op. cit. pp. 39-40.

ἐξουσίαι are spirit-authorities,[100] but the nature of their loyalty is not always clearly distinguished (cf. 1 Cor 15[24]). Colossians 2[15] clearly illustrates the relationship of the evil ἐξουσίαι to the Aeon. Their authority has been effectively challenged by the death and victory of Christ.[101] The importance of these invisible powers of the Old Aeon is clear from Ephesians 6[12], in which Paul declares that the Christian's warfare is in reality against τὰς ἀρχάς, τὰς ἐξουσίας, τοὺς κοσμοκράτορας τοῦ σκότους τούτου, τὰ πνευματικὰ τῆς πονηρίας ἐν τοῖς ἐπουρονίοις (cf. Eph 1[21], Col 1[16]), not flesh and blood (i.e. mankind). The idea behind these formulae is a gauged hierarchy of demonic forces[102] that have allied themselves in a rebellious mutiny against the supreme Authority of the universe. In this alliance they have become identified with the Aeon, and indeed, are the cosmic authorities and rulers of the universe. So effective is their control over nature, that Paul sees the creation in thraldom, that is, in subjection to the forces which control it (cf. Rom 8[19-23]).[103] The Christian is warned against their insidious activity, particularly as it reveals itself in erroneous doctrines (cf. 1 Tim 4[1]: πνεύμασιν . . . διδασκαλίαις δαιμονίων).

Over all the intermediary hierarchy of inimical forces is the sinister figure of Satan, ὁ ἄρχων τῆς ἐξουσίας τοῦ ἀέρος (Eph 2[2]).[104] Such a title implies the headship of all the personal opposition to God in the Old Aeon. He is king of legion intermediary and lesser cosmic spirits (cf. Matt 12[26], Mk 3[22], Lk 11[15-23])[105] adding unity and destiny to opposition against God. He demands

[100] *Christ and Time*, p. 194; cf. J. B. Lightfoot, *Colossians and Philemon*, p. 154. This notion is particularly important in 1 Corinthians 6[3] where Paul denounces the Christians' practice of going to court in suits against each other. 'Know ye not that we shall judge angels?' The courts, as the states which authorize them, are unconsciously controlled by spiritual forces. See O. Cullmann, op. cit. p. 193; J. Weiss, op. cit. p. 600. In Titus 3[1] Christians are encouraged to be in subjection to the ἀρχαῖς ἐξουσίαις, probably as a temporary measure.

[101] Cf. J. B. Lightfoot, *Colossians and Philemon*, p. 190.

[102] Cf. J. Armitage Robinson, op. cit. p. 49; H. A. A. Kennedy, op. cit. p. 40. In the words of G. H. C. Macgregor: '. . . κοσμοκράτορες is the very word which is used in the Hellenistic mystical writings of the seven supreme astral deities; it occurs in Orphic hymns, in inscriptions, in Gnostic writings, and even in Rabbinic literature.' 'Principalities and Powers: the Cosmic Background of Paul's Thought', *New Testament Studies* (Cambridge, 1954), I.21.

[103] Cf. E. Y. Hinks, op. cit. p. 191. Note that Stephen affirms that God '. . . turned and gave them up (i.e. Israel) to serve the astral host' (Acts 7[42]).

[104] Note the parallel phrase, ὁ ἄρχων τοῦ κόσμου τούτου (Jn 12[31], 16[11]). See further, G. H. C. Macgregor, op. cit. p. 18.

[105] The demonic view of Paul is the same as that of the Synoptics. N. P. Williams, *The Ideas of the Fall and of Original Sin*, p. 160. Cf. B. Weiss, op. cit. I.104, 332.

I

complete subordination to himself within the Aeon. 1 Corinthians 2¹² mentions τὸ πνεῦμα τοῦ κόσμου in antithesis to the
'Spirit from God'. The inference may be justified that Paul has
Satan in mind.[106] If this is the case, there is a comparable relationship of the devil to unredeemed humanity, as there is in the
manifestation of the Holy Spirit in the believer. In Ephesians 2²
there is an explicit reference to Satan as the 'spirit which is now
working in the sons of disobedience'. Thus, for Christians to leave
the faith is equivalent to 'turning after Satan' (1 Tim 5¹⁵. Contrast Heb 6⁴⁻⁵, where partaking of the Holy Spirit is to participate
in the power of the Age to Come), or falling into the judgement,
snare, and reproach of the devil (1 Tim 3⁶⁻⁷). In a striking reference to Satan as ὁ θεὸς τοῦ αἰῶνος τούτου (2 Cor 4⁴), the blind-
ness of the thoughts of unbelievers is ascribed to his devilish
activity. He is distinct from the 'rulers' (1 Cor 2⁶, ⁸, note the
plural τῶν ἀρχόντων) and 'sons of disobedience' (Eph 2²), but
he acts in and through them to effect the extension and main-
tenance of his dominion over the Old Aeon.[107] To secure this
objective, he is transformed into an angel of light even as the
'false apostles' are transformed into 'apostles of Christ' (2 Cor
11¹³⁻¹⁴). In a passage fraught with exegetical difficulty, Paul
told the Corinthian Church that the worship of idols or heathen
deities was in actuality the worship of demons (1 Cor 10²⁰⁻¹).[108]
In all probability the deity of Satan is of this same character,
namely, an assumed and derived divinity, secured through the
homage subscribed by lesser spirits and men.[109] Certainly, Paul
did not hold to Satan's deity in any comparable sense to that of
God; both Satan and his demonic retinue had been created by
Jesus Christ (Col 2¹⁶). The devil merely stands as a puppet over

[106] So B. Weiss, op. cit. I.332. Cf. H. W. Robinson, *Mansfield College Essays*, presented to A. M. Fairbairn (London, 1909), p. 285.

[107] Note 2 Tim 2²⁶: '. . . and they (those that oppose themselves) may recover
themselves out of the snare of the devil, having been taken captive by him unto his
will.' Cf. 2 Cor 11⁴.

[108] Cf. H. A. A. Kennedy, op. cit. p. 40; N. P. Williams, op. cit. p. 160; W. Morgan,
The Religion and Theology of Paul (Edinburgh, 1917), p. 13. A similar relationship
between demons and pagan gods is found in the Old Testament. 'They sacrificed
unto demons (שֵׁד, 'evil spirit', demon', according to L. Koehler and W. Baumgartner,

Lexicon in Veteris Testamenti Libros (Leiden, 1953), p. 949), not to God; to gods whom
they knew not, to new gods that came newly up, whom your fathers feared not'
(Deut 32¹⁷).

[109] Note the parallel idea in 2 Thess 2⁴; cf. Rev 13⁴.

the Old Aeon; God still rules over the whole Creation.[110] Consequently, Paul sees Satan as under the obligation to serve God, as when the incestuous man is delivered into the power of the devil for the destruction of the flesh (1 Cor 5[5]), or as Hymenaeus and Alexander are committed into Satan's tutelage to unlearn blasphemous speech (1 Tim 1[20]). Therefore, the dualism of the New Testament is only mediated and temporal (cf. 1 Thess 2[18], 3[5], 2 Thess 2[3-9]), not metaphysical.[111]

A problem is introduced in positing an alliance of spirit-forces in opposition against God and against the original *good* creation. The only commendable answer is the Fall of Satan and his cohorts, although there is no direct statement to that effect. The Fall of Adam was neither coincident with, nor did it precipitate the Fall of the evil spirits;[112] rather, it was the occasion through which the world was brought into subjection to them.[113] Through Adam's original transgression not only was sin able to gain a strangle-hold on mankind, but the whole cosmos (man and nature) became part of the Old Aeon. Thus, evil spirits, mankind, and the material creation were united in the direct violation of the original intention of the Creation. Paul refers to this thraldom as the subjection of the creation (κτίσις) to vanity (ματαιότης); it is in the 'bondage of corruption' (Rom 8[20-1]). 'Vanity' at once suggests a connexion with the heathen deities, in that μάταιος is a standing term for the gods of the Gentiles in the Septuagint.[114] An actual relationship was seen by Paul to exist between the demons, the heathen deities, and rest of creation. Man's subjection to

[110] This idea may be clearly grasped by comparing 2 Cor 4[4] with 1 Cor 15[24]. Satan's dominion over humanity was instituted through Adam (Rom 5[12-21]) who traitorously delivered the cosmos (i.e. humanity) into Satan's domain, the Old Aeon. Christ, the Second Adam, through His singular victory on the Cross (Col 2[15]) wrested humanity (Paul calls it the 'kingdom') from the Aeon and from Satan (cf. Rom 16[20]) to deliver it back to its rightful Owner (1 Cor 15[24]).

[111] Cf. O. Cullmann, *Christ and Time*, p. 196; J. S. Stewart, 'On a Neglected Emphasis in New Testament Theology', *SJT*, Vol. IV (1951), p. 300.

[112] The Genesis account of the Fall clearly maintains that evil existed before Adam's disobedience. Paul concurs apparently in saying that 'sin entered into the world' (Rom 5[12]) and asserting that Eve was subjected to external temptation (1 Tim 2[14]). H. J. Holtzmann, *Lehrbuch der Neutestamentlichen Theologie* (Tübingen, 1911), II.47, regards the phrase, 'sin deceived me', as a conscious reference to the Fall-story in conjunction with 2 Cor 11[3], '. . . the Serpent deceived Eve'. Cf. J. E. Thomas, *The Problem of Sin in the New Testament* (London, 1927), p. 80. In any case, as Brunner says, man is not astute enough to have invented sin; *The Christian Doctrine of Creation and Redemption*, p. 108.

[113] This view was held both before and contemporaneously with Paul by Jews; (J. Armitage Robinson, op. cit. p. 49).

[114] Cf. W. L. Knox, *St Paul and the Church of the Gentiles*, op. cit. p. 107.

the power of sin is the counterpart to the wilful offering of allegiance to pagan deities and its consequent corruption.[115] It is here that the true nature of sin appears as self-asserted rebellion against God.[116] For this reason, Paul saw the cosmos and all of its constituents involved in sin.

Κόσμος may have a narrower meaning than αἰών in some instances. It is used to designate the world of men as a totality (cf. Rom 5[12], 3[6], 1 Cor 6[2], 11[32], 2 Cor 5[19], 1[12]). The identification of the cosmos with the Aeon is clear from the fact that the term still bears the connotation of sinfulness.[117] The emphasis does not lie on humanity as such, but on man as a part of αἰών οὗτος,[118] and consequently sinful. For this reason, κόσμος is used as the antithesis to the New Humanity in a number of instances (cf. e.g. 1 Cor 1[20-1, 27-8], Eph 2[2], 1 Cor 6[2]). The significance of the believer's deliverance from the forces of the cosmos is readily seen in the earliest Christian confessions which refer to the defeat and subjection of these powers by Jesus.[119] Paul, therefore, warns against collusion with the 'world' lest his believing audience be included in its judgement (1 Cor 11[32]). Says R. Bultmann very much to the point:

This means that 'Kosmos' is an eschatological concept. It denotes the world of men and the sphere of human activity as being, on the one hand, a temporary thing hastening toward its end, and on the other hand, the sphere of anti-godly power under whose sway the individual who is surrounded by it has fallen. It is the sphere of 'the rulers of this age' (1 Cor 2[6, 8]) and of 'the god of this age' (2 Cor 4[4]).[120]

THE IMPLICATION OF MANKIND IN THE OLD AEON THROUGH ADAM

(1) *Mankind's Betrayal into the Domain of Death.* We have already discussed the corporate judgement of Adam, the decree that he and his posterity should all die. But the full significance of this

---

115 This is the theme of Romans 1[18-32]. 'God gave them up' repeatedly emphasizes the passing of man from the dominion of God to that of idolatry and sin. Cf. C. H. Dodd, *The Meaning of Paul for Today*, p. 59.

116 'Sin' in *Bible Key Words (TWNT)*, p. 78.

117 A. Nygren, 'Christ and the Forces of Destruction', *SJT*, Vol. IV (1951), p. 336.

118 Cf. E. C. Rust, op. cit. p. 199; B. Weiss, op. cit. p. 331. We may well agree with the latter that the pre-Messianic age (העולם הזה) of current Jewish thought affords the background of Paul's conception of the Aeon, since for Judaism also, this period was ungodly and wicked; ibid. pp. 331-2.

119 O. Cullmann, *Christ and Time*, p. 103.

120 *Theology of the New Testament*, p. 256.

judgement cannot be realized without seeing with Paul that sin and death are the bonds by which humanity is held in the thraldom of the Old Age. Death (as sin) was personalized in such a manner in the mind of Paul that he speaks of its domain as a realm over which it rules autocratically (cf. ἐβασίλευσεν in Rom 5[14, 17]). This realm includes Adam's corporate race.[121] Since it is the real ruler of man's particular part of the Aeon, it is called the 'last enemy'.

The Apostle further characterizes death as a sphere in which men are immersed. To be in the position of the heathen is to be dead in trespasses and sins (Eph 2[1-5], Col 2[13]. In this passage it is parallel to 'uncircumcision' indicating separation, cf. Eph 2[11-12]). The scope of death's kingdom is world-wide including the animate and inanimate creation (Rom 8[20]). Jews and Gentiles (the conclusion of the argument in Rom 1[18]–3[20]) and the Aeon itself are dominated by death (cf. 1 Cor 15[22-3]). Sin and death, which are, from the human standpoint, the fundamental characteristics of the Age, were united and established in Adam.[122] Only in Christ, the Last Adam, is the dominion of death relinquished in its moral (i.e. separation from God) and physical aspects. Because of Christ's victory over the power of death, Paul exults, ποῦ σου θάνατε τὸ νῖκος; ποῦ σου θάνατε τὸ κέντρον (1 Cor 15[55]) and foresees the abolishment of death altogether (2 Tim 1[10]).

(2) *Man's Subjection to the Power of Sin.* Besides the dominion of death in the Old Aeon, Paul posits regal authority to sin (Rom 5[21]; cf. 6[12, 14], 7[9, 11]). Sin is the sting, goad, or weapon (κέντρον) which is the means of death's continued dominion over mankind (1 Cor 15[56]). 'Like a harsh tyrant (it) holds men enslaved (Rom 6[6, 20], 7[14]), paying men for its service the miserable wage of death' (Rom 6[23]).[123] While one might be prone to consider the choice of evil as an evidence of human freedom, 'sin' actually took the part of determinism (Rom 7[17-20]).[124] Consequently, the significance of God's giving men up (Rom 1[24, 26, 28]) is that they were released into the power of sin which in turn leads to destruction. We must

---

[121] E. H. Wahlstrom, op. cit. pp. 26, 61; Sanday and Headlam, op. cit. p. 143. J. A. T. Robinson says appropriately: 'The universality of death as the destiny of man is thus not a natural fact like the mortality of the σάρξ'; op. cit. p. 35.

[122] A. Schweitzer, *Paul and His Interpreters*, p. 221.

[123] J. Weiss, op. cit. p. 515.

[124] Cf. J. A. T. Robinson, op. cit. p. 36.

be aware that Paul does not have in mind sinful acts or unrighteousness as a quality, but an active, powerful, external principle that organically produces its fruit, the evil deed (Rom 7¹⁷).[125]

Sin, by its very nature, acts in an organic way. Just as 4 *Ezra* saw the evil seed sown in the heart of Adam growing to bear the fruit of corruption in his progeny, Paul saw all human sin as the development of the details of the original transgression. It has organization and structure. It provides a spiritual κοινωνία of darkness (Eph 5⁸, ¹¹; cf. 1 Tim 5²², 1 Jn 1⁶, 2 Jn 11)[126] which exists in radical opposition to the light. It forms a kingdom whose extent embraces the whole human race. It is a force[127] which rules in such a manner that Paul may refer to the 'law of sin in my members' (Rom 7²⁵). Sin, moreover, produces a sphere in which the unredeemed dwell (ἐπιμένω, Rom 6¹); this realm is the domain of Satan (Acts 26¹⁸) and therefore identifiable with the Old Age.

Sin is the primary characteristic of the Old Aeon. Αἰών οὗτος is thoroughly and irremediably wicked; hence, redemption must be extended from without (Gal 1⁴, Eph 2⁵, Rom 8², Col 1¹³).[128] Sin is the expression and power of the age, providing the bonds whereby its subjects are brought into and kept in thraldom (cf. Rom 5¹², ²¹, 3⁹, Gal 3²²). In Romans 6–8, a glance will confirm the conclusion that Paul considered sin to be man's master. Slavery, bondage, legal power, among other ideas, characterize the nature of sin's control.

It is only in this context that one may see the significance of Paul's doctrine of sin and redemption. Again, it was his conception of the solidarity of mankind which allowed him to postulate the view that Adam was responsible for man's implication in the Aeon and his subjection to its external powers (Rom 5¹²). It is not Original Sin,[129] in its usual exposition, but mankind betrayed and betraying itself into the control of sin in the cosmos, which is Paul's doctrine.

[125] Cf. O. Pfleiderer, *Paulinism*, trans. E. Peters (London, 1877), I.38; *Primitive Christianity*, trans. W. Montgomery (London, 1906), I.289-90; J. S. Stewart, *A Man in Christ*, p. 105.
[126] L. S. Thornton, op. cit. p. 13.
[127] Cf. C. Weizsäcker, op. cit. I.148; H. Weinel, op. cit. p. 244; C. A. A. Scott, op. cit. p. 47. For the passages in point see 'Sin' in *Bible Key Words* (*TWNT*), p. 51.
[128] A. Schweitzer, *Paul and His Interpreters*, p. 57. C. A. A. Scott, op. cit. p. 29.
[129] See J. Caird's brilliant analysis of the problem in his Gifford Lectures, *Fundamental Principles of Christianity* (Glasgow, 1899), I.210-11.

(3) *'Flesh' Implicated in the Old Aeon.* We pick up now where we left off, to examine the second aspect of Paul's usage of the term σάρξ. Beyond the connotation of 'flesh' as a physical substance or human relationship is a designation of σάρξ as a continuum, a type of cohesive being which is the captive and seat of sin. This aspect concerns the flesh as a part of the Aeon and consequently its standing in opposition to God.[130] The flesh comes to symbolize mankind in thraldom to the ruling power of sin in the Aeon. Thus, to be ἐν σαρκί is to say that one is subject to the powers which control the flesh. 'In Romans 7⁶, "that wherein we were holden" refers to the σάρξ: it is that by virtue of which the powers have their grip over us.'[131] ἐν σαρκί is far removed from the Greek idea of the flesh as the material body or even the Old Testament where man is a manifestation of the totality of all flesh. In Paul's theology, 'flesh' is a sphere controlled by alien powers. As long as one remains in it, he is subjected to these forces. The end of life κατὰ σάρκα is death (Rom 8¹²). With the acquisition of the new life in Christ, the believer is no longer in the flesh but in the Spirit (Rom 8⁹; cf. Rom 7⁵). 'Flesh' and 'Spirit' are not two spheres in which one can live at the same time. Only one of these entities can determine man's existence.[132] Thus, Paul tells the Roman Christians that they are no longer 'in the flesh' but 'in the Spirit' (8⁹; cf. Gal 5¹³). Formerly, existence ἐν τῇ σαρκί meant the dominion of the passions of sin in our members (cf. Gal 5¹⁹⁻²¹) resulting in death (Rom 7⁵); now, however, there is no longer any condemnation for us who do not walk κατὰ σάρκα (Rom 8¹, ⁴).

The enmity of the Aeon against God is also ascribed by Paul to the σάρξ (Rom 8⁷, Gal 5¹⁷; cf. Rom 2²⁸⁻⁹, 7⁶). It is for this reason that Paul describes the flesh as σαρκὸς ἁμαρτίας (Rom 8³). Surely, to be 'in the flesh' obviates any possibility of pleasing God (Rom 8⁸, Gal 3³), and sowing to the flesh can only culminate in corruption (Gal 6⁸).

It is a most essential element in Paul's doctrine to conceive of

---

[130] See J. A. T. Robinson's admirable treatment, op. cit. pp. 24f.

[131] J. A. T. Robinson, op. cit. p. 22. By the flesh, the individual is connected with the cosmos; J. Weiss, op. cit. p. 606.

[132] R. Asting, *Die Heiligkeit im Urchristentum* (Göttingen, 1930), p. 193. The carnal Christian (σαρκίνοις, σαρκικοί, 1 Cor 3¹, ³) is living as though he still remained in the thraldom of the Aeon in spite of the redemption of Christ, which not only makes such an existence unnecessary, but utterly reprehensible (cf. Rom 6¹⁻²³, 7⁶, 8¹⁻¹³, Gal 5¹⁵⁻²¹).

the flesh (i.e. the sphere of human existence) as a sort of living or organic whole. When the Apostle comes to expound his doctrine of the atonement of Christ, he stresses the humanity of Christ. Through His assumption of a body and death, sin's control of the flesh was successfully challenged; consequently, those that are included in Him are extracted from the Old Aeon and its malignant powers, sin, death, and the Law (Rom 8³, 7⁴).¹³³ By this particular type of redemption, Christ was able to reverse the subjection of the flesh to sin which Adam inaugurated. This is the core of Paul's theology, a core so often misunderstood because our thought is so completely dominated by traditional Western individualism. Throughout the exposition of his doctrine, Paul's mind must be seen in its determination by Old Testament¹³⁴ and Early Jewish conceptions.

Paul's doctrine of man in the flesh, under the dominion of sin and death, is not merely a re-statement of the Old Testament and Jewish conceptions. The plight of man's involvement through the solidarity of the race in its distance from God¹³⁵ is more poignant to the Apostle because of the light which is cast upon it by the New Age. The striking nature of the human dilemma apart from redemption is two-fold. (1) Man, because of the weakness of the flesh, is completely unable to fulfil his responsibility to God. (2) Man, besides being frail, is engulfed in his solidarity with the race within the domain of powers too great for him to master. Both ideas characterize Paul's conception of the Aeon, the evil inversion of the New Aeon inaugurated by Jesus Christ. It is this same inversion which must explain the true nature of the Adam-Christ typology. Adam involved the race in the Aeon by virtue of his determinative headship; Christ, by incorporating

---

¹³³ Cf. J. Weiss, op. cit. p. 434.

¹³⁴ Of supreme importance is the conception of the σάρξ as a totality (cf. H. A. A. Kennedy, op. cit. p. 129) which harks back to the Old Testament conception of בָּשָׂר (cf. supra, pp. 28-9). But more than this is the concurrence of Paul and the Old Testament in the ascription of an ethical quality to the flesh, an idea altogether undeveloped by the Rabbis. W. D. Davies says: 'There are no expressions in Rabbinic Judaism which literally correspond to the use of σάρκινος, σαρκικός and πνευματικός and ψυχικός in Paul' (op. cit. p. 20). There are passages in Jewish literature which establish a connexion between the yetzer and the body in such a manner that the latter is completely under the domination of the former (cf. W. D. Davies, op. cit. p. 27, and supra, pp. 85-7). The Old Testament distinction between nephesh and ruah is analogous in some ways to the conflict between the σάρξ and πνεῦμα (Gal 5¹⁷); and ψυχικός and πνευματικός (1 Cor 2¹⁴⁻¹⁵). Cf. T. A. Lacey, op. cit. p. 243.

¹³⁵ Cf. J. A. T. Robinson, op. cit. p. 31. That is what N. Söderblom has called a mysterious solidarity of the individual and the race which is a 'solidarity of woe and of a curse'; op. cit. p. 10; cf. p. 27.

the New Humanity into Himself, brings them into the New Age (2 Cor 5¹⁷, Rom 8²¹, 1 Cor 15⁵¹⁻⁷).

(4) *'Law' Implicated in the Old Aeon.* As strange as it might at first appear, Paul, who taught that the Law which originated with divine approval and whose commands were holy, just, and good (Rom 7¹²; cf. 7¹⁴, 17, 18, 1 Tim 1⁸⁻¹⁰. Note also the practice of Paul according to Acts 16³, 21¹⁸⁻²⁷), also thought of the Law as being implicated in the Old Age. In this context the Law was one of the forces of the Aeon that had joined with sin and death in the subjection of mankind.¹³⁶ In the words of J. A. T. Robinson: 'If sin is the accomplice of death, the *law* is the instrument of sin.'¹³⁷ Paul calls the Law (subjectively, not objectively) 'the power (δύναμις, 1 Cor 15⁵⁶) of sin' that beguiled him (Rom 7¹¹). The Law κατεργάζεται 'works' wrath, for without it sin could not exist except in a submerged form.¹³⁸ The Law secures the bridgehead or footing (ἀφορμή, Rom 7⁸, ¹¹) whereby sin gains control over the whole man, thereby causing sin to abound (Rom 5²⁰). It gives sin's reign full power. It deceives those that put their confidence in it with the intent of securing eternal life through the fulfilment of its injunctions (Gal 3¹¹⁻¹²). And with this failure of the Law to give life, Paul found an empirically conclusive argument that subjection to the Law is worse than useless, an emphatic confirmation that it is one of the partners of the Old Aeon.

Paul does not hesitate to posit that, just as man is enslaved by sin and death, he is equally the thrall of the Law (Gal 4¹⁻⁷, 5¹), under it (Gal 4²¹, Rom 6¹⁴), and subject to its curse (Gal 3¹³). This latter point corresponds to the sentence of death under which all men in the Old Aeon live.¹³⁹ This contention is confirmed by Colossians 2¹⁴⁻¹⁵, where an unmistakable relationship is drawn between the 'principalities and powers' on the one hand, and the 'ordinances' (i.e. Law) on the other.¹⁴⁰ W. Morgan

¹³⁶ Cf. S. Hanson, op. cit. p. 63; A. C. Headlam, op. cit. p. 127; W. Bousset, *Kurios Christos*, p. 193.

¹³⁷ Op. cit. p. 36. Cf. T. Zahn, *Introduction to the New Testament* (Edinburgh, 1901), I.362.

¹³⁸ Cf. Rom. 3²⁰; N. P. Williams, op. cit. p. 132. 'Wrong actions done without knowledge that they are wrong are not imputed to the doer'; Sanday and Headlam, op. cit. p. 144.

¹³⁹ Cf. H. Weinel, op. cit. p. 248.

¹⁴⁰ Gal 4³ further indicates a relationship between the Law and the Aeon, in that it is identified with the στοιχεῖα τοῦ κόσμου. It has been impressed into the service of the forces of the Aeon; therefore, Paul says, ὅτε ἦμεν νήπιοι, ὑπὸ τὰ στοιχεῖα τοῦ κόσμου ἤμεθα δεδουλωμένοι.

suggests that the presiding of these powers over the Law implies a malicious interest in prosecuting both its demands and its condemnation to man's undoing.[141] Thus, Paul sees that the Torah, of divine origin, instead of acting to deliver man from the clutches of sin, is itself the instrument of the forces which delight in the destruction of man. As in the cases of the other powers of the Aeon, man's release from the bondage and curse of the law is effected through Christ.[142] Consequently, death (cf. ἀπέθανον, and its parallel identification with the crucifixion of Christ, Gal 2[20]) to the Law is the beginning of life unto God (Gal 2[19]).

But in what sense did Paul see Adam as the means by which mankind was implicated in the bondage and condemnation of the law? Although there are no explicit statements in the Epistles that Adam did involve man in legal subjection directly, at least symbolically, if not actually, Paul attributes to Adam the corporate responsibility for the legal subjection of mankind. Adam knew the will of God (although the Torah was not given until Moses, Rom 5[14]) which made transgression a possibility.[143] With Adam's betrayal of the race into the power of sin, the Law could have no other effect than to produce an antagonism to the will of God. It is interesting in this context to note that the major part of Romans 7 appears to be a personal paraphrase of the Eden temptation.[144] In any case, Paul does not divide responsibility for the subjection of mankind to the powers of the Old Age. Sin, death, flesh, and the Law are all inextricably interconnected in the Aeon in such a manner that the admission of one brings in the rest.

CONCLUSION

Our intended goal in this general section has been to unravel three dissimilar lines of thought which, more than likely, were not distinguished in Paul's mind.

(1) The first is Adam as the father of the race. As its ancestor, he is the origin (*Ursprung*) of all those general racial characteristics

---

[141] Op. cit. p. 71.

[142] Cf. A. B. Bruce, op. cit. p. 173; D. Somerville, *St Paul's Conception of Christ* (Edinburgh, 1897), p. 166.

[143] J. A. T. Robinson, op. cit. p. 35 note 1.

[144] So P. Feine, op. cit. p. 275. In that case, sin is equivalent to the serpent which tempts, deceives, and brings death (Rom 7[8-11]). The divine will is embodied in a commandment (ἐντολή, 7[8, 9-12]. It may be significant that Paul does not use νόμος as he normally does).

which distinguish mankind from the rest of Creation. One might profitably compare the race to a tree, which although possessing distinct leaves, gives to each leaf a common life and character, since the foliage is organically interrelated through the stem and the trunk.

(2) The second line of thought concerns Adam's role as the realistic representative of the race. This role implies the Hebrew conception of the corporate personality of the race in such a manner that all mankind is identifiable with one man; in Paul's doctrine this man is Adam. Because of his representation of the race, Paul posits a universal participation of the race in the original and archetypal transgression of Adam, culminating in the corporate judgement of the totality of men.

(3) The third aspect of Paul's doctrine may combine the first two lines of thought, but adds the horizontal solidarity of man under sin in united opposition to God. The Jewish idea of the two Aeons reached a heightened development in Paul's mind because he had personally experienced the contrast between the Old and the New (cf. Gal 3²²: '... συνέκλεισεν ἡ γραφὴ τὰ πάντα ὑπὸ ἁμαρτίαν').

Throughout our presentation of the Pauline views on the solidarity of the race, his dependence on the Old Testament and current Jewish thought has been more or less self-evident. Probably the most important single principle of solidarity used by Paul was the Old Testament conception of the corporate personality of the group. The application of this principle made it possible for Paul to go far beyond the current ideas of his day to postulate a doctrine of total human implication in sin as the foundation for his all-embracing doctrine of redemption. The debt of the Apostle to current theories of corporate justice, transferable demerit, the horizontal extension of life and flesh (which to the ancient Hebrew would correspond to the extension of personality)[145] as frail and yet a totality which may have more or less a psychic or organic life,[146] is self-evident. It is a debt which is primarily one of background. Paul may not be accused of parroting ideas of his Jewish contemporaries. Indeed, he makes more direct use of Old Testament conceptions than those of the Rabbis. But 'stimulus diffusion' is the phrase which best describes Paul's application of Old Testament and Early Jewish conceptions of the solidarity of the human race.

---

[145] Cf. J. A. T. Robinson, op. cit. p. 14; E. C. Rust, op. cit. p. 97.
[146] Cf. H. W. Robinson, *Mansfield College Essays*, op. cit. p. 286.

CHAPTER IV

THE SOLIDARITY OF THE NEW HUMANITY IN CHRIST

INTRODUCTION

IT is with the Church, the New Humanity, created and constituted through solidarity with Jesus the Messiah that the
theology of Paul is primarily concerned.[1] Eschatological to the
core are his declarations describing the nature of the 'New Man'
who reverses the role of the first Adam. The Messianic figures of
the Old Testament and Jewish Apocalyptic thought have been
realized in the Incarnation of the Son of God whose death and
resurrection bring into being the New Age. Over against the
sphere of death and the flesh dominated by sin is the new sphere
of the Spirit of life *in* Christ. Over against the archetypal act of
Adam and its catastrophic implications for the race is set the
obedient act of Christ with its more far-reaching consequences for
those united with Him. Through incorporation[2] and realistic
representation the elect 'chosen in Him before the foundation of
the world' (Eph 1⁴) realize even now the implications of their
redemption (Col 3³).

The burden of this chapter is to trace the relationship between
the fully developed teaching of Paul on the nature of the Church's
constitution through union with Christ to the Old Testament and
Early Jewish expectation and thought background. A necessary
step to this conclusion is the recognition of the Church as the New
Israel and Christ as the Epitome or Compendium of the people
of the New Covenant. Furthermore, it will be imperative to see
the implications of the Pauline doctrine of the Last Adam.
Finally, discussion will centre on the means of initiation into and
continuance within the sphere of Christ or the New Age. Throughout, the frame of reference in which the Pauline conceptions are

---

[1] In one sense, Israel after the flesh, occupies a middle position between the human
race 'in Adam' and the new Creation in Christ. See Appendix A.

[2] Says N. A. Dahl cryptically: '*Der Sohn Gottes ist die Verköperung des Volkes Gottes . . .*'
(*Das Volk Gottes*, p. 166); cf. P. Feine, *Theologie des Neuen Testaments*, p. 304.

cast will plainly depend on the Old Testament view of corporate personality as well as early Jewish ideas regarding the mysterious unity of the race and Israel.

THE CHURCH AS THE TRUE ISRAEL OF GOD

(1) *Direct Evidence*

That Paul in writing to the Galatian churches intended to refer to the Gentile Christian community as the Israel of God has been challenged (cf. 6[16]),[3] but the probable reference underlying the term is by no means either unique or unusual, for Paul thought of the Church as the New Israel having displaced the forfeited position of the Old Israel after the flesh (cf. Rom 9[6, 8]). Therefore, Paul emphasizes the first person: '*We* are the circumcision which worship God in spirit, boasting in Christ Jesus and have no confidence in the flesh' (Phil 3[3]). The implied contrast of the New with the Old is clear in that the older dispensation, Israel after the flesh, by its rejection of the Messiah whom the God of Israel had sent, 'had shown clearly that it could no longer serve the purpose for which God had originally brought it into being'.[4] There is a similar stress in Ephesians 2[11-22], where Paul discloses the purpose of God in calling the Gentiles. They had previously been aliens from Israel's citizenship, strangers to the covenants of promise (2[12]; cf. 4[18]); now, however, they are no longer aliens and foreigners, but fellow-citizens (συμπολῖται) with the saints (i.e. Israel as the true People of God) (Eph 2[19]).

Paul writes in the same vein to the Church in Rome. Using Hosea 2[23] as his text, the Apostle says: 'Us whom also he called, not alone of the Jews but of the Gentiles, as also in Hosea it says, I will call them my people which were not my people and her which was unloved, beloved' (cf. Rom 9[25]; Hos 2[1]). The conclusion cannot be avoided that Paul is thinking of the Gentiles as now part of Israel, for the original context refers exclusively to Israel and Judah. Paul's application of Hosea 1[10] in Romans 9[26], 'And it shall be that in the place where it was said unto them, Ye are not my people, There shall they be called sons of the living

---

[3] Cf. G. S. Duncan, *The Epistle of Paul to the Galatians* (London, 1937), p. 192 and E. D. Burton, *Galatians*, p. 358, while R. N. Flew, *Jesus and His Church* (2nd edn, London, 1943), p. 150, and J. B. Lightfoot, *St Paul's Epistle to the Galatians* (10th edn, London, 1890), pp. 224-5 disagree.

[4] W. N. Pittenger, *His Body the Church* (New York, 1945), p. 2; cf. T. M. Lindsay, *The Church and the Ministry in the Early Centuries* (London, 1902), pp. 34-5.

God' (*RV*), is identical. The idea of the Church's displacement of the position of Israel is clear in Romans 2²⁸⁻⁹: 'For he is not a Jew which is one outwardly. . . . But he is a Jew, which is one inwardly.'

The Apostle goes even further to point out that descent from Abraham is not the exclusive possession of the Jew. The promise that the Patriarch would be the father of many nations (πολλῶν ἐθνῶν, i.e. the Gentiles) had been fulfilled in their acceptance of the Gospel (Rom 4¹¹⁻²⁵; cf. Gal 3⁷). Paul does not hesitate to say that Abraham is the 'father of us all' (Rom 4¹⁶) since it is in Isaac that his seed should be called (Rom 9⁷). The true children of Abraham are those for whom the promise has become actual.⁵ This conception is the premise of the argument in the allegory of Galatians 4²¹⁻³¹. The children of Sarah (i.e. of the promise) inherit the New Jerusalem, the capital of the True Israel. The Jewish nation, in its bondage to the law are children of the slave, Hagar, and are content with an earthly Jerusalem as their capital.⁶

In the extended metaphor of the Olive Tree Paul clarifies his conception of the relationship between the Old and the New Israel. He uses the analogy of a tree to define the continuity of the People of God, a continuity which transcends both temporal and racial factors.⁷ This continuum is represented by the root or trunk into which believing Gentiles are engrafted (Rom 11¹⁷⁻²⁴).⁸ Israel's rejection of the gospel in no way pronounces a final judgement upon the tree. It merely results in the breaking off of some of its branches (11¹⁸; cf. 11²⁵). The whole continuum is the true Israel of God manifested in the Christian Ecclesia.⁹ 'Israel after the Spirit', says E. Lohmeyer, 'is the goal and culmination of the former Israel after the flesh and both are joined in one God-given continuity.'¹⁰ Paul's idea embraces the activity of God in Israel's redemptive history as a continuation and end of the

⁵ Cf. H. Weinel, *Biblische Theologie des Neuen Testaments*, p. 320.
⁶ Cf. E. Burton, op. cit. p. 263.
⁷ So M. M. Bourke, *A Study of the Metaphor of the Olive Tree in Romans XI* (Washington, 1947), pp. 82-5, 108-11.
⁸ ἐγκεντρίζω is a more technical word for grafting than σύμφυτος (Rom 6⁵) used to describe our union with Christ.
⁹ Cf. G. Johnston, *The Doctrine of the Church in the New Testament*, p. 77, note 3; B. H. Streeter, *The Primitive Church* (London, 1929), p. 47; R. N. Flew, op. cit. p. 151; Sanday and Headlam, *Romans*, p. 327.
¹⁰ *Grundlagen paulinischer Theologie* (Tübingen, 1929), p. 166. Cf. W. D. Davies, op. cit. p. 323.

original constitution of the People of God.[11] It is into this continuity that the Gentile Christians have been incorporated. It is for this reason that Paul says that they are borne by the root (Rom 11[18]), or speaks of the Exodus generation as the fathers of the Corinthian Church (1 Cor 10[1]).

It is on account of this sharing of Israel's privileged position that Paul speaks of the debt which the Gentile portion of the Church owes to the Jewish segment, for the Gentiles 'have been made partakers of their spiritual things' (Rom 15[27]). Any material contribution cannot compare with the spiritual benefits which accrue to the Gentiles through their being grafted into the stump of Israel.

(2) *Indirect Evidence*

Besides the more or less explicit reference to the Church as the Israel of the New Age, there are certain terms which indicate a conscious or unconscious conception of the continuity of the Church with the Covenant People of God. If they are unconsciously used by Paul it is due to the fact that he inherited these terms from the Christian community which preceded him and he had no mind to challenge them.

(a) *The Church as the Ecclesia of God.* The use of the term ἐκκλησία to designate the New Community points to its continuity with Israel.[12] P. G. S. Hopwood says quite categorically:

In adopting *ecclesia* or its Aramaic equivalent to denote itself, the primitive community showed that it was self-conscious as virtually belonging to the earlier 'ecclesia' of Israel, the Chosen People; it was aware of its social solidarity with the People of God.[13]

The adoption of this term by the Primitive Church may be presumed to have been influenced by the Septuagint which translates, קָהָל 'the congregation of Israel', with the term ἐκκλησία.[14]

---

[11] Cf. E. H. Wahlstrom, *The New Life in Christ*, p. xiv; G. E. Wright, *The Biblical Doctrine of Man in Society*, pp. 77, 79. (Note the distinction between λαός and ἔθνη in Acts 15[14].) This does not mean that the election of Israel is nullified (cf. Rom 11[26, 29]) since the incorporation of the Gentiles is providential. G. Johnston, op. cit. p. 78.

[12] C. A. A. Scott, *Christianity According to St Paul*, pp. 165-6. Cf. N. A. Dahl, op. cit. pp. 181ff; A. Schweitzer, *The Mysticism of Paul*, pp. 105-6.

[13] *The Religious Experience of the Primitive Church* (Edinburgh, 1936), pp. 230-1.

[14] Cf. A. G. Hebert, *The Throne of David* (New York, 1941), pp. 228, 233. ἐκκλησία occurs about 75 times in the LXX as recognized by E. Hatch and H. A. Redpath, *A Concordance to the Septuagint* (Oxford, 1897) (K. L. Schmidt, 'The Church', *Bible Key Words* [*TWNT*], says about 100 times), and shows that it is always a translation of קָהָל or a derivative of that noun (cf. ibid. p. 51). L. Koehler and W. Baumgartner,

The Hebrew term עֵדָה, also designates the general assembly of the whole people and is rendered indiscriminately as συναγωγή, and infrequently with other more or less synonymous terms.[15] In Psalm 73² (74²) the LXX renders עֵדָה with συναγωγή, but Paul changes this term to ἐκκλησία in an apparent allusion to this Psalm (Acts 20²⁸). This indicates that Paul goes beyond the Septuagint usage of ἐκκλησία to translate קָהָל by rendering עֵדָה as ἐκκλησία also.[16] In so far as a relationship is recognized between the New Testament usage of ἐκκλησία to refer to the Church and the LXX translation of the terms קָהָל and עֵדָה, it seems plausible to affirm that the writers of the New Testament saw an equivalence between Israel and the Church.[17]

To the Gentiles uninfluenced by the usage of the LXX, ἐκκλησία was a 'thoroughly secular word',[18] such as might designate a brotherhood, a political assembly, a club, or, even a mob (Acts 19³², ³⁹, ⁴¹). The choice was a natural one to denote the Church, for it was familiar to the Greek world but no longer carried a close association with συναγωγή which would have confused Christianity with Judaism. At the same time, as K. L. Schmidt says: 'This very word ἐκκλησία, with its natural worldly associations, voices the greatest claim of the Christian community over against the world.'[19] This was the universal appeal of Christianity to join the society of the Redeemed apart from any regard

Lexicon in Veteris Testementi Libros, give as one of the meanings of the term קָהָל, '*die (jüdische) Kultgemeinde*' (the Jewish congregation). Cf. BDB, op. cit. p. 874 for the usage of קָהָל to refer to the assembly and to the community. The whole argument gains force when it is recognized that Paul is what A. Deissmann calls 'a Septuagint Jew', *Paul, a Study in Social and Religious History*, trans. W. E. Wilson (London, 1926), p. 99.

[15] Cf. T. A. Lacey, *The One Body and the One Christ*, p. 229. This writer is not precisely correct in affirming that ἐκκλησία translates עֵדָה, since according to Hatch and Redpath, op. cit. I.433, it never does. While συναγωγή is usually used to render עֵדָה, the fact that קָהָל and עֵדָה are synonymous and that ἐκκλησία and συναγωγή are used more or less interchangeably (cf. Prov 5¹⁴, Judges 20¹, Joel 2¹⁶) in the LXX, indicates that the idea of the Congregation and not merely the Hebrew idea of congregating lies behind the New Testament term ἐκκλησία.

[16] In the later OT writings, עֵדָה almost disappears while קָהָל increases in prominence (cf. H. Cremer, *Lexicon of New Testament Greek*, pp. 330-1). Συναγωγή in the Intertestamental period and later came to refer almost exclusively to the Jewish place of worship.

[17] Note that Stephen, in referring to Israel, says, 'the Church (ἐκκλησία) in the wilderness' (Acts 7³⁸). Cf. K. L. Schmidt, op. cit. p. 5.

[18] K. L. Schmidt, op. cit. p. 4. Note Josephus' usage in *Wars*, 4.255 (Loeb Cl. edn, III.76).

[19] Op. cit. p. 28.

for considerations of race, position, sex, or creed. But the qualifying genitive 'of God' (cf. e.g. Gal 1¹³) establishes its distinctive character far above that of a club.²⁰ Thus, it is the 'Society of God', at once different from the ἐκκλησία of Judaism, yet at the same time, the fulfilment of the election of Israel in its role as the 'People *of God*'.²¹ According to T. A. Lacey, the very adoption of the word ἐκκλησία was paramount to the resounding claim that the New Society asserted its continuity and identity with the old *ecclesia* of God.²²

(*b*) *The Church as 'the Saints'*. The Church is composed of saints (ἅγιοι) which is therefore a definitive term. ἅγιοι and ἐκκλησία are used interchangeably²³ (2 Cor 1¹; cf. Rom 1⁷, 1 Cor 6¹⁻², 14³³, 16¹, ¹⁵, Eph 1¹, Phil 1¹, Col 1², 3¹² (ἐκλεκτοὶ τοῦ θεοῦ ἅγιοι) with 1 Cor 1², Gal 1², 1 Thess 1¹, 2 Thess 1¹). Since the Children of Israel were the 'holy ones' in the Old Testament (cf. Deut 14², Ex 19⁵, as well as the title in Dan 7¹⁸, ²²), the use of the term in the New Testament appears to be a conscious attempt to indicate the continuity between the 'saints' of all time. The New Testament adds, however, to the idea of separation unto God, that of the actualization of holiness in the Redeemed through the activity of the Holy Spirit (2 Thess 2¹³, 1 Cor 3¹⁶) in its contesting of the contemporary claim of Judaism that only Israelites were 'saints'.²⁴

Three basic ideas which first related to Israel as the 'holy race' by derivation apply to the Church.²⁵ (1) The conception of Israel as holy by separation unto God and for His purposes is axiomatic in the Old Testament and Early Judaism. (2) In an eschatological sense the 'holy' are those who have been delivered from the rule of darkness and share in the Messianic age (an idea which receives ample treatment in Paul's Epistles, cf. e.g. 1 Thess 3¹³). (3) There is finally the ethical sense in which it is implied that

²⁰ Ibid. pp. 7, 11. This distinction comes directly from the Old Testament; although generally omitted it is always understood. So also in Philo, the religious connexion is maintained through the addition of 'of God' or 'of the Lord' (cf. *Leg. All.*, III.81, LoClL I.354; *Ebr.* 213, LoClL III.428). Cf. G. Johnston, op. cit. p. 79 note 9.

²¹ C. H. Dodd, *According to the Scriptures* (London, 1952), p. 111.

²² Op. cit. p. 29. Contrast J. Y. Campbell, 'The Origin and Meaning of the Christian Use of the Word ἐκκλησία', *JTS*, Vol. LXIX (1948), pp. 130ff.

²³ But Paul refers to the holiness of the Church only once (Eph 5²⁷), a reference which later became common-place. The use of ἅγιοι does not refer to a quality but is bound up with Paul's conception of justification. K. L. Schmidt, op. cit. pp. 16, 22.

²⁴ The eschatological awareness of the Church that the Messianic Age had dawned is plain (cf. Ezek 37¹⁴).

²⁵ See further, R. N. Flew, op. cit. p. 102.

K

the Community will keep the commandments of God (cf. 1 Thess 4³⁻¹²). It is the continuity of the Church with the righteous remnant of the True Israel which forms the background of the passage in Colossians 1¹² where reference is made to the grace of God in making Gentiles partakers of the inheritance of the saints through their redemption from darkness into the kingdom (messianic) of Christ.

(c) *The Church as* ὁ λαὸς τοῦ θεοῦ. The designation of the Church by the term λαός indicates that it exists in continuity with the covenant people of God.[26] In the LXX, λαός is the term used to render עַם (more than 1,500 times, cf. 1 Cor 10⁷), and is an explicit designation of Israel when it is qualified as עַם הָאֱלֹהִים; עַם יְהוָה. In the Epistles it is the Church of Corinth (2 Cor 6¹⁶; cf. Lev 26¹², Jer 31¹, Ezek 37²⁷) or Gentile believers in general, which are called the 'people of God'. (Note that οὐ λαόν μου λαόν μου—Rom 9²⁵; cf. Hos 2²⁵, 2¹—is equivalent to the designation of ethnic Israel as ὁ θεὸς τὸν λαὸν αὐτοῦ in Rom 11¹, ²). In Romans 15⁸⁻¹² Paul declares that Christ became a minister of the Circumcision that the promises which God made to the Fathers might be fulfilled (cf. Gal 4⁴⁻⁵). These promises have been given explicit fulfilment in the call of the Gentiles and the confession of Christ among the heathen (cf. Ps 18⁴⁹, 2 Sam 22⁵⁰) so that they have been enabled to rejoice *with* God's people (Rom 15¹⁰). In the sacrificial offering of the blood of Christ there has been provided a cleansing from all sin (ἀνομίας) and the purification of a people for his own possession (ἑαυτῷ λαὸν περιούσιον, Tit 2¹⁴; cf. Deut 14², Ex 19⁵).

(d) *The Church as* οἱ ἐκλεκτοί. In the Old Testament period Israel was supremely conscious of its election by the free grace of God.[27] In the New Testament the Church has displaced national Israel's position as 'the elect' (οἱ ἐκλεκτοί).[28] Therefore, Paul speaks of Gentile Christians as ἐκλεκτοί (Rom 8³³, Tit 1¹, with the qualification of θεοῦ: Col 3¹², 2 Tim 2¹⁰). The election of the Church, like the choosing of Israel, was founded on the sovereign decision of God which long antedated its actualization in the formation of the church of Ephesus (1⁴), Thessalonica (2 Thess

---

[26] Cf. C. A. A. Scott, *The Fellowship of the Spirit*, pp. 75-6.

[27] Cf. N. H. Snaith, 'Choose', *TWBB*, p. 43. In the period of the Second Temple, such terms as 'Chosen People', or 'Elect of God', referred technically to Israel.

[28] This is the LXX rendering of בָּחוּר and בָּחִיר—note בְּחִירֵי יְהוָה said in reference to pious Israelites (Isa 65⁹, ¹⁵, ²³, Ps 104(105)⁴³); cf. *Sap* 4¹ indicating a connexion with the remnant concept.

2^{13}), or the Universal Church (2 Tim 1^9). It may be inferred that the election of Israel and the Church are identified in Paul's mind.

This election does not have individual emphasis in Paul, any more than it did for Israel in the Old Testament or the Early Jewish period. Rather, it implies a covenant-relationship through which God chooses for Himself a whole people. This collectivism is of supreme importance for the understanding of the implications of 'election in Christ' even as K. Stendahl concludes:

> ... How meaningless Paul's agonized theodicy in Romans 9-11 would be, unless one could consider the question of the Jewish people as a whole apart from that of its individual members. What application would the ultimate salvation of all Israel have to St Paul's Jewish contemporaries who died without knowledge of Christ? The collective entities St Paul is considering occupy whole aeons. . . . Election in Christ not only constitutes a new society; its meaning is to be found in the new society, and not in the status of individuals.[29]

In Paul's intricate argument recorded in Romans 9 he is not attempting to refute the notion of a corporate election, but the Jewish contention that this election was mediated only through the natural relationship of birth, thus identifying a man's pedigree with the election of God. It is just the opposite. God called Isaac (9^{7-9}) and loved Jacob (9^{13}) quite apart from their generic relationships. Election belongs to the secret purposes of God, before the individual is born or has done either good or evil (9^{11}). This is not, however, the whole story. God does recognize some relationship (a fundamental idea to the conception of a corporate election), for Isaac is chosen out of the descendants of Abraham and Israel out of Isaac's progeny.[30]

In this section we must again recognize our theme, for Paul does not think of any election for the Gentiles outside of God's 'Elect One', Jesus Christ. Paul asserts that it was 'in Him' that 'the elect ones' were chosen before the foundation of the world (Eph 1^4; cf. 1 Cor 1^{27}).[31]

---

[29] 'The Called and the Chosen', p. 69.

[30] It is of interest in this connexion that Paul alludes to (in acceptance) the Jewish conception of ancestral merit (note Rom 9^5, 11^{28}).

[31] Note that in Luke, Christ is 'the Elect' ($o\tilde{v}\tau\acute{o}\varsigma$ $\dot{\epsilon}\sigma\tau\iota\nu$ $\acute{o}$ $v\acute{\iota}\acute{o}\varsigma$ μov $\acute{o}$ $\dot{\epsilon}\kappa\lambda\epsilon\lambda\epsilon\gamma\mu\acute{\epsilon}\nu o\varsigma$, 9^{35}; $\acute{o}$ $\dot{\epsilon}\kappa\lambda\epsilon\kappa\tau\acute{o}\varsigma$ 23^{35}). This is an oft-repeated designation of the Messiah in the Book of Enoch, Chaps 39-71. In Isa 42^1, 'mine elect' is the designation of the עבד יהוה. Twice the 'Master of Justice' is called 'Elect of God' and his followers are the 'elect of God', in the Dead Sea Commentary on Habbakuk. Cf. A. Dupont-Sommer, *The Dead Sea Scrolls*, p. 32.

(e) *The Church as the 'Sons of God'.* As Israel through election and the Covenant became the 'son' of God (Ex 4[22-3], Hos 11[1]; cf. Deut 14[1], 'Ye are the children of the Lord your God . . .') and individual Israelites partook of that relationship, so Paul repeatedly refers to the membership of the Church as the 'sons of God'. It is on the basis of the New Covenant that the Church has been given divine adoption.[32] The Apostle refers to the sonship under the law as identical with servanthood (Gal 4[1-7]); a sonship 'after the flesh' is contrasted with the sonship of promise (Gal 4[22-31]). Through the Incarnation of the only-begotten Son and His implication in the human solidarity in its distance from God, the possibility of the adoption into divine sonship has been opened to us (Gal 4[4-5]). Apart from Christ, this adoption is not our privilege.[33] It is the Spirit of the Son which issues to seal the relationship and to make the believer conscious of a filial relationship to the Father (Gal 4[6], Rom 8[15-16]).[34] Rather than exemption from the inheritance due to the firstborn (a fate which the Judaizers were courting through their continued servant-relationship), the Community of believing Jews and Gentiles (Gal 3[26]) has been declared co-heirs with Him (Gal 4[6], Rom 8[17]).[35]

Participation in the Son (1 Cor 1[9])[36] is aligned with the idea of the sonship of Abraham in the Epistle to the Galatians. 'If ye be Christ's, then are ye Abraham's seed, and heirs according to the promise' (3[29]; cf. 3[16]). Both ideas were interchangeable in Paul's mind since Christ was both Israel (epitomized) and the Son of God. By incorporation into Christ the New Israel became sons of God as well as sons of Abraham. The title 'sons of God' is therefore, like 'saints', a collective term, which at the same time has special reference to the Church as the New Israel.

[32] E. H. Wahlstrom, op. cit. p. 75.

[33] D. Somerville, *St Paul's Conception of Christ*, p. 45; cf. E. L. Mascall, *Christ, the Christian and the Church* (London, 1946), pp. 94-5.

[34] Cf. W. Koester, *Die Idee der Kirche beim Apostal Paulus* (Münster, i.w., 1928), p. 40.

[35] Cf. L. S. Thornton, *The Common Life*, p. 51. We may note a counterpart to this idea in the oscillation between Israel as the son of God and the king of the elect people of God as pre-eminently worthy of this title in the Old Testament. Thus it is written of Solomon: 'I will be his father and he shall be my son' (2 Sam 7[14]).

[36] Κοινωνία retains its primary and common meaning 'participation along with others in something', J. Y. Campbell, 'Κοινωνία and its Cognates in the New Testament', *JBL*, Vol. LI (1932), p. 380. But note the views of Wm. Robinson, *The Biblical Doctrine of the Church*, p. 73, and T. F. Torrance, *The Atonement and the Oneness of the Church in the New Testament* (Edinburgh, 1954), pp. 10-11.

(f) *The Total Extension of the Whole Church in the Local Assembly.*
One more point deserves some attention. In New Testament
usage the Church is conceived in typical Hebrew terms of extension. Thus the local church(es) is thought of in an absolute
sense when Paul exhorts the elders of Ephesus to 'pasture the
ἐκκλησία of God' (Acts 20²⁸; cf. 20¹⁷).[37] The local church is
neither a part nor a fraction, but the whole Church locally embodied.[38] Says F. J. Hort to the point:

Of course in strictness the words belong only to the one universal
Christian Ecclesia: but here (Acts 20²⁸) they are transferred to the
individual Christian Ecclesia of Ephesus, which alone these elders
were charged to shepherd. In the Epistles we shall find similar
investment of parts of the universal Ecclesia with the high attributes
of the whole. . . . These attributes could not be ascribed to it as an
absolutely independent and as it were insular society: they belong to
it only as a representative member of the great whole.[39]

It is further true that the local church is also used in the plural
number to designate the different manifestations of the whole
Church (1 Thess 2¹⁴, Rom 16¹⁶)[40] by Paul, even as he used the
singular in an identical manner (cf. e.g. 1 Cor 1²; altogether
about ninety times in the New Testament).

Besides the conception of the transcendent unity of the Church
which this mode of expression indicates, there is a significant and
precise parallel in the contemporary Jewish use of the term
'synagogue' in referring either to Israel as a whole or to a local
assembly of Jews. The many synagogues were never considered
to be a denial of the inclusive unity of the one Synagogue
constituted by the Covenant People of God.[41] The Church

[37] This mode of expression is common as Acts 12⁵, 15⁴, ²² (of Jerusalem) and 11²⁶,
14²⁷, 15³ (of Antioch) will show. Note the striking illustration in Acts 15³ where the
church refers to the Christians of Antioch and in 15⁴ to the Christians of Jerusalem.
It is particularly clear in Acts 9³¹, ἡ μὲν οὖν ἐκκλησία καθ' ὅλης τῆς Ἰουδαίας καὶ
Γαλιλαίας . . . (the plural is very poorly supported, occurring in the Koine rescension
and Beza as over against all of the better MSS. witnessing to the singular).
[38] R. H. Fuller, 'Church', *TWBB*, p. 48; cf. T. Schmidt, *Der Leib Christi* (Leipzig-
Erlangen, 1919), p. 123; Wm. Robinson, op. cit. p. 61. It is identical with the Semitic
manner of thinking (pp. 26-32 *supra*).
[39] *The Christian Ecclesia* (London, 1908), p. 103. K. L. Schmidt, op. cit. p. 11.
[40] The use of the plural is no exception to the point contended. Says R. B. Rackham: 'If there were many local churches, there was only one church in one place; we
read of "the churches of Syria and Cilicia", not of "the churches of Antioch" ' (*The
Acts of the Apostles* (12th edn, London, 1939), p. 80).
[41] R. B. Rackham, op. cit. p. 80. In the Old Testament LXX there is only one
'synagogue' or 'ecclesia' (see Hatch and Redpath, op. cit. II.1309-10). Even as late
as 1 Macc (cf. 3⁴⁴) and Susanna (cf. verses 41, 59-60) 'synagogue' refers to the whole
nation or a part.

and Israel are both universal in extent and locally manifested.

(g) *Conclusion*. As long as the Church is the New Israel, it is not surprising to find that it is characterized by the distinctive attributes of the Covenant People such as holiness, election, divine adoption, extension, and even the technical titles of Israel.

This self-consciousness of the Church, namely, that it is the True Israel, has very important implications. The significance of the conception for Paul will become increasingly apparent. But, briefly, it is fundamental to recognize that the solidarity of Israel in both the Old Testament and post-biblical periods may be safely ascribed to the Church.[42] The attributes of corporate personality, continuity, group kinship, transferable merit and punishment, realistic representation, vicarious substitution, and so on, are thereby assumed to be applicable to the Church with the same rigour that they applied to Israel.

ELEMENTS IN THE FORMULATION OF PAUL'S DOCTRINE OF THE CHURCH AS THE NEW ISRAEL

We must now proceed to consider the presuppositions on which Paul built his doctrine of the Church as the New Israel completely apart from the elaborate initiation ritual required of Gentile proselytes in becoming Jews.[43] It was with rare insight that Paul cut the ties of the Christian Community to the very core of Judaism. Neither circumcision nor the Torah defines the limits of the New Israel. The question turns on faith by which a man is identified with Christ. To describe this identification, Paul (in complete agreement with the rest of the New Testament) uses certain Old Testament figures to represent Christ. Throughout this presentation, the Old Testament and early Jewish conceptions of solidarity determine the Apostle's thought.

(1) *Jesus Christ is the 'True Isaac'*

We shall first consider Paul's unique interpretation of Genesis 13[15-17] and 17[8]. He affirms that the 'seed' promised to Abraham was singular in reference and therefore represents Christ (Gal 3[16]). Now it is clear that the early Church thought of Christ

---

[42] Cf. S. Hanson, *The Unity of the Church in the New Testament*, p. 29; W. J. Phythian-Adams, *The People and the Presence* (Oxford, 1942), p. 200.

[43] On this subject, see the magnificent argument of L. Newbigin, *The Household of God* (London, 1953), Chap. 2, pp. 32ff. Cf. G. Johnston, op. cit. p. 81.

as epitomizing Israel,[44] but Paul goes farther to assert that He is the Son of Abraham *par excellence*. But the 'seed' of Abraham is not merely an individual but a corporate figure including in Himself all of the true sons of Abraham even as Isaac had incorporated ethnic Israel in himself. It is only by virtue of Gentiles acquiring a kinship relationship to Christ who is the Head of the new מִשְׁפָּחָה, that they are, as a matter of fact, given membership in Israel.[45]

It is this corporate figure to which Paul is referring in the Epistle to the Galatians: 'Ye are all one (εἷς—man)[46] in Christ; and if ye are part of Christ, then are ye Abraham's seed and heirs according to the promise' (Gal 3[28]). Christ is here viewed as a corporate personality who includes in Himself all of the true sons of Abraham thus annulling the age-old cleavage between Jew and Gentile, slave and freeman, male and female.[47] The contrast with the contemporary practices of proselyte initiation is self-evident. The True Israel is formed by incorporation into a person (i.e. the Body of Christ), not a community or society. This person in turn creates a community in fellowship with Himself. Paul is applying the Old Testament conception of realistic representation.[48] Through faith Gentiles have identified themselves with Christ who acts as their representative, 'that the blessing of Abraham might come on the Gentiles through Jesus Christ' (Gal 3[14]; cf. 3[8]). This all-important truth had been revealed to Abraham and was sealed in a covenant more than four centuries before the revelation of the Mosaic Law, making it obvious that the Torah could not therefore have any part in making Gentiles into Israelites (see the argument in Gal 3[14-21], 3[8], Rom 4[6-25]).[49] This is the basis for the remarkable passage in the Epistle to the Ephesians 2[13-15]. The Gentiles, formerly aliens to the citizenship (ἡ πολιτεία) of Israel, and excluded from the covenants of

---

[44] G. A. F. Knight, *From Moses to Paul*, p. 158. It is altogether natural that Matthew (2[15]) applies Hosea 11[1] to Jesus as long as Christ is equivalent to Israel (G. A. Danell, 'The Idea of God's People in the Bible', *Root of the Vine*, p. 35).

[45] Cf. G. A. Danell, op. cit. p. 35; M. M. Bourke, op. cit. pp. 56ff. Compare the Rabbinic pronouncement of the proselyte as a 'son of Abraham' through initiation into Israel.

[46] That is, masculine not neuter. Cf. G. S. Duncan, *The Epistle of Paul to the Galatians* (London, 1937), p. 124.

[47] Cf. S. Hanson, op. cit. p. 70; N. A. Dahl, op. cit. p. 214; L. S. Thornton, *The Common Life*, p. 54.

[48] Cf. T. Schmidt, op. cit. pp. 218ff.

[49] Cf. M. N. Bourke, op. cit. p. 38.

promise (made to Abraham), are all made nigh; through Christ a common citizenship with the saints (i.e. the faithful righteous down through history) and membership in the household of God have been freely awarded (Eph 2[12, 19]).[50] There are no longer Two Men, the privileged and the non-privileged, but the One Man united in peace. Hence, to be 'in Christ' is equivalent to being in the New Israel. A. E. J. Rawlinson has stated it well:

The New Israel, according to the New Testament thought, is 'in Christ' as the Jews were in Abraham, or as mankind was in Adam. The Messiah is at once an individual person—Jesus of Nazareth— and He is more: He is, as the representative and (as it were) the constitutive Person of the New Israel, potentially inclusive.[51]

(2) *Jesus Christ is the Messiah of the Eschatological Community*
We have already made more than one allusion to the Old Testament prophetic picture of the New Israel regathered under the Messiah and reconstituted through the New Covenant. In the post-biblical writings, especially among the Apocalyptists, this eschatological community was given a great deal of attention. It was the regathered Israel in the Age to Come under Messiah's benevolent rule which Jews in the first century were impatiently awaiting. In both the Old Testament and the Apocalyptic literature the Messiah is not infrequently identified with this eschatological community just as Israel was included in the corporate personality of King David or Solomon in the infancy of the monarchy. Various figures were used to designate the Messiah in this corporate role. It is natural that the New Testament writers should use these same figures to describe Christ and His relationship to the Church, especially when Jesus by His teaching gave them explicit warranty. We must look at the use which Paul made of these figures and what light they shed on his conception of the solidarity of the New Humanity with Christ.

(a) *Christ as the Rejected Stone.* One of the least complicated illustrations of the New Testament conception of an eschatological community finds its background in Psalm 118[22]: 'The stone which the builders refused is become the head of the corner.' While the

---

[50] Paul maintains vigorously the Old Testament idea that there is no salvation outside of Israel. See Wm. Manson, 'The Biblical Doctrine of Mission', *IRM*, Vol. XLII (1953), pp. 261-2.

[51] 'Corpus Christi' in *Mysterium Christi*, edn G. K. A. Bell and D. A. Deissmann (London, 1931), p. 235.

original intention of the figure may have been a designation of the People of God, in the New Testament it is unambiguously applied to Christ (1 Pet 2[4, 6-10], Acts 4[11], Mk 12[10], Lk 20[17]). Paul alludes to this figure in referring to Christ as the 'head of the corner' (Eph 2[20]). R. N. Flew grasps the thought of Paul when he says: 'The Stone by itself has little meaning. If it is "the head of the corner" there is contemplated a new house of Jacob (cf. Eph 2[19-22]).'[52] Israel, reduced to the one Man, is built again in the corporate Temple (a figure which we shall discuss later).

(b) *Jesus Christ as the Son of Man.* A much more complicated figure is that of the Son of Man. It is difficult to ascertain whether or not the figure of the *Bar enash* in Daniel (7[13-22]) influenced the later Messianic conception of the apocalyptic literature.[53] If the Son of Man in the Similitudes of Enoch is related to that of Daniel, there is a significant development, for the figure of the saints of the Most High denotes the pre-existent Messiah.[54] Moreover, in Enoch (Chaps 45-8) the 'congregation of the righteous', also called 'the elect' and 'the holy', appear together with the Elect, Righteous or Holy One, who is also the Son of Man.[55] In 4 *Ezra* (7[27-32]), there is a reference to the Messiah, who dies and thereby brings about the expiration of all who breathe. Later he is raised together with those who are identified with him.[56] In 4 *Ezra* (Chap. 13) 'the man' appears who is presumably the *Bar enash* of Daniel. C. C. Torrey argues that this figure is the Davidic Messiah[57] and to be contrasted with the Messiah *ben Ephraim* of 4 *Ezra* 7. Even if this evidence is not considered to be compelling, the figures of the Messiah (i.e. the Son of Man) and the Suffering Servant are found in close proximity to each other.

Nowhere in his extant Epistles does Paul use the title 'Son of Man'. But his familiarity with it (as well as its implications in terms of a Messianic community) is evident from a number of

---

[52] Op. cit. p. 65.

[53] Cf. A. Fridrichsen, 'Jesus, St John, and St Paul', *The Root of the Vine*, p. 42.

[54] Cf. C. H. Kraeling, *Anthropos and Son of Man*, p. 137. But this point is contested from another angle. J. Y. Campbell ('The Origin and Meaning of the Term Son of Man', p. 149) and H. H. Rowley (*The Relevance of the Apocalyptic* [London, 1944], p. 29) maintain that the title 'Son of Man' was not a Messianic designation prior to the adoption of this title by Jesus. W. F. Albright is just as certain that the title was identified with the Davidic Messiah before Christ with the result that it was recognized by the disciples (*From Stone Age to Christianity* (2nd edn, Baltimore, 1946), pp. 290ff).

[55] C. H. Dodd, *The Apostolic Preaching and Its Development* (London, 1936), p. 143.

[56] Cf. A. Schweitzer, *The Mysticism of Paul*, p. 98.

[57] 'The Messiah Son of Ephraim', p. 261; so also A. Schweitzer, op. cit. p. 87.

passages. Without the pretence of being exhaustive, we may note that judgement which the saints are given to exercise (Dan 7²²)[58] corresponds to the judgement of the world which Paul reminds the Corinthian Church they will exercise (1 Cor 6². Compare the irony of 1 Cor 4⁸ with Dan 7¹⁸). The reference to the 'second Man who is from heaven' (1 Cor 15⁴⁷) appears to be a certain allusion to the Son of Man in Daniel 7¹³.[59] C. H. Dodd observes in regard to the 'faithful saying' in 2 Timothy 2¹¹⁻¹²:

(It is) apparently from a confession of faith in the form of a hymn, expressing the ultimate Christian formulation of the meaning of the vision, in which the Son of Man is at once Christ Himself, and the Church as 'the people of the Saints of the Most High'; 'If we endure, we shall also reign with him.'[60]

A paragraph in Romans (8¹⁷⁻¹⁹) appears to correspond to the experience of the corporate figure in Daniel, in that suffering with Christ guarantees glorification together with him.[61] T. W. Manson contends that the suffering of Christ which Paul claims to 'fill up' by his own persecution (Col 1²⁴) reflects the suffering of the Son of Man in conjunction with the Saints. The sufferings of Christ overflow into the life of the believer (2 Cor 1⁵, Phil 3¹⁰) and the marks of persecution are the marks of the Lord Jesus (Gal 6¹⁷).[62] Paul's descriptions of the Second Advent apparently reflect ideas found in Daniel; the saints are manifested with Jesus Christ in the Parousia (1 Thess 3¹³; cf. 2¹⁹, 4¹³⁻¹⁷).

If Paul actually sees the Church as the fulfilment of Daniel's corporate figure, an obvious link is closed between the Old Testament conception of the 'righteous remnant' identified with the Messiah and the Church as the True Israel constituted through Christ. Thus, the saints which form the corporate personality of the Messiah before His death (i.e. of Jesus) are reconstituted after His resurrection as the reincarnation of the personality of Christ, which is His Body.[63]

Besides this controversial figure in Daniel, the title 'son of man'

[58] Cf. H. H. Rowley, *The Relevance of the Apocalyptic*, pp. 27-8.

[59] T. W. Manson, *The Teaching of Jesus*, pp. 233-4.

[60] *According to the Scriptures* p. 68.

[61] The phrase ἀποκάλυψιν τῶν υἱῶν τοῦ θεοῦ (Rom 8¹⁹) is reminiscent of the 'appearance' of the Son of Man (ἐθεώρουν ὡς υἱὸς ανθρώπου ἤρχετο, LXX, Dan 7¹³).

[62] *The Teaching of Jesus*, p. 232; cf. A. Schweitzer, *The Mysticism of Paul*, pp. 126-7; L. S. Thornton, *The Common Life* . . . p. 35. Albeit, the suffering is not expiatory in the sense in which Christ's is.

[63] Cf. O. Cullmann, *Christ and Time*, p. 118.

also appears in the Psalms in such a way as to attract the attention of the New Testament writers. He is the 'hero' (possibly the king; see verse 1) of Psalm 80, apparently a collective figure[64] which stands for the People of God or may be an individual such as the king who incorporates Israel through realistic representation. This 'son of man' is also called 'God's right-hand man' (80^{17}) who unites with himself the People of God in their oppression (80^{3-19}) only subsequently to be 'strengthened' (80^{17}). Here, as in Daniel, the 'son of man' is identified either with Israel as a whole or with a remnant.

There is still another reference to a 'son of man' in Psalm 8^{4-8} which was equated with Christ in the New Testament. The original intention of the Psalmist was the extolling of the dignity of mankind. Both Paul and the writer of the Epistle to the Hebrews equate this passage with Psalm 110^1 to describe the risen Lord. Philippians 2^{9-11} (describing the exaltation of Jesus who became Man) and Ephesians 1^{20-3} (describing Christ's supreme position as Lord of the whole creation) clearly indicate their dependence on these passages in the Psalter.[65]

In applying the 'son of man' described in Psalm 8 to Jesus Christ the New Testament breaks with the conception of an exclusively Jewish Messiah. This 'son of man' is mankind epitomized in the incarnation of Jesus Christ,[66] the 'Man who is from heaven'. Thus, it is strikingly apparent that the 'son of man' concept (i.e. as a title) in the Old Testament provides the basis of the New Testament conception of Christ as the One who incorporates the True Israel in Himself and is at the same time one with mankind apart from racial or national distinctions.

In extended discussions of the New Testament conception of the 'Son of Man' it has been fashionable to compare it with the Iranian 'heavenly man'.[67] While Jesus' self-designation appears

---

[64] C. H. Dodd, *The Old Testament in the New* (London, 1952), p. 11; *According to the Scriptures*, p. 101.

[65] The reference to the subjection of all things under the feet of Christ (1 Cor 15^{27}) is a direct quotation of Psalm 8^7 (cf. also Eph 1^{22}). The placing of all enemies under His feet (1 Cor 15^{25}) is an unmistakable allusion to Psalm 110^1. Hebrews 2^{6-11} quotes Psalm 8 at length only to arrive at the same conclusion, i.e. that Jesus is the 'son of man', that is, man. In both Hebrews and Philippians death is the prior experience to exaltation, nor is suffering far removed in 1 Corinthians (cf. 15^{20}) and Ephesians (cf. 1^{20}). Cf. C. H. Dodd, *According to the Scripture*, p. 20.

[66] Cf. Wm. Manson, *Jesus the Messiah*, p. 187.

[67] C. H. Kraeling maintains that the title 'Son of Man' is a conscious attempt to designate the 'Anthropos' (op. cit. p. 144). See also E. O. James, 'The Sources of Christian Ritual', *The Labyrinth*, p. 252.

to be totally unrelated since it places almost entirely a future significance on the title,[68] in the Epistles of Paul a number of striking parallels suggest a possible dependence on the Iranian myth. We may summarize some of these elements in Paul's Christology already pointed out by Wm. Manson:[69] (1) Christ's pre-existence (cf. e.g. Phil 2[6-7]), (2) Christ's cosmological significance (cf. Col 1[15-22]), (3) Christ's description as a victorious redeemer raised from death (cf. e.g. Eph 1[20]), (4) the reference to the Man who is from heaven (1 Cor 15[47]),[70] (5) Christ as the sole ground and source of the spiritual life of the Christian.

On the other side of the ledger there are some differences which argue strongly for the Apostle's independence of this oriental mythology. (1) Paul does not describe the pre-existence of Christ as a man, but as the eternal Son of God (cf. Phil 2[6], Col 1[13-19]).[71] (2) Christ's cosmological significance, in contrast to the Anthropos, is related to creation, never determined ontologically (cf. Col 1[16]). Christ's exalted position as Christus Victor has been but recently awarded (Eph 1[20-3], Phil 2[9-11]). (3) The union of the Body with Christ is effected through an act of creation, rather than the infusion of a divine principle which re-awakened the whole race. So great is the contrast that Wm. Manson considers it a possibility that Paul may be actually protesting the Iranian mystery (possibly in Jewish form) in his doctrine of Christ.[72]

Our conclusions have been presented as the discussion has progressed, but in summary form we have sought to establish that Paul fuses the figures of the 'Son of Man' in both Daniel and the Psalter to formulate his Christology. In this way Christ is identified with the righteous remnant, the True Israel, while at the same time He is the typical man and mankind's realistic

---

[68] Wm. Manson, op. cit. p. 184.

[69] Cf. ibid. pp. 186, 189-90.

[70] It is important to note that the Man from heaven is also the Last Adam in 1 Cor 15[45, 47]. The fusion of the Heavenly Man with the Second Adam might support Kraeling's contention that Jewish Adam-speculation was influenced by the Iranian myth (cf. also S. Hanson, op. cit. p. 116). J. M. Creed is not impressed with this idea: 'The Pauline doctrine of Christ as the Second Adam has nothing to do with the heavenly Man of the Apocalyptic or Philonic philosophy', ('The Heavenly Man', p. 134; cf. H. St J. Thackeray, *The Relations of St Paul to Contemporary Jewish Thought*, p. 49). Contrast D. Somerville, op. cit. p. 51; H. Lietzmann, *The Beginnings of the Christian Church*, p. 271, following Reitzenstein, *Podmandres*, pp. 109ff.

[71] Christ is Man only by acquisition or incarnation, but not so originally.

[72] Op. cit. p. 189. Cf. J. M. Creed, op. cit. p. 134; J. Moffatt, *1 Corinthians* (London, 1938), pp. 187-8; A. Schweitzer, *The Mysticism of Paul*, p. 167.

representative. This is the central theme in Paul's doctrine of unity in that Christ unites both Israel and the Gentiles in Himself, making of both one New Man. The eschatological character of this revelation leads Paul to refer to it as the 'mystery of this dispensation' (cf. Eph 2–3).

(c) *Jesus Christ as the Servant of the Lord.* Two Old Testament figures remain for our consideration in Paul's doctrine of Christ identified with the eschatological community, namely, the Suffering Servant and Adam.[73] These figures are inextricably interrelated with the picture of Christ as the Son of Man and the True Isaac to produce Paul's kaleidoscopic Messianic picture. In one passage (Phil 2[6-11]) the figures of Adam, the Son of Man, and the Servant of the Lord are inter-woven in a single configuration.

The great importance of the Servant of the Lord passages (Isa 40–53) is evident throughout the New Testament.[74] It was the basis for the interpretation of the life and death of Christ and undoubtedly held an important place in the earliest instruction of Gentile converts (cf. Acts 8[28-35]). On these grounds it is not surprising that Paul apparently assumes that his audience knows the significance of this passage, although there may be personal or apologetic reasons for his omission of any direct reference to Christ as the Servant.[75] Allusions to the Servant are plentiful, however.

Philippians 2[6-11] is largely determined by the fourth Song of the Servant.[76] Some of the points of contact are: (1) the use of the term 'servant' (2[7]), (2) the humiliation of the Servant (cf. 2[8] with Isa 53[8], 'in his humiliation', LXX), (3) the Kenosis of the Servant (cf. 2[7] with Isa 53[12], 'he emptied his soul'), (4) the death of the Servant (cf. 2[8] with Isa 53[10, 12]), (5) the exaltation of the Servant (cf. 2[9-11] with Isa 52[13], 'he shall be high and greatly exalted'). Elsewhere in the Songs, as God is glorified in His Servant (Isa 49[3]), Paul declares the establishment of the Lordship of Christ to be 'unto the glory of God the Father' (2[11]).

In Romans 4[25], Christ 'who was delivered up for our transgressions . . .' (cf. Eph 5[2], 'even as Christ . . . gave Himself up

[73] The importance of Paul's conception of Christ as the Second Adam has made it necessary to treat his doctrine in a major section.

[74] Cf. O. Cullmann, *Peter*, trans. F. V. Filson (London, 1953), pp. 66ff.

[75] Cf. Vincent Taylor, *The Atonement in New Testament Teaching* (London, 1940), pp. 95ff.

[76] Cf. T. H. Bindley, 'Fresh Light Upon Philippians 2:5-8,' *Expositor* (Dec. 1923), pp. 443-4; E. Lohmeyer, *Kyrios Jesus* (Heidelberg, 1928), p. 36.

for us') is a definite allusion to the sacrifice of the Servant (Isa 53[5, 6, 12]).[77] 'For he hath made him to be sin for us, who knew no sin' (2 Cor 5[21]), is a re-statement of the clause, 'thou shalt make his soul a sin-offering' (Isa 53[10]) and fits the spirit of the whole of the last Song.[78] The 'peace' which Christ has been made for us (Eph 2[14]; cf. Rom 5[1]) may be a contraction of the 'chastisement of our peace' which the Servant bears through his suffering (Isa 53[5]). The direct quotation of Isaiah 52[15], 'To *whom* no tidings of *him* came, they shall see; and they that have not heard shall understand' (Rom 15[21]), identifies Christ with the Servant. For this reason the report mentioned in Isaiah 53[1] is the gospel which Paul preaches (Rom 10[16]).[79]

Although Paul individualizes the figure of the Servant of the Lord as do the Songs of the Servant, there is another side to the issue. He in no way emasculates the corporate character of the Old Testament figure but gives it new meaning in the identification of Christ with the Church. The conception oscillates between the individual and the collective in the mind of Paul so that he does not distinguish between the experience of the Servant and that of the Community which He incorporates. Thus, in Romans 8[33-4], the justification or vindication accorded to the Servant (cf. Isa 50[8-9]) is ascribed to the 'elect', that is, the Church. In the next breath Paul asserts that this justification rests entirely on the merits of Jesus Christ who died and rose again to be exalted to the place of honour at God's right hand. The expanding and contracting figure of the Suffering Servant painted the ideal picture of Christ whom Paul saw as the Individual incorporating the Israel of God in Himself.[80]

There is still another aspect to Paul's identification of Christ with the Servant of Jehovah. It is his doctrine of the vicarious atonement of Christ for the New Israel. Just as the Servant stood

---

[77] Cf. Vincent Taylor, op. cit. p. 95.

[78] Cf. H. J. Schoeps, 'The Sacrifice of Isaac in Paul's Theology', trans. R. H. Pfeiffer, *JBL*, Vol. LXV (1946), p. 391.

[79] Wm. Manson makes an interesting correlation between the function of the Servant in the role of 'the light of the Gentiles' (Isa 42[6], 49[6]) and Paul's designation of Christ as the 'Wisdom of God' to the world (1 Cor 1[24, 30]). 'Mission and Eschatology', *IRM*, Vol. XLII (Oct. 1953), p. 393.

[80] The Old Testament principle of corporate personality which designated the Servant as at one time Israel and at another an individual is identical with Paul's interpretation of the promise to Abraham regarding the 'seed' (Gal 3[16]). There is an interesting terminological coincidence in Isa 41[8] where the Servant is called 'the seed of Abraham'.

in vicarious solidarity with Israel (emphasized repeatedly in Isa 53[4-12]), Christ stands in vicarious union with the True Israel.[81] In correspondence to the Old Testament idea of the identification of the offerer with his vicarious substitute, Paul declares that he himself has been crucified with Christ (Gal 2[20]). The vicarious death of Christ was the corporate experience of the New Humanity even as Paul declares: '. . . the love of Christ constrains us; because we thus judge, that one died for all, therefore all died' (2 Cor 5[14]). The way to forgiveness, life, and exaltation is through inclusion in Christ and through a realistic sharing in His death and resurrection.[82]

More explicitly, for Paul, the death of Christ is sacrificial. That Christ fulfilled the mission of the Servant of the Lord is important at this juncture. The Servant is explicitly described in terms of a sacrifice (*'asham*, 'guilt offering', Isa 53[10]).[83] It follows that the death of Christ should be interpreted as an expiation for sin. This doctrine is so completely interpenetrated with the vicarious mission of the Suffering Servant and so fundamental to the whole of his theology that no detailed list of the points of correspondence can be made. 2 Corinthians 5[21] is very explicit: 'Him who knew no sin he made to be sin on our behalf; that we might become the righteousness of God in him.' It is the sacrificial character of Christ's death which is presented to the Ephesians: 'Even as Christ also loved you, and gave himself up for us, an offering and a sacrifice to God for an odour of a sweet smell' (5[2]). For Paul the sacrifices of the Temple ritual have been displaced by the one, all-inclusive sacrifice of the Lamb of God for the New Israel, even as the Servant in his death bore the sins of a defiled Israel (Isa 53[6]). As the death of the Suffering Servant was not limited to national Israel in the scope of its effectiveness, Paul posits the potential extension of the atonement of Christ to the whole cosmos (cf. Rom 5[6, 8-21], 4[25]). The references to 'blood', 'reconciliation' (Rom 5[8-12]), 'propitiation' or 'expiation'[84] ($\iota\lambda\alpha\sigma\tau\eta\rho\iota\sigma\nu$, Rom 3[25]; cf. Eph 2[13]), arise directly out of the Jewish sacrificial system, but Paul's explicit claim that Christ

---

[81] Cf. Wm. Manson, *Jesus the Messiah*, pp. 117-18; T. W. Manson, *The Servant Messiah* (Cambridge, 1953), pp. 73-4.

[82] Cf. G. A. Danell, 'The Idea of God's People in the Bible', *The Root of the Vine*, p. 36.

[83] Cf. H. H. Rowley, 'The Meaning of Sacrifice in the Old Testament', p. 104.

[84] On this point see Vincent Taylor, op. cit. pp. 219-20 and Leon Morris, *The Apostolic Preaching of the Cross* (London, 1955), pp. 275-80.

died for our sins 'according to the Scriptures' (1 Cor 15³) can scarcely be justified by any other Old Testament reference than Isaiah 53.[85]

H. J. Schoeps in a recent article has argued cogently that the doctrine of the expiatory sacrifice of Christ reflects the Jewish teaching on the 'binding of Isaac', as it is interpreted in the familiar Rosh Hashana liturgy.[86] There is something to be said for this contention, especially when we remember Paul's interpretation of the 'seed' of Abraham as Christ who is, as a result, the real 'Isaac' (Gal 3¹⁶). There are other correlative points: τοῦ ἰδίου υἱοῦ οὐκ ἐφείσατο (Rom 8³²) is to be compared advantageously with οὐκ ἐφείσω τοῦ υἱοῦ σου (Gen 22¹⁶ LXX). Προέθετο in Romans 3²⁵ may well reflect Genesis 22⁸: 'God *will provide* himself a lamb.' In contemporary Jewish thought broad merits were believed to have issued from the 'Binding' to the advantage of all Israel.[87] The emphasis which the Rabbis placed on the voluntary submission of Isaac has its counterpart in the voluntary self-sacrifice of Jesus (cf. Rom 5⁷).[88] But Isaac is no more than the type (he was not actually sacrificed) of the real 'Isaac' whose vicarious death provides a full redemption for the New Israel.[89]

The Apostle's designation of Christ as 'our Passover' (1 Cor 5⁷) gains an added significance from this same area of Jewish thought. It was the blood of the Passover lamb, when applied to the doorposts of Israelites in Egypt, which derived its efficacy from the 'binding of Isaac'.[90] This has its counterpart in Paul's reference to the 'redemption (ἀπολύτρωσις, a term of deep religious significance for a Jew, as "redemption" was the mighty act of God which constituted Israel as a nation) through his blood' (Eph 1⁷; cf. Rom 3²⁴, 1 Cor 1³⁰, Col 1¹⁴). In Romans 5⁹ Paul writes of 'justification (a word containing greater ethical significance) in his blood'. In Paul's reapplication of the elements which were fundamental to the history of the Jewish nation, the redemption from Egypt only finds its true significance in the redemption from the thraldom of sin. Calvary is the juncture of the 'passing over'

---

[85] Cf. Wm. Manson, *Jesus the Messiah*, p. 124.
[86] Op. cit. pp. 385ff.
[87] Cf. H. St J. Thackeray, op. cit. p. 91.
[88] Cf. C. H. Dodd, *According to the Scriptures*, op. cit. pp. 118-19.
[89] Cf. H. J. Schoeps, op. cit. p. 392.
[90] H. J. Schoeps, op. cit. p. 391. Cf. *Mek* I.57; *Ex R.* 17.3.

of the New Israel incorporated in Christ from the Aeon of sin and death to the New Age of life and peace (cf. Rom 5[17]).[91]

In the eschatological interpretation of the death of Christ as the true sacrifice there is a radical contrast with the unreal and unprofitable sacrifices still carried on in the Jewish ritual.[92] In the death of Christ which was the anti-type of the sacrifice prefigured by Isaac, Paul saw the fulfilment of the original intention of the historical event on Mt Moriah as well as the prophetic picture of the atoning Servant.

Rudolph Otto, after accepting the proposition that Jesus interpreted His death in the light of the corporate experience of the Servant of the Lord,[93] adds the significant point that the Servant was 'the covenant' for the People of Israel. 'I will make you into a *berith* (a *diatheke*, a covenant) with the people of Israel' (Isa 42[6]), that is, into a mediator of the covenant between me and the people. And likewise in Isaiah 49[8]: 'I will preserve thee and give thee for a covenant of the people.'[94] Paul makes reference to this 'new covenant' in 1 Corinthians: 'This cup is the new covenant in my blood' (11[25]). It is impossible to be certain that Paul has the Servant passages in mind from his allusion to the Eucharist, but the sacrificial nature of Christ's death as the seal of the 'covenant' is clear. This is further shown in 10[18-21], where the 'cup' of the Lord is placed in direct contrast with the pagan sacrifices offered to Gentile deities.[95]

The Old Covenant was the foundation of the psychic bond which united Israel, transcending the distinctions between

---

[91] Cf. A. Nygren, *Commentary on Romans*, op. cit. p. 228.

[92] A. G. Hebert, op. cit. p. 204.

[93] *The Kingdom of God and the Son of Man*, trans. F. V. Filson, B. L. Woolf (London, 1938), pp. 250ff.

[94] Ibid. pp. 289ff; cf. Wm. Manson, *Jesus the Messiah*, p. 142.

[95] In Paul's contrast between the two covenants in Gal 4[24-31], the feature of sacrifice is omitted. But it must not have been far from his mind, since the free sons of the promise were accorded their blessed position only by the death of Christ, as Ephesians 2[12-13] specifically declares. In another context, Paul and his associates, through their missionary endeavours among the Gentiles, are the 'ministers of the New Covenant' (2 Cor 3[6]); they announce the message of reconciliation to all men apart from the consideration of ethnic distinctions (2 Cor 5[18-21]). The Apostle's reference to the New Covenant in Romans 11[27] is somewhat confusing. Here a quotation of Isaiah's prophecy touching the New Covenant (59[20-1]; cf. 27[9]; Jer 31[31-4]) is applied to national Israel. This raises the difficult question whether Paul oscillates between the fulfilment of the prediction of the New Covenant in (1) national Israel and (2) in the calling out of the New Israel. While the former is assured, the latter is less certain, there being no direct quotation from the Old Testament which would unequivocally support it. One encounters the same problem in interpreting Peter's sermon in Acts 2[14-36] (see R. N. Flew, op. cit. pp. 100ff).

individuals and the vertical distinctions between generations; it made Israel specifically the People of God. The identical features were extended to the New Israel through the New Covenant mediated by Jesus Christ.[96] The nucleus of the Church as an eschatological community of Jesus' disciples was united inseparably with Christ in the Last Supper.[97] In the undissected Event of the communal meal and the crucifixion a new covenantal relationship with God was secured with positive features distinguishing it from the old: 'First was inwardness: "I will put my law in their inward part"; second, individualism: "all shall know me"; third, forgiveness of sin: "their sins will I remember no more." '[98] In the same transaction each party to the New Covenant was conjoined in community with the whole,[99] but of this we shall have more to say later. In fine, '. . . by the connexion of this covenant with His (Jesus') atoning death, . . . He gives His disciples a share in that reconciling power',[100] and establishes a real, visible community (in which the Gentiles are given an option) known as the People of God.

Our theme has been repeatedly mentioned in the course of the discussion. In applying it to his doctrine of the Church Paul needed little originality, for the mission of the Servant involved those outside ethnic Israel. 'I will give thee for a covenant of the people, for a light of the Gentiles; to open the blind eyes, to bring out the prisoners from the dungeon, and them that sit in darkness out of the prison house' (Isa 42[6-7]).

(d) *Jesus Christ as the High Priest of the New Israel.* Paul, in contrast to the Letter to the Hebrews, gives very little emphasis to the priestly role of Christ. Nevertheless, the idea apparently does not lie far beneath the surface of his thinking.[101] One of the reasons for his omission may be his conception of the fusion of

[96] Cf. J. Bright, *The Kingdom of God*, pp. 228-9. Note that the sect which produced the Zadokite Fragments and the Dead Sea Scrolls were 'covenanters'; their name was 'New Covenant' (cf. A. Dupont-Sommer, op. cit. p. 33).

[97] Cf. R. N. Flew, op. cit. p. 65. As long as the Supper and the Crucifixion are regarded as a single 'event' all subsequent partaking of the 'cup of the covenant' is a memorial, a symbolic recollection of the original transaction. This seems to be Paul's intention in quoting the words of Jesus, '. . . this do ye, as oft as ye drink of it, in remembrance of me' (1 Cor 11[25]).

[98] R. N. Flew, op. cit. p. 73.

[99] Cf. C. A. A. Scott, *Christianity According to St Paul*, p. 187; S. Hanson, op. cit. p. 33.

[100] R. N. Flew, op. cit. p. 65.

[101] Cf. St Augustine, *Ep. ad Anatolium*, 4: 'Our Priest took from us what He offered for us: He took flesh from us; and in this flesh He was made a victim, He was made a holocaust, He was made a sacrifice.'

the roles of the officiating priest and the sacrificial victim. Far from there being any opposition between these two functions, Christ brings to fruition the Old Testament conception of the solidarity of the sacrifice and the one who offers it.[102] In Paul's doctrine Christ offers Himself (cf. Eph 5[2], quoted above), a feat which the High-priest could accomplish only symbolically. In 1 Timothy 2[5-6] Paul refers to Christ as the Mediator[103] between God and men, serving as a ransom ($\dot{a}\nu\tau\dot{\iota}\lambda\upsilon\tau\rho o\nu$)[104] for all. Titus 2[14] adds to our understanding of this mediation the conception of a redeemed community which is a peculiar people (cf. Ezek 37[23]) gaining through solidarity with its self-sacrificed Saviour the benefits of redemption and cleansing from iniquity.

The probable background of the image of Christ as the Mediator is the impressive ritual of the Day of Atonement. A first principle of Judaism was that neither the individual Israelite nor the Community could gain access to God without the High Priest as a 'go-between'.[105] This dogma is heightened in the New Testament doctrine of access into the divine presence. In Christ, who is God's Mediator, both the individual Christian and the Church find ready access to a personal relationship with God.[106]

There is an important transition in Paul's thought in Ephesians 5[26-7]. It is no longer Christ as an individual[107] who is the sacrifice (contrast 5[25], 'even as Christ also loved the church, and gave himself up for it'), but as the Priest who offers His Body (the Church) to Himself (not, however, a sin or guilt offering). There is

---

[102] Cf. E. L. Mascall, op. cit. p. 75.

[103] It is by no means certain that $\mu\epsilon\sigma\dot{\iota}\tau\eta s$ in this passage means a priest. In Gal 3[19.20] the 'mediator' is clearly designated as Moses, indicating a covenantal concept rather than a priestly function. The same idea is found in Heb 8[6], 9[15], 12[24], where Christ is repeatedly the Mediator of the New Covenant, contrasting with the covenant proffered by angels (cf. Gal 3[19]). In Hebrews this is quite natural, for the writer sees Christ as the fulfilment of the priesthood of Melchizedek (cf. 8[1-6]).

[104] A derivative of $\lambda\dot{\upsilon}\tau\rho o\nu$ (cf. Tit 2[14]) denoting the idea of the manumission of slaves. The Old Testament background is the emancipation of Israel from Egyptian bondage.

[105] The sinlessness of Christ (emphasized in Rom 8[3], 2 Cor 5[21]) may be an antithetical reference to the embarrassing requirement of the High Priest to offer a sacrifice of atonement for himself on the Day of Atonement (Lev 16[11]), although of course there are other reasons (cf. D. Somerville, op. cit. p. 37).

[106] 'In strict accord with Hebrew thought he (Paul) has nowhere spoken of a direct fellowship with God: "relationship to God, in the Old Testament, was established through the altar (10[18])"; St Paul represents it as mediated through Christ.' G. V. Jourdan, '$Ko\iota\nu\omega\nu\dot{\iota}a$ in 1 Corinthians 10[16]', *JBL*, Vol. LXVII (1948), p. 113 (cf. Hauch, *TWNT*, III.804).

[107] The context is characterized by the idea of the Church as the Body of Christ, meaning that both Christ and the Body are one.

a fusion of the roles of priest, victim, and accepting Deity fulfilled in Christ. The Church is implicated in the holiness of Christ since it is identified with His sacrifice which has rendered it without blemish. Colossians 1^{22} is more concise in its presentation of the idea of Christ's death as a reconciling sacrifice which makes the Church presentable to God.

The theme of Christ as the realistic representative of the sinful community is the theme of the New Israel. Christ comes from the seed of Abraham (Rom 9^5), from which the priests of God must come; nevertheless, in His identification with all flesh,[108] Israel's repeated Day of Atonement was given a universal and final fulfilment. Gentiles and Jews are included together in an offering made once (ἐφ ἅπαξ, cf. Heb $9^{26, 28}$, 1 Pet 3^{18}) for all sins in the 'end of the ages'.

THE SOLIDARITY OF THE CHURCH AS THE NEW HUMANITY

Introduction

We must now turn to Paul's doctrine of the Church as the New Humanity through its identification with the Last Adam. This designation of Christ is supremely important for his doctrine of the Church and is all the more remarkable for its uniqueness.[109] As we have already considered, the use of the historical figure of Adam as a type of Christ is both comparative and antithetical.[110] In this respect the doctrine of the Last Adam belongs to the same category as the figures which we have already discussed in that it is the Church united with its Head as an eschatological community which is indicated by the idea of the New Humanity created through the Second Adam.[111] More explicitly, the ideas of the aeons and their respective heads find their contrasting

---

[108] Cf. M. J. Sheeban, *The Mysteries of Christianity*, trans. C. Vollert (London, 1946), p. 438.

[109] Cf. E. Hoskyns and N. Davey, *The Riddle of the New Testament* (London, 1931), p. 192. Although the first and the last man appear together for the first time in the writing of Paul, the casual introduction of the figure suggests that he is not presenting a new theologoumenon but is appealing to a traditional teaching (H. Lietzmann, *An die Römer (HBZNT)* (3 Auf., Tübingen, 1928), p. 63; C. H. Kraeling, op. cit. p. 161).

[110] Cf. J. Jeremias, *TWNT*, I.141-2; A. Nygren, op. cit. pp. 218-19.

[111] This is possibly true for another reason than that the New Israel has been manifested in the New Age. It is because as J. Weiss has said: 'In his (Paul's) way of thinking, there lies the presupposition that the events of the primitive times—only in a reverse sense—must be repeated at the end of time, a conviction which elsewhere plays a great role in Apocalyptic' (op. cit. p. 434). Cf. W. D. Davies, op. cit. p. 49.

parallels in Christ and Adam. The one brought sin and death; the other brought the converse, righteousness and life.[112] In Paul's theology Christ is therefore the Representative Head and source of the common nature and life possessed by the Christian Community which is also the Body of Christ.

CHRIST IN THE ROLE OF THE LAST ADAM

(1) *The Representative Role of the Last Adam.* D. Somerville has cited an opinion expressed by Nösgen[113] that Paul's designation of Christ as the Second Adam denotes Soteriological rather than Christological truth.[114] Although the statement is too extravagant, the Soteriological aspects are more clear and less subject to misrepresentation. In Paul Christ is indeed the Author of Salvation, but this title is not given to Him to carry the same conception with which a Gnostic might have described Him. Nor does it have kinship with the myth of the *Urmensch* or a salvation offered by the Mysteries in which through emanation or union with a deity the Cosmos finds redemption. The Incarnation of Christ has no benefits for the race apart from the determining act of obedience which stands over against the determinative transgression of Adam.

The antithetical parallel between Adam's disobedience and the archetypal Act of Christ is specifically drawn in Romans 5[18-19]:

So then as through one trespass the judgement came unto all men to condemnation; even so through one act of righteousness the free gift came unto all men to justification of life. For as through the one man's disobedience the many were made sinners, even so through the obedience of the one shall the many be made righteous (*RV*).

As all men were included in the corporate judgement of Adam for the one act of transgression, so all men (doubtless relative in its scope) share in the free gift which is the reward of the one act of righteousness. As the first act of disobedience brought mankind into the slavery of sin (ἁμαρτωλοὶ κατεστάθησαν), the positive act of obedience wrought by the Second Adam has rendered all the members of the New Race righteous. The enmity between man and God incurred through the first man (cf. Rom 8[7]) has been abolished in the reconciliation of the New Humanity with the

---

[112] Cf. F. C. Baur, *Paul: His Life and Works*, pp. 215-16. K. Barth, *Romans*, p. 164.
[113] *Christus der Menschen und Gottessohn*, pp. 110-15.
[114] D. Somerville, op. cit. p. 52 note 1; cf. W. D. Davies, op. cit. p. 53.

Creator (2 Cor 5$^{18-21}$). The first sin was judged by the infliction of the death penalty on Adam and his race; the righteous deed has brought in its wake the prospect of eternal life, confirmed through the resurrection of Christ which all who are in Christ will share (1 Cor 15$^{22-3}$). Throughout the contrasting parallel there is a corresponding identification of the 'many' (i.e. the Church) with Christ to the identification of the 'many' (i.e. the cosmos of men) with Adam. Both acts are crucial for the races which Adam and Christ represent. Although the incidents are historical, they have an eternal significance co-extensive with the aeons which they have founded.

The frame of reference in which the Pauline doctrine of the transferred merit of Christ is cast is familiar from the Old Testament and Early Jewish conceptions of solidarity. It is no more than the re-application of the conception of corporate personality which conceived of the guilt or blessing of the one involving the group in his own representative acts. As strange and mysterious as this type of thought is to us, it is increasingly clear that many commonly encountered interpretations of Paul's doctrine of atonement are quite beside the point. Any theory which stresses the 'forensic' or a purely insular substitution is as inadequate to support Paul's doctrine of atonement as it is to explain his teaching on the implications of Adam's transgression for the race. Such explanations suffer from the lack of realism and subjectivity in their attitudes toward the solidarity which was basic in the Jewish background of Paul. It is only because one is 'in Christ', implying a very real sense of solidarity, that any benefits accrue to the Christian. There is nothing here which can be construed as a mechanical transfer of merit.[115]

(2) *The New Humanity Implicated in the Nature of the Last Adam.* Because Christ stands in the same relationship to the New Humanity as Adam did to the old, not only is the archetypal act of obedience corporately rewarded, but the nature of Christ is shared by the Church. In contrast to man's subjection to the powers of the Old Aeon—sin, death, spirit-forces, all active in the flesh—the new character common to the New Humanity is described in terms of life, righteousness, and the partaking of the Holy Spirit, active in the Body of Christ.

[115] Cf. D. Somerville, op. cit. pp. 93-4.

For this reason to be 'in Christ' is for Paul a formula expressing the solidarity between Christ and the community members. It carries the assurance of 'life' in the present (Eph 2[1-10], cf. Rom 6[5-11], Gal 3[27])[116] and for the future[117] (1 Cor 15[22, 50-7], 1 Thess 4[13-17]). It is in this vein that Paul declares the purpose and grace of God to have been manifested in Jesus Christ, 'who hath abolished death, and hath brought life and immortality to light through the gospel' (2 Tim 1[10]).

In Christ the believer has also been made the 'righteousness of God' (δικαιοσύνη θεοῦ, 2 Cor 5[21]; cf. Rom 1[17], Phil 3[9]). This phrase is more emphatic than the expected adjectival description, 'made righteous' (δικαιωθέντες, Rom 5[1, 9]; cf. 2[24, 28], Gal 2[17], 3[24], 1 Cor 4[4], 6[11], etc.).[118] The determining characteristic of the Adamic race—sin—has been displaced in the New Race through solidarity with its righteous Head. 'There is therefore now no condemnation to them that are *in Christ Jesus*; for the law of the Spirit of life in Christ Jesus has made me free from the law of sin and death' (Rom 8[1]), exults the Apostle. This is the 'gracious gift' which 'superabounds' in its displacement of the banal influence of Adam's sin on the nature of the race.[119]

In Christ the believer is made a partaker of the Holy Spirit (πάντες ἓν πνεῦμα ἐποτίσθημεν, 1 Cor 12[13]), the determinative personal force of the New Age. He and His work correspond very clearly to Satan and his activity in the Old Aeon. According to the Gospels, Jesus taught that the giving of the Holy Spirit would be effected only subsequently to the resurrection (Jn 7[39], Lk 12[12], Jn 14[26-30]). Paul's doctrine of the Holy Spirit is also elaborated in a close relationship to the resurrection through which Christ, the Last Adam, became a 'life-giving Spirit' (1 Cor 15[45]). The apparent identification of Christ with the Holy Spirit, although not absolute,[120] is close enough for Paul to say: 'The Lord is the Spirit' (2 Cor 3[17]). For this reason the main point is seen in 1 Corinthians 12[12-31] if one recognizes that because Christians have

---

[116] That is, in the sense of being the converse of 'living death' meaning reconciliation with God.

[117] Cf. O. Pfleiderer, *Paulinism*, I.18ff.

[118] Cf. A. C. Headlam, *St Paul and Christianity*, p. 131.

[119] Cf. A. Nygren, *Romans*, p. 221; H. Lietzmann, *An die Römer*, p. 63.

[120] Cf. J. S. Stewart, *A Man in Christ*, p. 156. Contrast J. Weiss, *The History of Primitive Christianity*, p. 356; C. Weizsäcker, *The Apostolic Age of the Christian Church*, I.145; H. Lietzmann, *The Beginnings of the Christian Church*, p. 120. G. Johnston has better fathomed Paul's enigma: 'God is the Father of the Lord Jesus Christ; God's Spirit therefore is Christ's Spirit' (op. cit. p. 99).

the Holy Spirit, they are united in a connexion with Christ 'which may be compared to the relation of the body to the spirit'.[121] In the Hebrew mind such a relationship is indivisible—the body being the outward manifestation of the spirit or soul.

The burden of Paul's reference to Christ as a life-giving Spirit is that there now exists a new order of life. The manifestation of this resurrection life is made effective through the working of the Holy Spirit who represents Christ on earth (cf. Rom 8[2, 9, 11]). Jesus, following His resurrection, lives in His followers through the Holy Spirit (Rom 8[11], Gal 4[6]). 'For on account of having received the Spirit, man comes into a new, inner communion with Christ, so that Christ fills and rules him completely. Who is joined to the Lord is one spirit with him' (1 Cor 6[17], Eph 2[18]).[122] This forms the antithesis to Adam who lives on in the extension of physical life throughout the human tree. For Paul such life is no more than death in comparison with the life of the new order. Thus it comes that as Adam includes the Old Aeon within his corporate personality, the Holy Spirit incorporates the New Race, for the Spirit is one with the New Aeon.[123]

The Apostle bolsters his argument for the common spiritual nature of the resurrection body[124] by using the analogy of the 'firstfruits'. That which characterizes the dedicated portion cannot be essentially different from the whole. Christ is the First-fruits of those who sleep, who are Christians (1 Cor 15[20]). 'And what applies to the First, the Head, also applies to all the following, the rest of the race. To Paul, this is an absolutely conclusive proof'[125] (cf. Rom 11[16]). But such a proof has no meaning apart from the solidarity which characterizes the community with its Author.[126] Such a solidarity involves the sharing in the heavenly nature of the living Christ (1 Cor 15[46-56]). With a view toward

---

[121] R. Asting, *Die Heiligkeit im Urchristentem*, p. 211; cf. F. A. Christie, 'One Body in Christ, Rom 12, 1 Cor 12', *JBL*, Vol. XVI (1897), p. 128.

[122] R. Asting, op. cit. p. 192; cf. p. 215; C. H. Dodd, *The Meaning of St Paul for Today*, pp. 134-5.

[123] S. Hanson, op. cit. p. 96; cf. T. Soiron, *Die Kirche als der Leib Christi* (Düsseldorf, 1951), p. 181.

[124] On the corporate connotations of the 'resurrection body' see J. A. T. Robinson, *The Body*, Chap. 3, pp. 49ff.

[125] S. Hanson, op. cit. p. 99. Cf. A. Schweitzer, *The Mysticism of Paul*, p. 98. This corresponds to what C. H. Dodd refers to as the indivisibility of 'history and post-history' in the writers of the Old Testament (*The Old Testament in the New*, pp. 18-19).

[126] This is unmistakable in Romans 11[16] where the firstfruits is originally a part of the lump (*terumah*) just as the root and the branches are related to each other. They must partake of the same nature (cf. Matt 7[17-20]).

the future, Paul speaks of Christ as bearing the image of the heavenly and the incorruptible as the First from the resurrection; but, the same lies in store for the community (1 Cor 15⁴⁹). The Apostle does himself look forward to the reception of the newly fashioned body conformed to the body of His glory (Phil 3²¹).

By virtue of His position as 'firstborn (πρωτότοκος) from the dead', Christ has been accorded the Headship of the new creation which is His Body (i.e. the New Humanity) (Col 1¹⁸). To be 'in Him' means to share in the supra-mundane type of life which is His; it means that one becomes a participant in the 'new creation' (2 Cor 5¹⁷).

The assurance that the New Humanity in fact does share in the common nature of the risen Christ is provided through the common possession of the Holy Spirit.[127] He is the seal (σφράγις) of the salvation of the believer, a downpayment (ἀρραβών) on the inheritance of eternal life (Eph 1¹³⁻¹⁴, 4³⁰, 2 Cor 1²², 5⁵). This seal of the Holy Spirit makes the hope of the resurrection and the final vindication of the promise of the gospel absolutely certain. It is not wishful thinking, but a sure hope which saves us (Rom 8²³⁻⁴), a hope which the fruit borne in us by the Spirit confirms (Gal 5²²; cf. Eph 5⁹).

Paul uses the term 'New Man' to designate his conception of the Christ-collectivity and its characteristic nature. In antithesis to the Old Man which denoted the Adamic humanity and its defiled nature, the New Humanity has been re-created through solidarity with Christ, the Second Adam. The character which mankind received from its ancestral source brought in its wake the disruption and divisions which plague the race.[128] In each mention of the 'New Man' in Paul's Epistles these divisions are declared abolished in the unity of the New Man which is the incorporation of the personality of Christ (cf. Col 3¹⁰⁻¹⁷, Eph 2¹⁵⁻²², 4²⁴, Gal 3²⁸,(¹²⁹)).[130] The passage in Colossians joins to the idea of abolished

---

[127] Cf. A. Schweitzer, *The Mysticism of Paul*, p. 119; W. Beyschlag, *New Testament Theology*, II.87.

[128] This conception receives sustained emphasis in S. Hanson, op. cit. *passim*.

[129] Note that some ancient manuscripts (P46, ℵ*, A) have ἐστε χριστοῦ for εἶς ἐστε ἐν χριστῷ. If the former reading is correct, this passage must be removed from the list of those which contain the idea of the 'New Man'. The sense would be simply, you are united because you *belong* to the common Lord.

[130] Cf. S. Hanson, op. cit. pp. 80, 119, 144-5; A. G. Hebert, op. cit. p. 235; T. W. Manson, *The Teaching of Jesus*, pp. 233-4. Paul's doctrines of the New Israel and the New Humanity coincide in the conception of the 'New Man'. The mystery of the New Israel, that is, the provision for the inclusion of the Gentiles, is integrally related

boundaries that of the new nature which characterizes the New Humanity. There is a connexion with Adam suggested by the phrase, 'after the image of him who created him' (3^{10}). Adam, who was originally made in the image of the Creator, through sinning, lost any resemblance to the Holy God. By 'putting on the new man' the Colossians are already renewed in the image of Him (i.e. God) who created Him (i.e. Christ) (3^{10}, Eph 2^{15}).[131] As Christ, being the Son and Image of God (cf. Phil 2^6,[132] Col 1^{15}), incorporates in Himself the New Humanity, they are as a unit restored to the glory of the original creation of Adam. From a human standpoint it is the corporate Society which by ensphering itself in Christ produces the extension of the personality of Christ upon the earth. This is the representation of the character of God, for it reflects the image of Christ.[133]

Paul's doctrine of Christ as the Last Adam presents a studied attempt to show that Christ more than counteracts all the influence and consequences of Adam's solidarity with the human race in the New Humanity. In the place of death comes the influx of the new life of the Spirit which flows from Christ (Col 3^4). As F. A. Christie says: 'The Spirit in us is for Paul more than an ethical reality. The new life is new existence, new being, as well as a new character.[134] In the place of the determinism of sin's power in the flesh is the new nature characterized by righteousness. In brief, the original creation of mankind in the image of God has been restored in the New Humanity through its new relationship to Christ. Therefore, Paul does not hesitate to affirm that the corporate body of the redeemed forms a 'New Creation' or 'New Creature' (2 Cor 5^{17}).[135] Just as Adam was head and lord of the first creation, Christ, the Second Adam, is Head and Lord of the New Order.

to the description of the constitution of the New Humanity into the 'New Man' (cf. G. V. Florovsky, 'Sobornost' *The Church of God*, ed. E. L. Mascall [London, 1934], pp. 54-5).

[131] Cf. C. A. A. Scott, *Christianity According to St Paul*, pp. 261ff.

[132] See E. Lohmeyer, *Kyrios Jesus*, pp. 8ff, 18ff, who notes that μορφῇ may be translated as '*demoutha*' in Syriac, meaning image. The Peshitta uses '*demoutha*' in translating Phil 2^6 (cf. A. M. Hunter, *Paul and His Predecessors* [London, 1940], p. 49).

[133] See further D. Somerville's excellent discussion of this idea, op. cit. pp. 127ff, 160ff; cf. C. A. A. Scott, *Christianity According to St Paul*, p. 262.

[134] Op. cit. p. 123.

[135] See H. Lietzmann's good summary in *An die Römer*, p. 66; cf. E. L. Mascall, op. cit. pp. 77-8.

THE LAST MAN AND THE BODY OF CHRIST

We must turn to examine the nature of the solidarity by which the New Humanity is united with Christ. We have spoken of a common sharing of the resurrection life of Christ through the Holy Spirit and of Christ's realistic representation of the community. We have found fault with those views which describe the relationship of Christ to the Church as forensic and unrealistic. In the interpretation of the Body of Christ concept, where the conception of Paul describing the solidarity of the Christ-collectivity finds its most explicit expression, an opposite extreme is equally objectionable.[136] Thus A. Schweitzer explains Paul's conception of the nature of the Body as a quasi-physical solidarity with the risen Christ.[137] J. A. T. Robinson also follows this line of thought too far in his chapter on the 'Body of the Resurrection'.[138] It is quite true that Paul teaches that a common corporeity on the human family level sanctifies (ἁγιάζει) the unbelieving partner in the Christian community as well as making the children of the mixed pair holy (ἅγια, 1 Cor 7[12-16]), but it does not make them members of the Body of Christ; otherwise, Paul would not continue: 'For how knowest thou, O wife, whether thou shalt *save* thy husband? or how knowest thou, O husband, whether thou shalt *save* thy wife' (7[16]). In this passage Paul's emphasis is made not apart from the question of faith (cf. 7[12-14]); 'holy' can refer only to a position of privilege guaranteed by the solidarity of the family, an idea which is thoroughly Hebraic.

(1) *The Problem of the Source of the Body-concept*

W. D. Davies has made a most significant contribution to the understanding of the nature of the solidarity of the Body of Christ by relating the conception to the Rabbinic Adam-speculation.[139]

---

[136] Roman Catholic interpreters are frequently open to this charge. Thus, T. Soiron assumes that the unity between Adam and humanity is biological (op. cit. pp. 85-6, 91). By analogy to this doubtful explanation of the Adam-collectivity, Christ and the Christian are a biological-spiritual community (ibid. pp. 86, 91). Other Catholic writers interpret the Body of Christ with varying degrees of realism.

[137] *The Mysticism of Paul*, pp. 116ff; cf. p. 127. Schweitzer thus speaks of a 'corporeity (*Leiblichkeit*) which is common to Christ and the Elect' (pp. 118, 121). It is too physical as A. Raymond George, *Communion with God*, London, 1953, p. 159, correctly observes.

[138] Op. cit. pp. 49ff. A preferable interpretation is given in E. Best's, *One Body in Christ*.

[139] Op. cit. pp. 53ff.

We may briefly notice that there are some parallels which appear to be more than coincidental. (1) As the original man was created from the dust of all the earth and filled all the space between earth and heaven, so the Body of Christ is not confined to one single location but incorporates all of the redeemed and vitally joins them with Christ. (2) As Adam embodied all the souls of his race and individual men formed limbs and parts of his body, so Paul describes the Body of Christ as corporal; individual Christians form the members of Christ (cf. 1 Cor 12[12-27]). (3) The first man was androgynous, composed of varied colours of clay; the New Man incorporates Jew and Gentile, male and female, without distinction (Gal 3[28]). (4) As Christ and the Church are closely enough identified for Paul to refer to the 'body' as 'Christ' (1 Cor 12[12]), so 'Adam' in the Old Testament stands generically for mankind; in Judaism he is the typical representative of mankind.[140]

These parallels and others which might be adduced do not, however, of themselves justify any assumption that Paul simply adopted the Jewish Adam-speculation and with a new Christian aura presented it as his doctrine. There is no immediate assurance that such speculation is the original source of the body-concept. One is certain to be given cause to reconsider any simple answer to the problem of the source of the concept when note is taken of the imposing list of defenders of theories which are greatly at variance.[141]

Completely severed from his Jewish heritage, but lying right at hand, was the Stoic doctrine of the organic nature of the universe. The proximity of this conception to the Body-concept will be readily apparent from S. Hanson's summary:

In the *Stoa* the interest in unity is central. . . . Cosmos is conceived as ζῷον, a living being, an organic unity. The world is a σῶμα, a body where the individual parts have grown together and suffers with the other, so that they conjointly form an organic unity. The factor creating unity in this universal organism is the λόγος ὀρθός of the universe, which constitutes its essence, its laws, and its bond, and conjoins the various parts of cosmos into a living unity.[142]

[140] Cf. ibid. p. 57 note 4. On the whole of the subject of the Adam-speculation see Chapter 2, *supra*.

[141] W. L. Knox, *St Paul and the Church of the Gentiles*, pp. 160ff; S. Hanson, op. cit. p. 137; cf. pp. 52-3; J. A. T. Robinson has provided a convenient list of the main views and their defenders, op. cit. p. 55.

[142] Op. cit. p. 52.

Even more striking parallels such as Seneca's eulogizing reference to Nero, 'You are the soul (*animus*) of your community, which is your body', are to be found.[143] In Plato's metaphor describing the state as a body there are analogies drawn between functions of the members of a body and those of the arms of the body-politic.[144] As T. W. Manson says: 'The uniqueness of the phrase is not in the word σῶμα but in the qualifying genetive. The body is not τὸ σῶμα τῶν Χριστιανῶν but τὸ σῶμα τοῦ Χριστοῦ.[145] It is essential to note that Paul's use of the figure is violent and not merely a simile or metaphor, or as J. A. T. Robinson has stressed: 'something not corporate but corporal.'[146] It is plainly evident that the problem of the realism of the conception of the Body of Christ must be solved in the light of Paul's sources and background as indicated by the usage which he made of the figure. As long as the parallels in Hellenistic and early Jewish thought appear to be equally suited to provide such a source, we are forced to re-examine the development of the body-concept in the Epistles themselves.

(2) *The Development of the Body Concept in Paul's Thought*

In the impasse which we encounter in attempting to find the source of Paul's doctrine of the Body of Christ, we may do well to re-state a hypothesis suggested by Dillistone, namely, that the 'Body' may well be the result of Paul's own creative thinking.[147] In any case it is of more profit to our understanding of the character of the figure if we look for Paul's authorization and purpose in the use of the body-concept instead of its origin only. The development of Paul's teaching on the 'Body' suggests that he found this authorization within the Old Testament just as he did for the figures which we have discussed so far.

(*a*) We may commence our study of the development of the

---

[143] See further J. B. Lightfoot, *Philippians*, p. 286, and T. Schmidt, op. cit. pp. 128-9 as well as G. C. Richards, 'Parallels to a New Testament Use of σῶμα', *JTS*, Vol. XXXVIII (1937), p. 165.

[144] *The Republic*, Bk. 5.462d (see J. Moffatt, 1 *Corinthians*, p. 187, for a translation). C. Chavasse thinks that this is the source of Paul's use of the term (cf. *The Bride of Christ*, p. 17).

[145] 'A Parallel to a New Testament Use of σῶμα', *JTS*, Vol. XXXVII (1936), p. 385. See J. A. T. Robinson, op. cit. pp. 49-50.

[146] Op. cit. p. 50; so A. E. J. Rawlinson, 'Corpus Christi', p. 231. Cf. M. Goguel, 'L'Idée d'Église dans le Nouveau Testament', *Origine et Nature de l'Église*, p. 64; J. Armitage Robinson, op. cit. p. 103.

[147] *The Structure of the Divine Society* (London, 1951), p. 63.

conception with the assumption that 1 Corinthians is the earliest Epistle to mention the figure of the 'Body of Christ'. In the first reference (6^{15-17}) which has an ethical motivation, Paul refers to the bodies of Christians as the members ($\mu\acute{\epsilon}\lambda\eta$) of Christ ($6^{15}$). It is important to note that the context involves the Old Testament marriage injunction which declares that husband and wife become one 'flesh' (cf. Gen 2^{24}). From this passage Paul concludes that the union between a believer and a harlot incorporates both into one body (6^{16}). Overlooking any distinction between the terms 'flesh' and 'body'[148] he says: 'He that is joined to a harlot is one body.' It follows that the community of flesh produced in marriage is comparable to the believer's union with Christ. But the transition to the term 'body' is important for the understanding of 6^{17}: 'But he that is joined unto the Lord is one spirit.' By the term 'spirit', Paul actually means, 'spiritual body' (or person),[149] to correspond to the union between the harlot and the Christian. 'For him "body" and "spirit" are not related to "personality" as image to reality. The image and the reality are one.'[150]

(*b*) In the second mention of the idea of the Body, found in 1 Corinthians 10^{16-17}, an allusion is made to the participation in the Body through the Eucharist. As the loaf is a unity, so also is the Body.[151] Although the evidence is indirect, the inference that the union of the Body is based on the New Covenant commemorated in the Communion fellowship is probably justified.

(*c*) The third reference to the Body (1 Cor 11^{29}) declares that judgement is sustained by those who do not discern ($\mu\grave{\eta}$ $\delta\iota\alpha\kappa\rho\acute{\iota}\nu\omega\nu$) the Body.[152] While the reference is debatable, C. A. A. Scott's interpretation of the term $\sigma\hat{\omega}\mu\alpha$ as a reference to the Church is

[148] Distinctions which elsewhere have a great deal of importance (cf. J. A. T. Robinson, op. cit. p. 31; this author gives numerous instances in which Paul did use the term interchangeably, however).

[149] Cf. R. Bultmann, *Theology of the New Testament*, p. 209. On this whole section see A. Schweitzer, *The Mysticism of Paul*, pp. 127-8. In this connexion the sequence of 6^{15} is important. One is amputated ($\check{\alpha}\rho\alpha\varsigma$) to become a member of a harlot.

[150] F. A. Christie, op. cit. p. 122.

[151] Against the *RV*, *AV*, and many interpreters, 6^{17} does not intend to say that the Church is one bread or loaf (cf. L. S. Thornton, *The Common Life*, p. 335). J. Weiss has a commendable translation: 'Because one bread (is present) we, the many, are one body; for we all have part in the one bread' (op. cit. p. 640). So also C. H. Dodd, *The Meaning of Paul for Today*, pp. 142-3; S. Hanson, op. cit. p. 89; C. A. A. Scott, *Christianity According to St Paul*, p. 195 (note the reference to the Didache (9^4).

[152] C. Chavasse thinks the word 'discerning' has a nuptial connotation (op. cit. p. 64, note 1; cf. p. 72).

acceptable.[153] Since the Body is mentioned in instructions regarding the Eucharist we may again relegate this occurrence of the term to the conception of the New Covenant.

(d) The advance found in the fourth occurrence of the term σῶμα (1 Cor 12[27]) is the designation of the Body specifically as belonging to Christ (Χριστοῦ). While the emphatic ὑμεῖς and the anarthrous σῶμα denote a specific reference to the Church of Corinth,[154] Paul's characteristic understanding of the local manifestation of the universal Church in no way denies the unity or uniqueness of the one Body. This passage is of particular interest because of its treatment of the conception of the unity of the Body effected through the agency of the Holy Spirit. Every aspect of the organic life of the Church has an inter-relationship and inter-dependence with every other aspect.

(e) The fifth passage to mention the Body (Rom 12[3-8]) produces yet another distinction. Rather than the 'Body of Christ', it is here, 'one Body in Christ', that is, in whom the members are one body.[155] The intention of this passage, as that of the preceding (see above), is to describe the unity of the Body despite the diversity of the gifts exercised by its members.[156]

(f) The progression indicated by the use of the formula 'in Christ' in Romans is carried farther by Ephesians and Colossians in the distinction drawn between the Body and the Head.[157] While we cannot in this limited space treat the multiplicity of ideas which Paul relates to the conception of the Church as the Body of Christ, the most extensive passage (Eph 5[22-33]) contains a significant point. In this hortatory passage, Paul makes it abundantly clear that he is thinking of the relationship of the Head (Christ) to the Body (the Church) in terms of the relationship of authority which the husband rightfully exercises over the wife. With a specific application of Genesis 2[24] to the Church as the Bride of Christ, Paul affirms that the unity of 'flesh' effected through marriage is the answer to the riddle of the relationship

---

[153] *Christianity According to St Paul*, pp. 189-90. Cf. G. Johnston, op. cit. p. 90; F. C. Baur, *Paul*, II,170.

[154] Cf. F. J. Hort, op. cit. pp. 145f.

[155] Cf. E. Percy, *Der Leib Christi* (Lund, 1942), p. 5.

[156] Cf. ibid. pp. 5-6.

[157] There are other distinctions: (1) the articular use of σῶμα; (2) σῶμα refers directly to the Ecclesia, not 'ye' or 'we', and indicates the universal Church; (3) there is no comparison drawn with the human body; (4) there is no appeal to the idea of unity in spite of diversity. Note the phrase, ἔσμεν ἀλλήλων μέλη (Eph 4[25]).

between the Head and the Body (cf. Eph 5²⁸⁻³³). To be sure it is a great mystery (5³²), but the analogy comes as near as possible to disclosing the nature of the solidarity between the Church and Christ. It is significant that Paul goes on to indicate that the bond of this union is love just as it is in marriage. 'Nevertheless do ye also severally love each one his own wife even as himself; and let the wife see that she fear her husband' (5³³ *RV*).¹⁵⁸

We have stressed certain points to make our conclusion self-evident. It appears that Paul draws on the Old Testament declaration that marriage creates a unity of flesh between two partners to authorize if not originate his doctrine. The Church is the Bride united to Christ through the New Covenant and in consequence forms the 'flesh' or the 'body' of Christ (terms rendered ambiguous if they reflect the Hebrew conception of בָּשָׂר. Note that this term already has the concept of a totality so that the 'many' members are 'one' as the redeemed flesh).

Whether Paul thought of the Church as the Second Eve, who had been created for Christ, the Second Adam, is uncertain.¹⁵⁹ There are, however, some indications that the Church is the anti-type of Eve in its capacity as the Bride of Christ. Thus, in Paul's appeal to the creation account to establish his rules for feminine attire and decorum in public and private worship, the context refers to the headship of Christ over the man (i.e. the constituent element of the Church): 'But I would have you know, that the head of every man is Christ; and the head of the woman is the man; and the head of Christ is God' (1 Cor 11²⁻¹⁶). Men, constituting the representative membership of the Church united in the New Covenant relationship to Christ, are united to Him in the same manner as the wife is to her husband.

In 1 Timothy 2¹²⁻¹⁵ Paul refers again to the First Parents and the implications which their roles have in the conducting of the affairs of the Church. The position of women is determined by the gullibility of Eve; the position of authority given to men stems from Adam's choice of a self-determined course of action. This passage may have further significance if an inference is allowed. It is clear that if Adam sinned, although aware of the consequences, he must have done so out of love for Eve. The

---

¹⁵⁸ J. A. T. Robinson makes the same point in his interpretation of Romans 7⁴ where the metaphor describing the union with Christ is, εἰς τὸ γενέσθαι ὑμᾶς ἑτέρῳ denoting sexual union (op. cit. p. 52).

¹⁵⁹ See E. Best's discussion, *One Body in Christ*, Chap. 10, pp. 169ff.

possible parallel with Christ's relationship to the Church is instructive. In the passage where Paul most explicitly refers to Christ as the fulfilment of the contrast with Adam (Phil 2⁶⁻¹¹), not to mention others where this Christological figure is missing, there is a manifest correspondence. Christ became a sin offering for His Bride; He was completely aware of the implications of His choice but willingly took upon Himself the penalty incumbent upon the Church because of His love for her (Eph 5²).¹⁶⁰

In a more elaborate argument, C. Chavasse has isolated more technical evidence for this conclusion. He notes that the Hebrew text reads: 'The rib which the Lord God had taken from the "man" builded (בָּנָה) he into a woman' (Gen 2²²). It is possible that when Paul describes the 'building up' of the Body through the ministry of the leaders of the Church (Eph 4¹²) he has this term in mind. This passage continues:

> . . . But speaking truth in love, may grow up in all things into him, which is the head, even Christ; from whom all the body fitly framed and knit together through that which every joint supplieth, according to the working in due measure of each several part, maketh the increase of the body unto the *building up* of itself in love (4¹⁵⁻¹⁶ *RV*).¹⁶¹

It might be suggested that around the Rib, that is, the flesh of the Last Adam crucified (Col 1²²), was built up the new Bride, the Second Eve (cf. Col 3¹⁰, Eph 4²⁴ with Rom 7⁴).¹⁶² By this analogy, the Body of Christ is the extension of the personality of Christ in the same way in which Eve was the projection of the body of Adam out of which she was formed.¹⁶³ As Adam and Eve were 'one flesh' in a unique sense, so Christ and the Church in an equally unique sense (i.e. spiritual)¹⁶⁴ form the Body of Christ.

Finally, there is a strong inference that the Church described

---

¹⁶⁰ See A. Nygren, *Agape and Eros*, trans. P. S. Watson (London, 1953), p. 120. By fusing the figures of the Suffering Servant and the Last Adam, Christ does what the First Man could not do, namely, reverses the divine sentence against humanity by undeservingly exhausting the penalty in Himself (cf. A. G. Hebert, op. cit. p. 171).

¹⁶¹ In the term 'build' and its derivatives, there is an ideological tie made between the figures of the Body and Temple (which we shall discuss later). In a strange switch, Paul speaks of the Temple growing in the Lord (Eph 2²¹). Both growth and building occur in Eph 4¹⁶ (see S. Hanson, op. cit. p. 133).

¹⁶² Cf. C. Chavasse, op. cit. p. 79.

¹⁶³ Ibid. p. 70. R. V. G. Tasker says: 'She (the Church) is only the Body of Christ because she is primarily the mystical Bride of Christ' (*The Old Testament in the New Testament*) (2nd edn, London, 1954), p. 98.

¹⁶⁴ Cf. L. Newbigin, op. cit. p. 71.

M

as the 'chaste virgin espoused to one husband (Christ)', is the Second Eve, for Paul in this same context warns that the Church may be corrupted just as Eve was seduced through the craftiness of the Serpent (2 Cor 11²⁻³).

In summary, it appears that Paul's doctrine of the Church as the Bride of Christ is prior to His postulation that it is the Body of Christ. The idea of the corporate Bride came directly from the Old Testament where Israel is designated as the 'wife of Yahweh'.[165] This marriage was consummated through the Old Covenant and finds its counterpart in Paul's reference to Israel married to the law. When Christ died, the Old Covenant was dissolved and the marriage bond broken, making Israel again free to marry (Rom 7¹⁻⁶). Through the New Covenant, a new betrothal vow has been contracted between Christ and the New Israel. The union has made of both one spiritual *basar*, that is, one Body. This is again another example of the mystery of the New Israel. No longer can racial and religious ties form a barrier for the Gentiles. Adam and Eve were created and united before there were any such distinctions. The New Age reverses the subsequent characteristics of the Old Aeon in the dissolution of all distinctions in Christ, in (or out of) whom the New Man is *created* (Eph 2¹⁵; cf. 4²⁴).

It is possible that Paul may have resorted to either Rabbinic or Hellenistic 'body-concepts' to embellish his doctrine of the Body of Christ.[166] On the other hand, we cannot subscribe to the opinion that Paul found his authorization in either of these general sources, where in most cases the body is used either as a symbol[167] or simile and rarely is more than a simple metaphor. Paul uses the figure of the Body to designate a reality which goes beyond figurative speech. It involves the Hebrew conception of the Word of God, calling into existence that which is not actual. Thus the election of Israel and the Church are realities apart from their visible evidence. In the historical Genesis account of

---

[165] G. E. Wright suggests that the origin of the 'Bride of Christ' is to be found in an allegorical interpretation of the Song of Songs (applied realistically to Israel by Jewish commentators) or in Hosea, op. cit. p. 82; cf. A. Lods, 'Les Antécèdents de la Notion d'Église en Israël', p. 50.

[166] Cf. e.g. 1 Corinthians 12 with Aristotle, *Politics*, Bk. 2, par. 2.2-3. (LoClL, trans. H. Rackham [London, 1932], pp. 84ff.) The Rabbinic doctrine of the creation of Adam has already been mentioned. They also used the simile of the body to describe the principle of corporate suffering.

[167] Cf. R. M. MacIver, *Community*, pp. 68ff, especially p. 81.

the creation of Eve, the realism of the conception of the sharing of a common flesh and life was evidently appropriated by Paul to describe the realism of Christ living in His Body. Christ, as Adam did, exists in His Bride, yet apart from her.[168] The Church exists literally only through the life which it derives from Christ; it is therefore identifiable with the Source of that life (1 Cor 1[13]) but distinct from it. The personality of Christ receives, so to speak, an extension in the life of the Body on earth,[169] while He continues to be an Individual Personality. The doctrine of the Body of Christ is therefore an explicit application of the Hebraic conception of corporate personality.

(3) Christ, the Last Adam, as the Head of the New Aeon

We must now direct our attention to the cosmic implications of Paul's Adam-typology. In this section we are reminded again that Paul, in direct continuity with his Jewish heritage, did not think of mankind as isolated within the broad confines of the universe. Beyond the solidarity of individuals within the race, we learned through our examination of the doctrine of the Fall that there is an extension of this principle of solidarity to include the whole animate and inanimate world. Paul's doctrine of Christ as the Last Adam is the converse of the picture of Adam as the head of the Old Aeon. The cosmic implications of Christ's headship are correspondingly greater because of the majesty of His person. The identification of Christ with the Old Aeon begins with His pre-existence and subsequent incarnation. He, being the Son of God (Gal 4[4]) and existing in the form of God, emptied Himself of the divine form (μορφῇ) to become as a man (ἐν ὁμοιώματι ἀνθρώπων γενόμενος, Phil 2[6-7]; cf. Gal 4[4]). Christ's incarnation through the medium of human birth (γενόμενον ἐκ γυναικός) realistically identified Him with the totality of mankind. This identification could not have been made without Christ's becoming a member of the group which He represents. He, who was formerly outside the community of men, became,

---

[168] Cf. J.-L. Leuba, The New Testament Pattern, trans. H. Knight (London, 1953), p. 136. This is the direction in which we must look for the solution of the problem raised by G. Johnston, op. cit. pp. 88-9, 93-4. The 'I and thou' relationship continues to hold true within the Body. Cf. J. S. Stewart, A Man in Christ, p. 167; D. Somerville, op. cit. p. 128.

[169] Cf. C. H. Dodd, The Apostolic Preaching and Its Development (London, 1936), pp. 147-8.

through the process of birth, a part of the human family.[170]

It is essential to understand Paul's view of the 'flesh' at this juncture. When he speaks of Christ coming in the 'likeness of sinful flesh' (Rom 8[3]), he is implying a great deal more than human appearance. One might say that Paul considered the flesh to be a sort of metaphysical substance in which all men share. 'Thus, a blow struck at Sin by any human being who partakes of the "flesh" is struck on behalf of all.'[171] It is the same totality which allowed Sin to gain mastery of the whole of the race through Adam's sinning. It is true that Christ is different from the rest of the race of men, in that He committed no sin (Rom 8[3], 2 Cor 5[21]), but that does not mean that He did not live a truly human life, indeed, the only truly human life. Thus He fulfilled the original intention of God in the creation of Adam and merits the designation of the 'image of God' (1 Cor 15[49], Phil 2[6]). Yet with all this, Christ is not a separate creature as the Son of God incarnate; but He was completely identified with human existence in its distance from God, immersed in the totality of the 'flesh'.[172]

Now, this corporate totality which mankind constitutes had become a part of the Old Aeon and its consequent subjection to the nefarious forces at work therein. The original creation of God, although marred by the incursion of Sin, was not destroyed. In place of that possibility, a plan of redemption was imposed upon it which corresponded to the manner in which it was brought into thraldom. Therefore, human nature which was no longer a neutral element in its corporate identification with the powers of the Old Aeon had to be redeemed through Christ's defeating each of these hostile forces in Himself. According to Paul's doctrine, Christ had to become identified with Sin, 'Flesh', Death, Law, and rebellious spiritual forces[173] to effect the redemption of the entire Creation. These ideas find more or less explicit mention in the Epistles.

(a) *Sin.* In 2 Corinthians 5[21], '. . . he was made to be sin on our behalf', specifically teaches that Christ was identified with

---

[170] Cf. W. Koester, op. cit. p. 31; E. L. Mascall, op. cit. p. 75.

[171] C. H. Dodd, *The Meaning of Paul for Today*, p. 95. Cf. H. Lietzmann, *An die Römer*, p. 79; J. Denney, *Studies in Theology* (3rd edn, London, 1895), pp. 79, 99.

[172] Cf. further J. A. T. Robinson, op. cit. p. 38.

[173] On this subject see J. A. T. Robinson, op. cit. pp. 34ff. G. H. C. Macgregor, 'Principalities and Powers', p. 23, and C. H. Dodd, *The Meaning of Paul for Today*, pp. 89-90.

sin.[174] Although Christ was one with humanity in every other relationship to Sin, He nevertheless did not consent to its dominion. Sin which had heretofore reigned unchallenged was defeated in the sinless life of our Lord. This passage further implies the death of Christ. As death cannot reign over a dead subject, those who are united in Him (through death) are thereby also made free from Sin's reign (Rom $6^{2, 10}$).

(b) *Flesh.* The Incarnation unavoidably meant that Christ participated in the 'flesh' (1 Tim 3^{16}, 'who (Christ) appeared in flesh' implies humanity apart from God, for the next phrase refers to His 'justification (vindication) in the Spirit'). 'God, sending his own Son in the likeness of sinful flesh and for sin, condemned sin in the flesh' (Rom 8^3), means that 'He was so truly man that the flesh He bore was human flesh as it had come to be, an appanage of sin, the open field of sin's activity'.[175] Not only did Christ successfully repel the attack of Sin in His flesh, but through His death He deprived the hostile forces, which held human 'flesh' in subjection, of their point of attack.[176] The integral relationship of the 'flesh' to the Old Age and its control was wrested by Christ through His realistic representation of those who are identified with Him.[177]

(c) *Death.* On the Cross, Christ completely and voluntarily identified Himself with the plight of the Aeon under the dominion of Death. The victory of this 'last enemy' over Him was only temporary. In the resurrection lay the seeds of the complete overthrow of Death's dominion in the Aeon (cf. Rom 6^9). In the New Age, inaugurated through the resurrection of Christ, it is Life that reigns (Rom 5^{17}). The grave is no longer the dismal goal of human existence (1 Cor 15^{50-7}). To those who are given to participate in the resurrection life of Christ through the Holy Spirit, a glorious emancipation has been proclaimed. Its guarantee of fulfilment is placarded in the resurrection of Christ, the Firstfruits (1 Cor 15^{20-3}).[178]

(d) *The Law.* Paul explicitly affirms that Christ was born under the Law that He might redeem those who are under the Law

---

[174] L. S. Thornton, *The Common Life*, p. 45.
[175] C. A. A. Scott, *Christianity According to St Paul*, p. 248.
[176] J. A. T. Robinson, op. cit. p. 45.
[177] Cf. F. Prat, *The Theology of St Paul*, II.208; E. Loymeyer, op. cit. pp. 137ff, 168.
[178] Cf. C. H. Dodd, *The Meaning of Paul for Today*, pp. 104ff. For this reason, death is not significant as entrance into the New Aeon, but the dissolution of the Old (ibid. p. 79).

(Gal 4⁴⁻⁵).¹⁷⁹ As the Law had become implicated in the Old Age (Gal 4³; cf. *supra* pp. 123-4) it was essential that Christ should become identified with it that He might successfully fulfil its claims upon mankind as well as throw off its shackles.¹⁸⁰ In life, Christ perfectly fulfilled the Law; through His death came the end of the demands of the Law for both Christ and those identified with Him (Rom 7⁴). Legal injunctions have no binding force after one's death (Rom 7¹⁻⁶; Col 2²⁰⁻³);¹⁸¹ therefore, dying to the Law makes possible 'life unto God' (Gal 2¹⁹).

(*e*) *Hostile Spirit-forces.* Climactically, Paul declares of Christ:

... Having blotted out the bond written in ordinances that was against us, which was contrary to us, . . . and he has seized it from the midst (i.e. removed it) nailing it to the cross, having disrobed himself of the principalities and authorities,¹⁸² he made an open show of them, triumphing over them in himself (Col 2¹⁴⁻¹⁵).

The stage is the Aeon. Its spirit-rulers had drawn up a list of charges against man who was thoroughly guilty, particularly of the transgression of the Law. On the Cross, the claims of the accusers (i.e. the principalities of the Aeon) were satisfied. At the same time as Christ divested them of any rights over Himself (involved in the word ἀπεκδυσάμενος) He earned the reprieve of the New Race incorporated in Him. Through Christ's identification with humanity enslaved in the Aeon He was obliged to meet the specific forces which held man in their sway with the result that Paul says, '. . . Jesus Christ, (was) giving himself for (ὑπέρ) our sins, so that he might extract (ἐξέληται) us out of this present evil age' (τοῦ αἰῶνος τοῦ ἐνεστῶτος, Gal 1⁴).

The whole of this discussion throws into striking relief Paul's own conception of the solidarity of the race, for the actuality of the redemption depended entirely on the realistic identification of Christ with human existence so that He might reverse the archetypal role of Adam in the Old Aeon. But the question of

¹⁷⁹ Cf. S. Hanson, op. cit. p. 72.
¹⁸⁰ Cf. F. Prat, op. cit. II.208; W. Grundmann, 'Sin', *Bible Key Words* (*TWNT*), pp. 76-7.
¹⁸¹ This is the recurrence of the theme of the New Israel in that the penalty incurred through Gentile sin and the curse fallen on Jews who failed to keep the Law (both ideas are inter-related as we have seen) are both absolved in the one self-sacrifice of Christ. Thus, in Christ, the New Israel has fulfilled the Law (Rom 3³) even as it is dead to the Law through the body of Christ (Rom 7⁴).
¹⁸² Following Ellicott, Lightfoot, and contrary to Abbott, *Ephesians and Colossians* (Edinburgh, 1897), pp. 258-9.

the extent of this reversal quite naturally arises. The delimitation of the extent of the New Aeon must be approached from two sides: (1) the cosmic significance of man in the universe, and (2) Paul's conception of the cosmic significance of Christ and His victory. The very character of the Apostle's doctrine forced him to conclude that in the New Age the restoration of the Creation to a proper relationship to God would be as complete as was the corruption of the original intention of creation in the Old Age. This restoration was not a complete event effected at one instant in the Passion and Resurrection of Christ, yet this Event was the guarantee of the future consummation of the reconciliation. In the words of C. H. Dodd: 'What He wrought on our behalf is also wrought into the very fabric of the universe in which we live.[183]

The skeleton of Paul's conception of the restoration is the principle of selective representation.[184] From the selection of the Apostles by Christ as His *shaliachim*,[185] and the nucleus of the original Church baptized with the Holy Spirit at Pentecost, the process of inclusion moves from the One (Christ) to the Many (the Church). This constitutes the present spacial centre of the Lordship of Christ in the universe.[186] From the constitution of the New People of God, the process of reconciliation increases to involve the whole creation in a final restoration[187] (Rom

[183] *The Meaning of Paul for Today*, p. 105.

[184] Cf. J. A. T. Robinson, op. cit. p. 61.

[185] That is, envoys, authorized agents, who go in the name of Him who sends them; in this case, the risen Christ (cf. K. H. Rengstorf, 'Apostleship', *Bible Key Words* (*TWNT*), p. 29). While the grounds of apostleship were limited by an encounter with the risen Lord and a personal commission (ibid. p. 43), and could not be passed on, it was the Apostles who were the missionary representatives of the Church. Thus, it was through them that the larger group of the Church are called. See also C. T. Craig, *The One Church* (London, 1952), pp. 57ff.

[186] O. Cullmann, *Christ and Time*, p. 151.

[187] Cullmann adds a fourth category between the Church and the whole Creation, seeing a redemption of all of humanity in the Kingdom of God (ibid. p. 117). C. H. Dodd after rendering Romans 11[32] as 'God has consigned all men to disobedience, that he may have mercy on all', concludes that Paul considered it to be the will of God that all men should ultimately be saved (*Romans*, p. 183; note the chart on p. 187). But this universalism has difficulties. The πάντας may be relative or, as Sanday and Headlam suggest, collective (so also W. Morgan, *The Religion and Theology of Paul*, p. 249). Paul does not mention any implications which the resurrection will have for the wicked dead or of their inclusion in the eschatological kingdom (cf. 1 Cor 6[9]: 'Know ye not that the unrighteous shall not inherit the kingdom of God?' He continues by giving a list of those which are to be excluded). Paul's reference to the πλήρωμα τῶν ἐθνῶν (Rom 11[25]) cannot well mean all Gentiles any more than can πᾶς Ἰσραήλ (11[26]) refer to every individual in the historical existence of Israel. As the latter refers to Israel at a point in history in which the nation will be reconciled to God, the 'fulness of the Gentiles' refers to the complement of the gracious election of

8[19-25]) until Christ is all in all (Col 3[11]), because all things are subjected under Him (1 Cor 15[28]).

Paul saw the New Aeon in the process of replacing the Old. The acceptance of the gospel is the temporary means of the advancement of the New Age because of its identification with the New Humanity (the present manifestation of the restoration of the creation; cf. Col 1[23] with 2 Cor 5[17], Col 3[11]). Increasing significance of the New Aeon lay in the future. Therefore, Paul looks to the return of Christ or to the time immediately preceding it for the salvation of all Israel (cf. Rom 11[26])[188] and the inclusion of the 'fulness' of the Gentiles. Apparently he is referring to a great surge of converts from among the Gentiles at the time of the turning of the Jews (Rom 11[15]).[189] The salvation of Israel will be the signal of the resurrection ($\zeta\omega\grave{\eta}$ $\grave{\epsilon}\kappa$ $\nu\epsilon\kappa\rho\tilde{\omega}\nu$, Rom 11[15]); that, in turn will bring the work of the reconciliation of the New Israel to its completion (Phil 1[6], 3[12-21], Col 1[22]; cf. Rom 8[23]).

Passages in Ephesians and Colossians refer to the cosmic significance of Christ's death and resurrection in His consequent exaltation. In the 'fulness of times' all things will be 'summed up' or 'comprised' ($\grave{\alpha}\nu\alpha\kappa\epsilon\phi\alpha\lambda\alpha\iota\acute{\omega}\sigma\alpha\sigma\theta\alpha\iota$) in Him (Eph 1[10]). Through the atoning work of Christ the unity of creation destroyed by sin is restored. The kingdom of the Son is brought into actual existence out of the realm of darkness (Col 1[13]). The unity is eschatological; as yet, not every knee has bowed in acknowledgement of the Lordship of Christ (Phil 2[10]), nor has every enemy been brought into complete subjection under Him (1 Cor 15[25-8]). Nevertheless, every intelligence shall confess that Christ is Lord, whether it be of the earthly, heavenly, or subterrestrial sphere (Phil 2[10-11]).

God who are predestined to be saved (cf. Rom 11[20-1]). The lack of clarity arises out of the imminence of the Parousia, so that Paul apparently refers to his own generation as *all* that will exist. In this passage Paul does not consider the fate of the wicked and unbelieving, nor does he elsewhere. They are like the Old Testament Israelite, 'cut off' from life and from the Community.

[188] Note the quotation of Isaiah 59[20-1] referring to the coming Deliverer. Evidently Paul is thinking of the Parousia.

[189] The phrase 'reconciliation of the world' is perforce to be understood by the principle of representative universalism. Thus, Paul can state that a large part of his task is completed and that there is no longer any place for him in the East—the West alone remains an open field for his activity (Rom 15[18-23], especially 15[23]; cf. Col 1[23]). But there are few Christians and few churches even in the East. The acceptance of the Gospel has been representative, meaning that completeness is sure to follow (cf. J. Munck, 'Israel and the Gentiles in the New Testament', *JTS*, New Series, Vol. II [1951], p. 8).

Paul's most extensive treatment of the conception of the cosmic restoration in Christ is found in Colossians 1[14-22]. The argument is founded upon Christ's role in the New Creation. Chiefly He is 'the beginning, the firstborn from the dead'. Christ is then in the position of the 'ancestor' of a new race. Christ has been given the Headship of the New Humanity in His Body; so also does He include representatively all that has been created because He is the 'Firstborn of *all* creation'.[190] As He is the Source of all existence as the Creator, it is by Him that all things consist and continue to exist. But the Fall brought opposition and rebellion into the very fibre of the universe. It must be removed through a reconciliation effected through the propitiatory sacrifice of Christ on the Cross[191] which will find its complete achievement in the eschatological goal. As Lightfoot says: 'It must end in unity, as it proceeded from unity: and the centre of this unity is Christ.'[192]

It is difficult to ascertain to what extent Paul thinks of the terms 'reconciliation' ($\dot{a}\pi o\kappa a\tau a\lambda\lambda\dot{a}\xi a\iota$, Col 1[19]) and 'subjection' ($\dot{v}\pi o\tau\dot{\epsilon}\tau a\kappa\tau a\iota$, 1 Cor 15[27], Eph 1[22]) as synonymous. In 1 Corinthians 15[24-8] the latter emphasis is clarified by the 'abolishing' ($\kappa a\tau a\rho\gamma\dot{\eta}\sigma\eta$) of every (opposing) $\dot{a}\rho\chi\dot{\eta}\nu$ $\kappa a\dot{\iota}$ $\dot{\epsilon}\xi o\upsilon\sigma\dot{\iota}a\nu$ $\kappa a\dot{\iota}$ $\delta\dot{\upsilon}\nu a\mu\iota\nu$ (meaning powers of the category of Death and Sin, but not necessarily Discarnate Intelligences) which are the enemies brought under His feet in the eschatological Kingdom (15[24-5]). If the powers mentioned here are inclusive of the spiritual powers referred to in Ephesians and Colossians (i.e. the principalities and powers), the question revolves on the meaning which Paul intends in using the word 'abolish'. By comparing Philippians 2[10-11] with 2 Thessalonians 2[8-11] (referring to the destruction of the Lawless One by the breath of His mouth (cf. Isa 11[4])), two acceptable alternatives emerge. (1) The acknowledgement of Christ to be Lord is forced upon all beings ('every tongue') after which the wicked Intelligences are destroyed (2 Thess 2[8-12]). (2) All mankind along with the Discarnate Intelligences will be given opportunity to share the benefits of the atonement and receive the reconciliation of Christ (Eph 1[10], Col 1[20]). If they fail to appropriate these gifts of mercy, they are thoroughly discounted or destroyed so that universal unity is realized in the Kingdom delivered up to God (1 Cor 15[24]).

---

[190] Cf. W. Wrede, *Paul*, pp. 102f; D. Somerville, op. cit. p. 67.
[191] Unity through the atonement is the theme of Colossians (S. Hanson, op. cit. p. 107). See further D. Somerville, op. cit. pp. 163ff.
[192] *Colossians and Philemon*, p. 153.

Paul's view of the restoration of the material creation is some-what clearer. Even as Old Testament prophets had pictured the implications of the coming Messianic Kingdom in the animal-world and a cosmic return to an Eden-like peace (cf. e.g. Isa 11, 65[25], Mic 4[1-8]), Paul saw the future release of the Creation from the 'bondage of corruption' (Rom 8[21]).[193] In the New Aeon, the vanity (ματαιότης) to which the creation has become subjected through its control by subordinate and partly hostile powers awaits the revelation of the 'sons of God', which is the Second Advent of the Son of Man in the company of the saints. This points to the Parousia as the decisive event in the consummation of the restoration of the whole Creation. The dissident elements, rebellious spirit-forces, and wicked men are either destroyed or put out of the way. The solidarity of the Creation including men and everything outside of humanity is thus influential in the final actualization of the original intention of God in creating the universe. The New Age is superseding the Old, only in the end to displace it entirely. In brief, the reconciliation of the world through Christ (2 Cor 5[19]) 'has reference beyond the limits of the human race, and the vague phrase of 1 Corinthians 15[28] "that God may be all in all" receives a more precise and fuller meaning'.[194]

(4) Conclusion

We must point out in summary that the Christology and Soterio-logy which Paul expresses in the Epistles is not one of his own creation. Like Old Testament and inter-testamental Messianism the Apostle proposes an eschatological significance in his doctrine of Christ. Jesus Christ as the Son of God (cf. Ps 2[7-12]) and as the Son of Man is the Second Adam (1 Cor 15[45]) or, as we might say in current language, the eschatological Adam. He bears the image of God (2 Cor 4[5]), and he is the New Man (Col 3[9-11]). He is monogenēs, prōtotōcos, archē. In Christ there is a new creation (2 Cor 5[17]).'[195]

[193] We follow the opinions of Cullmann (Christ and Time, p. 103) and Bultmann (Theology of the New Testament, pp. 251-2) in opposition to various interpreters, that the 'creation' in this passage does not refer to man in unbelief but to the universe (cf. E. C. Rust, Nature and Man in Biblical Thought, pp. 235-6).
    [194] C. H. Dodd, 'The Mind of Paul: Change and Development', Reprint from the BJRL, Vol. XVIII 1 (1934), pp. 41-2.
    [195] A. Fridrichsen, 'The Theology of Creation in the Old and New Testaments', The Root of the Vine, p. 22.

The universalism of the New Covenant predicted by Isaiah (42$^{6-17}$) has been fulfilled in the Servant and in His constitution of the New Community of the Elect from among all nations of the earth (Eph 2$^{11-22}$, Col 3^{11}, Gal 3^{28}). The fountain 'for sin and separation for uncleanness' of which Zechariah spoke (13^1) has been provided in the shed blood of the unique and actual sacrifice of the True Isaac (Rom 3^{25}, Eph 1^7, 5^2; cf. Titus 2^{14}, 3^5). The out-pouring of the Holy Spirit foretold by Ezekiel (36$^{24-7}$) and Joel (2$^{28-32}$) has been experienced by the New Israel in the New Age.[196] The prophecy of the nations coming to worship the Lord in the 'house of the God of Jacob', seen by Micah (4$^{1-8}$) and Isaiah (2$^{2-4}$), is in the process of fulfilment in the increasing acceptance of the gospel by the Gentiles (Rom 9$^{24-30}$, 10$^{12-21}$, 15$^{8-23}$), and in the creation of the corporate Temple (Eph 2$^{20-2}$). As Micah predicted that the proclamation of the judgement of the Lord from Zion would bring peace to the world (Micah 4$^{3-8}$), Paul sees the Headship of Christ uniting the communities of Jews and Gentiles together in peace (Eph 2$^{13-22}$; cf. Ezekiel 37$^{15-28}$).

This revolution is going on apace. The resurrection foretold by Isaiah (26^{19}) and Daniel (12^3) has already had 'firstfruits' fulfilment in the risen Christ (1 Cor 15$^{20, 23}$). The completion of its fulfilment awaits His return in the company of the saints (1 Thess 4^{14}). The subjection of the forces of evil is effectively being realized (Col 2^{15}, 1 Cor 15$^{25-6, 28}$). Even now they are unable to 'separate us from the love of God' (Rom 8$^{38-9}$). As Wm. Manson says, this incompleteness 'gives rise in Christianity to a new eschatology of the things-which-are-not-yet-seen, an eschatology of glory which looks to the final victory, or Parousia, of Christ'.[197] Still lying in the future is the redemption of the cosmos from the bondage of corruption incurred through the lust of Adam and his race. Isaiah's new world (Chap. 11) will be seen in the reconciliation of all things under the reign of Christ (1 Cor 15^{28}) who in turn asserts His subjection to the Father, that God may be all in all (1 Cor 15^{28}). The original unity of all the Creation is thereby restored and the universal reign of God will continue without further challenge.

[196] Cf. Wm. Manson, 'Mission and Eschatology', p. 390.   [197] Ibid. p. 391.

METAPHORICAL FIGURES DENOTING THE SOLIDARITY
OF THE NEW HUMANITY

We must turn back to discuss some of the omitted metaphors used in Paul's conception of the solidarity of the Church. Pfleiderer has noted that the nature of the Christian Community is only indicated by figurative comparisons,[198] a conclusion which is strikingly borne out in Paul's teaching on the mysterious unity of the Church.

(I) *The Corporate Temple*

Among the figures which Paul adopts to indicate the nature of the Church, that of the 'Temple' and the equivalent 'Building of God'[199] are especially significant. The first representation of the community as a corporate temple occurs in 1 Corinthians 3[16-17]: 'Know ye not that ye are God's temple and the Spirit of God dwells in you? If any man destroy the temple of God, this one God will destroy, for the temple of God is holy, which temple ye are.' Paul's interest in reminding the Corinthian Christians that they are the House of God is purely to promote unity in the community. The schism which has split the Church into numerous cliques is not consonant with the unity of the one Temple in which God has chosen to dwell through the one Spirit. If any man destroys this unity through his divisive influence, he will be removed from the picture.[200] The declaration that the holiness of the corporate Temple is destroyed by division is in line with Old Testament injunctions against local sanctuaries which would violate the sanctity of God's designated place of worship (note Deut 12[13-14] and Josh 22[10-34]).

In his succeeding second reference to temple-typology, the

[198] *Paulinism,* pp. 229-30.

[199] It is not altogether certain that Paul's reference to the 'building of God' (1 Cor 3[2]) is an allusion to the Old Testament or Jewish temple. The phrase is couched among other metaphors which do not suggest a relationship to the temple-typology. On the other hand, the succeeding verses (although transferring the figure from a building as incorporating the Church, to a structure composed of the actions of the members of the Church) suggest the imagery relating to the building of the Tabernacle or Temple and all of the required precious elements (cf. 1 Cor 3[10-15]; cf. A. Deissmann, *Paul,* pp. 212-13).

[200] 'The repeated $\phi\theta\epsilon\text{\'{\i}}\rho\epsilon\iota\nu$ expresses the spontaneous reaction from God's side, a reaction which corresponds to the kind of offence' (R. Asting, op. cit. p. 207; holy, then, is inviolable, ibid. pp. 209ff).

Apostle says: 'Or know ye not that your (ὑμῶν) body (τὸ σῶμα)[201] is a temple of the Holy Spirit which is in you, which ye have from God?' (1 Cor 6[19]). It is difficult to know whether Paul intends that we should understand τὸ σῶμα to indicate the corporate Body (i.e. of Christ) or the individual bodies of believers. In any case the second Epistle to Corinth clears up the difficulty: 'We are a temple of the living God;[202] even as God said, I will dwell in them, and walk in them; and I will be their God, and they shall be my people' (6[16]; cf. Lev 26[11], and Ezek 37[27-8] where the prophet relates the idea to the Messianic Age). Following a direction of thought mentioned in the address on Mars Hill, that is, the denial that God dwells in temples of human construction (Acts 17[24]), Paul concludes that the true Temple is composed of what Peter refers to as 'living stones' (1 Pet 2[5]).

The climax of the doctrine of the corporate Temple is found in Ephesians 2. In 2[14] the distinctive feature of the old Jewish Temple is removed through the abolition of the middle wall separating the areas accessible to the outside world. 2[19-22] describe the New Temple, composed of the united 'household of God' founded on the apostles and prophets, fitted together in agreement, and growing into a holy temple in the Lord. Jesus Christ is the chief corner or key stone (a shift from 1 Cor 3[11] where Christ is the foundation rock).[203] The whole Temple provides a dwelling-place for God in the Spirit (2[22]) who actualizes the presence of God in the corporate Temple.[204]

In Paul's Bible, בָּנָה and בַּיִת were used to refer to Israel (cf. Ruth 4[11], Jer 24[6], 31[4], 42[10]).[205] There too, he found the conception of the Tabernacle and Temple as the locus of the presence of God. For the Judaism of Paul's own day there was only one Temple, occupying Mount Zion in Jerusalem. There the Shekinah rested in undiminished reality. The Temple area was the

---

[201] That is, in the singular, the difficulty of which may have prompted the correction in MSS. L33, 69pm. If this passage refers to the individual body it is equivalent to the οἰκοδομὴν ἐκ Θεοῦ ἔχομεν (2 Cor 5[1]) which is probably also individual in reference.

[202] Without apparent reason, Calvin takes this reference to apply to the bodies of individuals (*The Epistle to the Ephesians*, trans. Wm. Pringle [Grand Rapids, 1948], p. 245).

[203] Cf. J. Y. Campbell, 'Corner-stone', *TWBB*, p. 53.

[204] Corresponding to the Shekinah in the Temple (cf. Wm. Robinson, op. cit. pp. 47-8).

[205] Cf. S. Hanson, op. cit. p. 130. For numerous references, see BDB, pp. 124-5, 108-9.

epitomization of the Land of Israel, the place from which Israel derived its characteristic holiness. To the Temple was ascribed a cosmic significance which would be realized particularly in the Age to Come. Since Paul thought of the Church as the New Israel constituted through the advent and sacrifice of Jesus the Messiah, as well as being endowed with the Holy Spirit who effected the indwelling of the presence of God in the Church,[206] the figure of the Temple most aptly described the New Community.

In using the figure of the Temple, Paul does not fail to emphasize the theme of the New Israel. It is Christ, the chief stone, who unites the diverse elements composing the Temple through a union with Himself. He stands apart from the Sanctuary as the corner-stone, but is at the same time an integral part of the whole Temple as its determining feature.[207] As Phythian-Adams says: 'Christ is not a part but at once the whole transcendent to its parts.'[208]

(2) *The Corporate Tree*

Paul's most explicit reference to botanical imagery is his use of the Olive Tree to denote the continuity of the true People of God. We have already discussed this point under the Church as the New Israel. Another incidental reference to a tree is made in Colossians 2[7], where the Church is 'rooted' in Christ.[209] It is impossible to draw the full implications of an organic relationship uniting the Church with Christ such as the metaphor of the Vine and Branches does in John 15[1-8]. Such an organic connexion is amply brought out in the body-concept. With the same disregard of a consistent imagery which allowed the Apostle to

[206] Cf. R. N. Flew, op. cit. p. 152; R. Asting, op. cit. p. 206; L. S. Thornton, *The Common Life*, p. 13; T. K. Abbott, p. 76.

[207] Cf. S. Hanson, op. cit. p. 133; Abbott, op. cit. p. 71.

[208] The source of Paul's temple-typology is almost as difficult to ascertain as that of the body-concept. It may have its roots in Ezekiel's eschatological temple (Chaps. 40-8) or other prophetic utterances regarding the restoration of the temple in the Messianic Age (cf. e.g. Zech 14[16-21], especially 14[21]). The more immediate source, however, would be the statement of Jesus calling Himself the real Temple (ναός, cf. Jn 2[20-2], Matt 26[61]). In that case Paul's doctrine of the Body of Christ may come from this source; that is, if the conception of the Church as the corporate Temple is prior to the body-concept. But it is impossible to determine whether Jesus' statement influenced Paul's choice and use of either the figure of the body or of the Temple. We might profitably ask what John means when he states that the Apostolic Church understood this reference to Jesus' body as the destroyed and raised Temple (cf. 2[21-2]).

[209] In 1 Cor 3[6-8] there may be a reference to organic imagery as in a tree or crop. In 3[9] the Church is the 'field of God'.

speak of a Temple growing, this passage adds to the idea of being 'rooted' that of being built up and established in Christ. This would indicate that the figures of the Temple and tree belong together. The common denominator of these figures of growth and building is quantitative increase involving geographical expansion and organic structure.[210]

(3) *The Lump of Dough*

Paul uses a unique Scriptural metaphor in describing the Church as a lump of dough. 'Your glorying is not good. Know ye not that a little leaven leaveneth the whole lump? Purge out the old leaven, that ye may be a new lump, even as ($\kappa a \theta \dot{\omega} s$) ye are leavened' (1 Cor 5[6-7]; cf. Gal 5[9]). This metaphor in itself portrays more than any other Paul's conception of the solidarity of the Church. The sin of one member (in this case the incestuous man) implicates the whole community. Any Jew knew that a very limited amount of leaven would corrupt any quantity of dough used in the preparation of the unleavened bread for the feast. As the holiness of the corporate Temple was violated through the sin of immorality (1 Cor 6[19]) and the yoking of members with unbelievers (2 Cor 6[14-18]), so the purity of the dough is violated through the impurity of a member. It is related to the idea which underlies Paul's warning to Timothy: 'Lay hands hastily on no man (i.e. ordain), neither be a partaker ($\kappa o \iota \nu \dot{\omega} \nu \epsilon \iota$) of other men's sins: keep thyself pure' (1 Tim 5[22]).[211]

INCORPORATION INTO THE SOLIDARITY OF THE
NEW HUMANITY

Introduction

We must now turn to consider the question of incorporation into the fellowship ($\kappa o \iota \nu \omega \nu \dot{\iota} a$) of the New Humanity. Since the Church is the New Israel of God, it is not strange that incorporation into

---

[210] Cf. E. L. Mascall, op. cit. pp. 120ff. Hanson suggests that $a \ddot{\upsilon} \xi \epsilon \iota$ may have in addition a qualitative meaning. Note also O. Cullmann, *Baptism in the New Testament*, p. 32.
[211] Cf. T. A. Lacey, op. cit. pp. 247ff. There are two other figures used to describe the Church but they have little significance. In Ephesians 5[27], the Community is the sacrificial victim cleansed from any blemish and holy for presentation to God. Again the corporate holiness of the whole is the main feature. The other metaphor is the reference to the Church of Corinth as a letter ($\dot{\eta} \epsilon \pi \iota \sigma \tau o \lambda \dot{\eta}$, 2 Cor 3[2-3]). 'Ye are an epistle of Christ, ministered by us, written not with ink, but with the Spirit of the living God; not in tables of stone, but in tables that are hearts of flesh' (3[3], *RV*). There is no apparent idea of solidarity involved in the use of the corporate metaphor.

the New Community may be profitably compared to the initiation of aliens into the constituting covenant of ethnic Israel.

Paul's doctrine of the constitution of the New Humanity has two basic propositions. (1) The first we have already discussed in connexion with the question of the identification of Christ with humanity through the Incarnation, involving His incorporation into the body of flesh, sin, and death. In His representative victory over the Old Aeon, the New was given actuality. This victory was potentially the victory of the race. The keyword is 'potentially', otherwise redemption would be universal and the role of the human recipient purely passive. All humanity would automatically belong to the Elect People of God; a doctrine which has manifestly little support in the New Testament. (2) The second fundamental factor in redemption embraces the medium of inclusion into the New Community through faith and baptism.[212] This involves the free choice of the individual without any violation of the corporate predestination and election of the whole People.[213] While the original decree of God assures the existence of the whole Community (Eph 1[14]), the gospel is preached and must be believed for the election to find its historical fulfilment (Rom 10[8-21]).

Now, gaining a place in the community is not secured through the simple desire to have it; rather, 'our life must be incorporated in the Saviour and His work'.[214] This incorporation involves aspects which are both inward and outward,[215] not in a dualistic sense but in an indivisible unity. These two aspects which essentially belong to the medium of identification with Christ are faith and baptism.

Faith as the Medium of Identification

The inward identification of the initiate with Christ is realized through the acceptance of the propositions of the gospel relating to the significance of the historical Event of the life, death, and resurrection of Christ. By faith, the novice makes the decision to walk according to the direction of the Holy Spirit (Rom 8[9, 14]).

[212] Cf. W. Koester, op. cit. p. 35; C. A. A. Scott, *Christianity According to St Paul*, pp. 98-9. Note the sustained emphasis of L. Newbigin, op. cit. *passim*.

[213] We cannot in this study attempt to solve the inconsistency in these opposing propositions. They are not altogether clarified by Paul but suggest an excellent example of his organic thinking. See L. Newbigin, op. cit. pp. 100ff.

[214] N. Söderblom, *The Mystery of the Cross*, p. 50.

[215] Cf. C. A. A. Scott. *Christianity According to St Paul*, pp. 98-9.

While we cannot deal with the great mass of material and the features which belong to Paul's doctrine of faith, one thing cannot be emphasized out of proportion, namely, that faith, in the New Testament sense of trust in someone or something (*fiducia*), is the medium of identification with the risen Lord. By it, the benefits of salvation are appropriated,[216] and the living Christ is experienced. Faith is the bridge by which the Adamite passes from the dominion of sin and death to the New Aeon of life and peace with God (Rom 5[1]).

Because Paul has so much to say about justification by faith, we may do well to consider his doctrine of faith as it is found in just one passage in Galatians 3. In a crucial debate with the Judaizers, Paul makes explicit the necessity of faith for consideration of oneself as a member of the New Community. (1) Faith is the medium by which the true Children of Abraham are constituted (Gal 3[7]. Paul supports this proposition by appealing to Gen 18[18], and 12[3] in Gal 3[8]). (2) Faith is the only means by which the Holy Spirit is received; He is the real bond of the Community (3[14]).[217] (3) Faith secures the promises (of salvation) which the Law could not do (3[18]). (4) Faith realistically identifies the believer with Christ; this means sharing in His righteousness and victory over the forces of the Aeon, involving one in justification (3[23-4]; cf. Rom 3[21-31], Eph 2[8]). (5) Through this identification 'we are made the children of God by faith in Christ Jesus' (3[26]). So much is clear from this passage. Elsewhere, Paul points to faith as the contracting medium of the New Covenant (Gal 4[21-31]); it is the means by which Christ dwells in the hearts of the members of His Body (Eph 3[17]) and the channel of the new life which Christ offers to those who have died and risen with Him (Gal 2[20]).[218] Faith, then, incorporates the believer into the corporate personality of Christ.

Although this list is not exhaustive, it will serve as an introduction to Paul's conception of the absolute necessity of that inward

---

[216] Cf. D. Somerville, op. cit. pp. 93-4.

[217] Cf. E. Best, op. cit. p. 73. Along with this passage must be placed all those which indicate that the Holy Spirit is given through baptism (cf. H. Lietzmann, *An die Römer*, p. 66). L. Newbigin has stressed a much forgotten New Testament emphasis that it is the Holy Spirit that constitutes the Church (cf. op. cit. pp. 87ff).

[218] In Ephesians 4[13], for the Church to attain to the unity of the faith and knowledge of the Son is to effect the completion (τέλειον) of the corporate 'Man' (εἰς μέτρον ἡλικίας τοῦ πληρώματος τοῦ Χριστοῦ). The principle justifying the elimination of the natural branches of the Olive Tree and the grafting in of the wild slips contrary to nature is the principle of faith (cf. L. Newbigin, op. cit. pp. 44-5).

N

relationship of the Christian with its Object (i.e. Christ) which faith provides. Thus, apart from many other involved ideas, when Paul speaks of faith, he stresses its importance in identifying the Community with its Lord. This factor alone sufficiently explains Paul's opposition to Judaistic legalism which gave little if any place to faith in the attainment of righteousness before God.[219] In a direct correspondence to Christ's identification with human existence through participation in human flesh, the initiate into the body of Christ is identified with Him in a new resurrection existence through the reception of the Holy Spirit by faith. This is not a simple opposition between grace and works, but involves actual participation in the life of Christ, or in His corporate personality.

For the Apostle, faith is exercised in the individual's response to join the *koinonia* of the Elect. Since it is the Community which is the dwelling-place of the Holy Spirit, it is there that grace superabounds to the dissolution of the Old Aeon and its penalties (Rom 5[15-21]). Through faith a union is born between Christ and the believer; therefore, the term 'saints' (οἱ ἅγιοι) is equivalent to 'believers (πίστοι) in Christ Jesus' (Eph 1[1]). By faith in Him, the Community is to reckon itself to be dead to sin (Rom 6[11]) and henceforth bears about in the body the dying of the Lord Jesus (2 Cor 4[10]). In faith-submission to the Lord of the Community, believers are made one with Him in such a way that His personality and character become theirs in the same manner that the Church shared in the archetypal experience of its Lord. Goguel speaks of faith as a mystical phenomenon uniting the believer to Christ,[220] but it is more than this, for it has very distinctive social implications. C. Ryder Smith has spoken incisively:

It is really a unique relation—transcending other social relations, ever while it is like them. The best way to approach it is to recall that Jesus chose His disciples one by one. Between Him and each Christian there is a link called 'faith'. His followers are one with each other because by 'faith' each of them is one with Him.[221]

Lest we be tempted to place an undue emphasis on the role of baptism as the medium of incorporation into the Body of

---

[219] H. St J. Thackeray, op. cit. p. 85.
[220] *The Birth of Christianity*, trans. H. C. Snape (London, 1953), pp. 237f.
[221] *The Bible Doctrine of Society*, p. 258.

Christ, we must recognize that Paul uses the aorist of the verb ($\pi\iota\sigma\tau\epsilon\acute{u}\omega$) six times absolutely (cf. e.g. Rom 13[11]) and once with $\epsilon\acute{\iota}s$ to denote the beginning of the Christian life, indicating that faith is the paramount factor (cf. Eph 1[12-13], 2[8-9]).[222] In reality, faith is the inward and baptism the outward or objective side of the same event. Baptism without faith is completely invalid.[223] Even as G. Johnston affirms, it is not baptism but faith active in love (Gal 5[6]) that realizes membership in the community.[224]

Faith is the New Testament equivalent and fulfilment of Jeremiah's predictive prophecy regarding the inward bond of the New Covenant (31[33]) and the promise of God through Ezekiel touching the 'heart of flesh' to be created within His people (11[19], 36[26]). Faith centres on a new awareness of the inward triangular relationships of the Community; its vortex touches the risen Christ; its horizontal plane embraces the full extent of the *koinonia*. Faith is the perception of the eschatological nature of the Community formed by the outpouring of the Holy Spirit. By linking the believer with Christ, he is incorporated into the Messianic Age heralded by the prophets; there the new deathless order of existence is already present in moral experience.[225] In conclusion we may echo Bishop Newbigin's statement: 'Here it is sufficient to draw attention to the overwhelming weight of argument in favour of the statement that faith is, from the human side, the constitutive fact of membership in the people of God.'[226]

Baptism as the Outward Means of Identification with Christ

(1) *Introduction*

Following the contemporaneous Jewish practice of proselyte baptism as an initiatory rite,[227] the primitive Church required baptism in 'the name of the Father, and of the Son, and of the

---

[222] A. Nygren well says, that $\pi\acute{\iota}\sigma\tau\iota s$ denotes a receptive attitude to the offering of God (*Agape and Eros*, p. 130).

[223] R. N. Flew rightly points out that, 'The chief argument against the view that *ex opere operato* Baptism itself effected a change in the substance of the soul is the unvarying Pauline emphasis on faith' (*The Idea of Perfection in Christian Theology* [London, 1934], p. 58). Contrast F. Prat, op. cit. I.223; A. Schweitzer, *The Mysticism of Paul*, p. 23; A. Plummer, 'Baptism', *HDB*, I.244.

[224] Op. cit. p. 89.

[225] R. N. Flew, *The Idea of Perfection in Christian Theology*, p. 58. Cf. C. H. Dodd, *Romans*, p. 126; L. Newbigin, op. cit. p. 45.

[226] Op. cit. p. 45.

[227] See A. Plummer, op. cit. I.239-40.

Holy Ghost' (Matt 28¹⁹) or in 'the name of Jesus Christ' (Acts 10⁴⁸, 19⁵; cf. Rom 6³) for admission to the Christian Community. As such an initiatory rite, baptism is mentioned only once in the Pauline Epistles: 'For in one Spirit were we all baptized into one body, whether Jews or Greeks, whether bond or free' (1 Cor 12¹³). To the non-Christian world, whether of Jews or Gentiles, the Christian practice of immersion must have appeared as a conscious attempt to incorporate proselytes into a Jewish sect.²²⁸ As such it provided a link between the Old and the New Israel.

(2) Baptism as a Rite

In Paul's conception, baptism merely as a rite had little significance, if any. In writing to the Corinthians he says that he is thankful that he did not baptize more converts than he did (1 Cor 1¹⁴⁻¹⁵. This is said because the schismatic groups were naming themselves after apostles). His commission was specifically to preach the gospel, not to baptize (verse 17). He warns the same church that baptism is not a magical rite which can guarantee that the novice will reach the 'promised land'.²²⁹ Just as Israel of old had its sacraments²³⁰ and historical events with spiritual significance (1 Cor 10²), yet perished in the wilderness, so the believers of Corinth must beware of unbelief and of the accompanying pitfalls of the Congregation. Baptism of itself cannot assure anyone's escape from divine punishment (1 Cor 10⁵⁻⁶; cf. Heb 3⁶⁻¹⁹).²³¹ Thus, it is fundamental to recognize that according to the teaching of the Apostle, true baptism is received only in conjunction with the response of faith.

²²⁸ Both the baptism of John and that of the New Covenantors belonged to this category.

²²⁹ Cf. A. E. J. Rawlinson, op. cit. p. 230; H. A. A. Kennedy, *Theology of the Epistles*, p. 133 note 1; E. Best, op. cit. p. 73.

²³⁰ These are in Barth's words, a representation (*Abbild, Darstellung*), a seal (σφραγίς) or a sign (*signum*), a type (*Entsprechung*) or a copy (μίμησις) of the spiritual reality (*The Teaching of the Church Regarding Baptism*, trans. E. A. Paine (London, 1954), pp. 13-14). See also A. M. Hunter, op. cit. p. 80, and H. A. A. Kennedy, *St Paul and the Mystery-Religions*, p. 247.

²³¹ Cf. J. Moffatt, *1 Corinthians*, pp. 129-30; R. V. G. Tasker, op. cit. pp. 90-1; K. Barth, *The Teaching of the Church*, p. 63; F. C. Baur, *Paul*, II.177; A. E. J. Rawlinson, op. cit. p. 232; A. D. Nock, *St Paul* (London, 1938), p. 240. Unfortunately the evidence is too inconclusive for us to penetrate the intention of Paul's reference to the Corinthian vicarious baptism for the dead (1 Cor 15²⁹). Did he see the bond of solidarity extending across the gulf of death or is it an argument *ad hominem*? See H. G. Marsh, *The Origin and Significance of New Testament Baptism*, p. 167, and J. A. T. Robinson, op. cit. p. 54.

For Paul, the sacrament is what we might designate 'faith-baptism'. This is clear from Galatians 3^{26-7}: 'For ye are all sons of God, through faith, in Jesus Christ. For as many of you as were baptized into Christ did put on Christ' (*RV*). So also Romans 10^{8-9}: 'But what saith it? The word is nigh thee, in thy mouth, and in thy heart: that is, the word of faith, which we preach: because if thou shalt confess with thy mouth Jesus as Lord,[232] and shalt believe in thy heart that God raised him from the dead, thou shalt be saved.' Through the confession of faith in baptism, the novice is incorporated into the new Israel; he becomes part of the New Man, that is, he is 'saved' ($\sigma\omega\zeta\epsilon\hat{\iota}\nu$).

(3) *Paul's Doctrine of Baptism*

Baptism in the New Testament is aligned with a wide variety of meanings. These have been summarized by C. T. Craig:

First of all it involved a washing or cleansing (1 Cor 6^{11}, Acts 22^{16}, Rev 22^{14}, Heb 10^{22}), not the putting away of the filth of the flesh but the interrogation of a good conscience (1 Pet 3^{21}). Accompanying this washing was the forgiveness of sins (Acts 2^{38}). It meant also the gift of the Spirit. 'For by one Spirit were we all baptized' (1 Cor 12^{13}). Occasionally in Acts the gift of the Spirit is separate from baptism (Acts 8^{12}, 10^{47}), but according to the usual view they are brought together. This meant nothing less than a new birth. We are told that it is impossible to see the kingdom of God unless a man is born of water and the Spirit (Jn 3^5). It is therefore a washing of regeneration (Tit 3^{5-7}) which brought illumination (Heb 6^4, 10^{32}). Furthermore, baptism could involve 'putting on Christ', or dying and rising with Christ (Gal 3^{27}, Col 2^{12}, Rom 6^{4-6}).[233]

It is clear from the references that many of these meanings have been exemplified in the Epistles of Paul. But we must more particularly notice the meanings which Paul emphasizes. One among these is the alignment of baptism with incorporation into the fellowship of the Holy Spirit (1 Cor 12^{13}, quoted above).[234] The significance of the point is noted in that it is the one Spirit which

---

[232] It is quite possible that Paul has in mind the baptismal confession here.

[233] *The One Church* (London, 1952), pp. 69-70. It is most important to notice that in at least two instances, the gift of the Spirit which is the constituting factor in the creation or manifestation of the Church (cf. L. Newbigin, op cit. pp. 96-7) is granted apart from Baptism, meaning that submission to the rite is not necessarily the condition for inclusion into the Body of Christ (cf. K. Barth, *The Teaching of the Church Regarding Baptism*, pp. 23ff).

[234] Cf. R. N. Flew, *Jesus and His Church*, p. 119, for the same conception in the Gospels and Acts.

is the source of the unity of the Church, even as He is the ground
of the new life in Christ.[235] The vital connexion which baptism
has with the κοινωνία πνεύματος ('participation in the Spirit')
probably arose out of the fact that the Holy Spirit was given at
the Baptism of the convert.[236] This point is explicitly made in
Acts where Paul encounters twelve disciples previously baptized
by John but who did not possess the Holy Spirit (19^{1-7}). After
Paul had re-baptized them and laid hands upon them, they received the gift of the Spirit (19^6). The New Testament clearly
says that the difference between the baptism of John and that
of Christ (i.e. in His name) lay in the latter's bestowing the Holy
Spirit (cf. Lk 3^{16}). So Paul says correspondingly of the Church:
'Not by works in righteousness which we did, but according to
his mercy he saved us, by the washing (λουτροῦ) of regeneration
and renewing of the Holy Spirit whom he poured out abundantly
upon us through Jesus Christ our Saviour' (Tit 3^{5-6}).[237]

Baptism did confer upon the initiate the right of admission
into the visible community of the Church, the Body of Christ.[238]
Since the Body is also the dwelling-place of the Spirit, incorporation into it meant incorporation into the Spirit.[239] This eluci-
dates the phrases ἐν πνεύματι ('in the Spirit') (cf. 1 Cor 12^{13},
Rom 8^9, Gal 3^{25}, 1 Tim 3^{16}) and κοινωνία τοῦ πνεύματος ('fellowship of the Spirit') (2 Cor 13^{14(13)}). In this sense, baptism is
equivalent to the immersion of the proselyte in Judaism, although
the symbolism or meaning is radically different. Speaking of baptism, H. Sahlin writes:

The Christian is consequently 'in Christ'. He is virtually incorporated
into the body of Christ. Hence, by the Pauline formula 'to be in Christ'
there is meant, strictly speaking, no kind of mystical union with
Christ; it states the purely objective fact that through baptism a person
has been 'planted together with Christ' (Rom 6^5). To St Paul this
was evidently an objective reality just as it was an objective reality to
Judaism that through circumcision and proselyte baptism the proselyte

---

[235] W. Koester, op. cit. p. 34.

[236] Cf. J. Y. Campbell, 'Κοινωνία and its Cognates in the New Testament', p. 378,
and H. G. Marsh, op. cit. p. 141.

[237] Cf. L. Newbigin, op. cit. p. 99. It also corresponds to the counterpart of this
idea in Judaism, in which a proselyte through initiation into Israel was brought into
the sphere of the Shekinah (i.e. under its wings).

[238] Cf. C. T. Craig op. cit. pp. 70-1; A. M. Hunter, op. cit. p. 79; A. E. J.
Rawlinson, op. cit. p. 227:

[239] Cf. M. Goguel, 'L'Idée d'Église dans le Nouveau Testament', p. 70. Note Irenæus,
Adv. Haer, III.24.1.

was admitted into the Exodus generation and becomes a partaker of its salvation.[240]

We must examine still more closely Paul's understanding of the implications of the ἐν βάπτισμα ('one baptism') (Eph 4⁵) which embraced the undissected event of the death and resurrection of Christ involving the βάπτισμος ('baptism') of the individual in the Church. Two passages are paramount for this purpose; therefore, we shall quote them more or less in full:

We who died (οἵτινες ἀπεθάνομεν) to sin, how shall we yet live in it? Or are ye ignorant that as many of us as were baptized into Jesus Christ were baptized into his death? Therefore we have been buried with him (συνετάφημεν αὐτῷ) through baptism into death, in order that (ἵνα) as (ὥσπερ) Christ was raised from the dead by (διά) the glory of the Father, even so (οὕτως) we might walk in newness of life. For if we have been united (σύμφυτοι) in the likeness (ὁμοιώματι) of his death, but also we shall be (united in the likeness) of the resurrection. Knowing this, that our old man has been crucified, in order that the body of sin might be destroyed that we should no longer be in thraldom to sin (Rom 6²⁻⁶).

In whom also ye have been circumcised with the circumcision enacted without hands in the putting off of the body of the flesh (cf. Rom 2²⁸⁻⁹) in the circumcision of Christ, being buried with (συνταφέντες) him in the baptism, in which also you have been raised through the faith of the working of God who raised him from the dead; and you having been dead (in) the trespasses and uncircumcision of your flesh, he vitalized (συνεζωοποίησεν) with him, forgiving (χαρισάμενος) us all trespasses (τά παραπτώματα) (Col 2¹¹⁻¹³; cf. 2²⁰ and 3³, ἀπεθάνετε γάρ, καὶ ἡ ζωὴ ὑμῶν κέκρυπται σὺν τῷ Χριστῷ ἐν τῷ θεῷ, Col 3³).

In baptism the initiate shares in the ἐν βάπτισμα of Christ through union (σύμφυτας)[241] in the likeness (ὁμοίωμα) of His death. Thus, Paul sees the Christian proselyte bath as a purely derived event. It was the sharing in the whole Event (ἐν βάπτισμα) which contracted the New Covenant with the true

---

[240] 'The New Exodus of Salvation According to St Paul', p. 92. Cf. E. Best, Chap. 4, passim. op. cit. pp. 65ff.

[241] This word may derive from φύω ('born together', 'congenital', 'grow together') or it may stem from φυτεύω ('planted together'). F. Prat argues that it means to share the same life principle (op. cit. I.222-3) but Bourke's examination of usage prior and contemporary to Paul, forces him to reject any botanical associations. It means only 'united with' (cf. op. cit. pp. 112ff and especially p. 124). Both roots φύω and φυτεύω are used in grafting; either very close union or growth together (cf. Jn 15¹⁻⁷) appear to be in Paul's mind. See E. Best, op. cit. pp. 51ff.

People of God.[242] But it is more than an acknowledgement of the Covenant. It has also the elements of a contemporaneity of experience made so familiar by the Jewish Passover observance. Thus, what happened to Christ has through baptism happened to us (cf. Rom 6[4], and the use of ὥσπερ . . . οὕτως).[243] The concrete reality of the redemptive Experience (suffered by Christ)[244] has been offered to us in such a way that by baptism we participate in it. Thus, in Romans 6, baptism into Jesus Christ, burial with Him, grafting or union with Him, and a concrete incorporation into Him are all embraced within the conception of baptism made effective through faith.

In the second passage quoted (Col 2[11-13]), Paul relates spiritual circumcision to baptism. It was circumcision which sealed Abraham's 'righteousness of faith' (cf. Rom 4[11]). In succession Spirit baptism is the seal (σφραγίς) of a Christian's incorporation into the New Aeon (cf. 2 Cor 1[22], Eph 1[13], 4[30]). The general background of Paul's thought appears to be the two-fold requirement of the Gentile proselyte coming into the Jewish covenant.[245] The differences are self-evident, however. Incorporation by faith-baptism into the sphere of the New Covenant (i.e. Jesus Christ) frees one from the 'flesh' and its antagonism against God; it removes one from the Old Aeon and places him in the New Age[246] inaugurated by Christ and mediated through the Holy Spirit. Therefore, 'those that are of Christ Jesus have crucified the flesh and its lusts. If we live in the Spirit, by the Spirit let us walk' (Gal 5[24-5]).

---

[242] Even as Israel was baptized in the Red Sea to receive the Old Covenant. According to H. Sahlin, Jesus Christ is the New Moses (the starting point is the death and resurrection of Christ) which has the same meaning for the Church as the crossing of the Red Sea had for Israel (op. cit. p. 91). See further P. Carrington, *The Primitive Christian Catechism* (Cambridge, 1940), pp. 6-7, and W. J. Phythian-Adams, op. cit. pp. 184-5.

[243] Cf. further S. Hanson, op. cit. p. 85.

[244] Ὁμοίωμα signifies much more than mere likeness (cf. Rom 5[14], Phil 2[7], where it means the 'concrete embodiment' of our humanity) and is to be contrasted with ὁμοιότης.

[245] Baptism removed the filth and uncleanness of Gentile associations and idolatry (including the filth of the Serpent); in Christian baptism, the Church has been freed from πάντα τὰ παραπτώματα (Col 2[13]) through incorporation into the New Covenant through the circumcision of Christ, that is, His death for it. Because baptism is the symbol of the death and resurrection of Christ, the seal of circumcision has been displaced. Circumcision, in the New Age, becomes for Paul the symbol of trusting in the flesh which has no part in the attainment of the salvation which is purely of grace (see L. Newbigin's excellent discussion, op. cit. pp. 36ff).

[246] Cf. E. H. Wahlstrom, op. cit. p. 17; J. A. T. Robinson, op. cit. pp. 79-80. See E. Best, op. cit., Chap. 4.

In another passage in the Epistle to the Galatians, Paul states: 'For as many of you as have been baptized into (ϵis)[247] Christ have put on ($\epsilon\nu\epsilon\delta\upsilon\sigma\alpha\sigma\theta\epsilon$) Christ' (3[27]). This is another reference to the counterpart of the putting off 'the body of the flesh' (Col 2[11]).[248] The corporate clothing of the two opposing communities (i.e. 'flesh' and 'Spirit' or 'Body of Christ') is a witness to its unity (cf. Gal 3[28]). O. Cullmann remarks well:

The connexion of the two texts Rom 6[3ff] and 1 Cor 12[13] is not arbitrary. An inner bond exists between them, in so far as the Body of Christ into which we are baptized is at the same time the crucified body of Christ (Col 1[24], 2 Cor 1[5], 1 Pet 4[3]) and his resurrected body (1 Cor 15[20-2]). On the basis of a like connexion of thought between death and resurrection with Christ on the one hand, and the building up of a community of Christ on the other hand, Paul in Gal 3[27-8] . . . says also: 'as many of you as have been baptized into Christ . . . have put on Christ . . . ye are all one in Christ'.[249]

In Ephesians 5[26], Paul again refers to the whole Church: 'even as Christ also loved the church, and gave himself up for it; that he might sanctify it, having cleansed it by the washing ($\tau\hat{\omega}$ $\lambda o\upsilon\tau\rho\hat{\omega}$, 'laver') of water by the word. . . .' In his favourite way, Paul posits the corporate character of baptism.[250] The baptism of Christ, the baptism of the Church, and the baptism of the individual believer form one transcendant reality. Baptism includes one in the sphere of the corporate personality of Christ. This in turn produces His character manifested in His cleansed Body. This is the New Man in which all disunity of race, creed, and position is obviated (Gal 3[28]).[251] The Body, through baptism, shares in the obedient sacrifice of Christ and realistically experiences the revitalization of the risen Lord. This point has been well made by T. F. Torrance:

To be baptized is to be planted into that judgement, to be engrafted into the Body of death, inserted into the sphere of union where judgement and crucifixion are enacted as saving operation. It is therefore

[247] S. Hanson argues cogently for the local interpretation of ϵis when it refers to baptism in the Epistles, in the sense of incorporation into the personal representative sphere of Christ (1 Cor 1[13, 15]). Op. cit. p. 81. See J. A. T. Robinson, op. cit. p. 62.
[248] Cf. J. A. T. Robinson, op. cit. pp. 63-4.
[249] *Baptism in the New Testament*, pp. 30-1.
[250] Cf. C. A. A. Scott, *Christianity According to St Paul*, op. cit. p. 118. See the proper emphasis of K. Barth, *The Teaching of the Church* . . . , op. cit. pp. 31f. 'In principle, baptism cannot be celebrated as a private act . . . '. Cf. C. Chavasse, op. cit. p. 105.
[251] Cf. A. Schweitzer, *The Mysticism of Paul*, p. 118.

through baptismal incorporation into Christ that our sinful divisions
are brought under mortification of the Cross and are destroyed in
Christ. If through this Baptism the Church participates in that action
for it, is sacramentally incorporated into the one Body of Christ, then
Baptism is the primary enactment and expression of the oneness of the
Church.[252]

Because baptism is into (ϵἰς) Jesus Christ (Rom 6^{3-4}), it is
incorporation into His name.[253] It is He who is gathering the
sealed community of those 'who name the name of the Lord'
(2 Tim 2^{19}). By this is meant no less than incorporation into the
family of Christ, the household of faith, which is the sphere of
the Lordship of Christ (i.e. where He is *baal*). As such it offers
both privilege and obligation, as did the ancient Semitic kin-
group within its social structure. Neither the use of the 'name'
(i.e. Jesus Christ) nor the involuntary baptism of Israel into
Moses (ϵἰς τὸν Μωυσῆν) in the Red Sea (1 Cor 10^2) are examples
of primitive magic. On the contrary, it represents inclusion into
the representative sphere of a leader, whether it be Christ or
Moses.[254] 'They had become Moses' people and the obligation
was imposed upon them not in consequence of any ceremonial
but because they had *participated* in the supernatural deliverance.'[255] Besides experiential identification, baptism is concerned
with the act of grace in which God made a covenant with His
people. In the redemption of the New Israel from the Old Aeon,
the New Exodus had taken place, but at the same time it brought
the Community into the corporate sphere of the New Moses, and
under the aegis of the New Covenant.

(4) *Summary and Conclusion*

The core of Paul's conception of the meaning of baptism is a
realistic experiencing of the death and resurrection of Christ.
Through baptism the initiate shares in the penalty paid for sin
as he bows in vital union with Christ to receive the judgement of

[252] Op. cit. p. 22; cf. F. Prat, op. cit. II.298.
[253] P. G. S. Hopwood, op. cit. pp. 284-5. Cf. A. E. J. Rawlinson, op. cit. p. 234.
R. N. Flew, *Jesus and His Church*, p. 119; R. Bultmann, *Theology of the New Testament*,
I.138. It is equivalent to the name of יהוה upon Israel (Num 6^{27}); cf. F. Gavin,
op. cit. p. 63; A. M. Hunter, op. cit. p. 83.
[254] Cf. S. Hanson, op. cit. p. 81.
[255] C. A. A. Scott, op. cit. p. 116 (italics ours). Cf. Wm. Manson, 'The Biblical
Doctrine of Mission', p. 259.

God.[256] This penalty is death, the universal judgement of God upon all transgression (cf. Col 2[20]). Out of death, God re-creates through His power and for His glory (δόξα in Rom 6[4]) the New Man through the infusion of the resurrection life of Christ mediated through the Holy Spirit (cf. 1 Tim 6[13]—τοῦ Θεοῦ τοῦ ζωογονοῦντος τὰ πάντα). Thus, the ἐν βάπτισμα corresponds to the one transgression (ἐν παράπτωμα).[257] The βάπτισμος of the believer in faith is the vindication of the extension of the reward of God offered for the one archetypal act of obedience since we share in it (cf. 2 Cor 5[14]), just as we formerly shared in the corporate judgement of God on the disobedience of Adam and vindicated it through our individual sinning. The new life also counteracts the destructive powers of the Aeon, freeing the initiate from any bond with sin.[258] So also is all condemnation absolved for those who are in Christ Jesus (Rom 8[1]; cf. 5[16]). 'In Him' includes deliverance from 'this evil age' (Gal 1[4]). Paul's doctrine of baptism is summed up in one passage: 'Faithful is the saying: For if we died (συναπεθάνομεν) together (with him) we shall live together: if we endure we shall reign together (with him)' (2 Tim 2[11-13]).

The Eucharist as Communal Fellowship

In Paul's Epistles, the Lord's Supper is largely governed by corporate considerations. It is fundamental to the life of the Church as a means of maintaining the awareness of the psychic unity originally constituted through faith-baptism. This unity is described as a participation in[259] and fellowship with[260] the Head of the Redeemed Community. Regarding the need for this fellowship, F. J. Hort has well said: 'All life in the higher sense

[256] Cf. K. Barth, *The Teaching of the Church*, pp. 21, 55-6. Professor Torrance speaks of baptism as the sacrament in which we step out of our inadequacy into Him. He gives us repentance, brings us to obedience; He is our acquiescence to God.

[257] If this conclusion is correct, it is not merely coincidental that Romans 6[1-11] follows 5[12-21].

[258] W. Koester, op. cit. p. 39; cf. C. Weizsäcker, op. cit. I.169-70. This release from sin must be apprehended by the will in faith (cf. Rom 6[6] with 6[11]). The Christian's task is: '*Werde was du bist.*'

[259] Cf. L. H. Seesemann, *Der Begriff κοινωνία im Neuen Testament* (Giessen, 1933), pp. 4, 34 (note that he refers to 1 Cor 10[16], 1[9], 2 Cor 13[13], 8[4], Phil 1[5], 3[10], Philemon 6, as examples of an *Anteilhaben, Teilnahme*). See also J. Y. Campbell, 'Κοινωνία and its Cognates in the New Testament', *passim*. The realism of the idea of participation or sharing is obvious in the series of synonyms used for κοινωνία in 2 Cor 6[14-18]: μετοχή, κοινωνία, συμφώνησις, μερίς, συγκατάθεσις.

[260] Cf. L. H. Seeseman, op. cit. pp. 86ff. It is a religious term for Paul (ibid. p. 99).

depends on some fellowship, an isolated life is a contradiction of terms.'[261] Fellowship is to the higher spiritual life what food is to the natural life.

Two passages are particularly important for our understanding of Paul's conception of the Eucharist:

(1) The cup of blessing which we bless, is it not participation (κοινωνία) in the blood of Christ? The bread which we break, is it not a participation (κοινωνία) in the body of Christ? Because there is one loaf, we, who are many, are one body, for we all partake of the one loaf[262] (ὅτι εἷς ἄρτος, ἓν σῶμα οἱ πολλοί ἐσμεν· οἱ γὰρ πάντες ἐκ τοῦ ἑνὸς ἄρτου μετέχομεν) (1 Cor 10[16-17]).

In this same passage, Paul continued his argument with the postulation that participation in the sacrifices of Gentile idol worship mediates a communion with demons. Participation in the Eucharist of the Lord and in the 'table of demons' is therefore mutually exclusive.

Paul is apparently thinking in terms of a psychic relationship made familiar in the Old Testament conception of solidarity. Thus, the Jewish priest through his close association with the altar (verse 18) partakes of the holiness of the altar (cf. Matt 23[16-21]).[263] The pagans in their heathen sacrifices join in a partnership with demons. The Christian Community, in the same way, does not partake of the actual body and blood (cf. 2 Sam 23[17]) of Christ,[264] but in a sacramental way is brought into a κοινωνία relationship with one another and with Christ. The contradiction between the fellowship of Christ and that of demons was self-evident to Paul[265] and is reminiscent of the gulf separating Israel from the idolatrous Gentiles. To join in the heathen liturgical worship is the very essence of the return to the Old Aeon and its slavery to demonic forces. But the κοινωνία of the

---

[261] *The Way the Truth the Life* (2nd edn, Cambridge, 1894), p. 194.

[262] Against *RV* and *AV*. It does not mean that the Church is one loaf (cf. L. S. Thornton, *The Common Life*, p. 335).

[263] Cf. C. A. A. Scott, *Christianity According to St Paul*, p. 185. This holiness, of course, comes from God to whom the altar belongs.

[264] Cf. J. Weiss, op. cit. p. 641; W. Morgan, op. cit. pp. 222f, N. Micklem, *A First Century Letter* (London, 1921), pp. 64ff. As J. Jeremias says, 'Eating together implies equality of position' (*The Parables of Jesus*, trans. 3rd G. edn, S. H. Hooke (London, 1954), p. 49 note 10), and provides the basis of κοινωνία as share-giving and share-receiving.

[265] Cf. A. E. J. Rawlinson, op. cit. p. 229.

body and blood of Christ conveys the conception of a 'vital relation with Christ Himself as the Crucified Saviour'.[266]

The meal is a commemorative representation of the sacrifice by which Christ inaugurated the New Covenant which constituted the New Israel. As such it is a confession of the covenant bond which makes the Community the People of God, while at the same time it produces a fellowship among those who partake of the elements in common.

(2) The second passage of vital concern to us is 1 Corinthians 11[23-9]:

... The Lord Jesus, in the night in which he was betrayed (or delivered up) took bread and after blessing it broke (it) and said: $\tau o \hat{v} \tau \acute{o} \mu o \acute{v}$ $\acute{\epsilon} \sigma \tau \iota \nu \tau \grave{o} \sigma \hat{\omega} \mu a \tau \grave{o} \acute{v} \pi \grave{\epsilon} \rho \acute{v} \mu \hat{\omega} \nu$. This do in my remembrance ($\epsilon \acute{i} s \tau \grave{\eta} \nu$ $\acute{\epsilon} \mu \grave{\eta} \nu \grave{a} \nu \acute{a} \mu \nu \eta \sigma \iota \nu$). So also the cup, after dinner, saying, this cup is the new covenant in my blood: this do, as often as you drink (of it) in my remembrance. For as often as you eat this bread and you drink this cup, you proclaim ($\kappa a \tau a \gamma \gamma \acute{\epsilon} \lambda \lambda \epsilon \tau \epsilon$) the death of the Lord until He come. Wherefore whoever eats this bread or drinks this cup of the Lord unworthily, he shall be guilty ($\acute{\epsilon} \nu o \chi o s \acute{\epsilon} \sigma \tau a \iota$) of the body and of the blood of the Lord.

In this passage the solidarity of the New Humanity as the $\sigma \hat{\omega} \mu a$ $\tau o \hat{v} X \rho \iota \sigma \tau o \hat{v}$ is paramount. Some of the Corinthian Christians by their selfish practices despised ($\kappa a \tau a \phi \rho o \nu \epsilon \hat{\iota} \tau \epsilon$) the Ecclesia of God (verse 22). Later, Paul warns the assembly: '. . . He that eateth and drinketh (unworthily), eateth and drinketh judgement unto himself not discerning the Body (of Christ) ($\mu \grave{\eta} \delta \iota a \kappa \rho \acute{\iota} \nu \omega \nu$ $\tau \grave{o} \sigma \hat{\omega} \mu a$)' (verse 29). As W. D. Davies has said:

Here he refers to those who in their conduct at the Holy Communion forgot their unity with their fellow Christians and with Christ, who failed to recognize that to partake in the Lord's Supper was not merely to participate in Christ but also in their fellow Christians who are one with Christ.[267]

Thus, it is not the sacrament which is itself holy, but the unity of the Body.[268] To violate it is to bring condemnation upon oneself.

It is preferable here to see Paul's conception of the unity of

[266] Vincent Taylor, *Jesus and His Sacrifice* (London, 1937), p. 211.
[267] Op. cit. p. 55.
[268] This is the same point as we have emphasized relative to the violation of the holiness of the corporate Temple in 1 Corinthians 3 (see above).

the Church as covenantal, mediated in personal experience, rather than sacramental.[269] It is a solidarity which corresponds to the corporate personality of Israel, even though the bond is the living κοινωνία of the Holy Spirit. It is He, as He extends the character and personality of Christ, who creates the solidarity of the New Humanity. It is for this reason that Paul speaks of the guilt of despising Christ when one pays no heed to the unity of the Community which bears His name. To sin against the Community is therefore to sin against the Lord of the Community who constitutes the basis of its unity (1 Cor 8[12]).[270] As Christ is present and alive in the members of His Body, the celebration of the Eucharist is the repeated witness to and confession of the presence of Christ within the Church.

But this common sharing of the life of Christ through the Holy Spirit in no sense destroys the individuality of its members which maintain full responsibility and value as the objects of Christ's redeeming love.[271] As it was in the case of the solidarity of Israel in the periods of the Old Testament and Early Judaism, Paul maintains the priority of the Community and the subordination of the individual member in love for and responsibility to the whole (cf. Col 2[19] *RV*, 1 Cor 12[14-31]). 'It implies a new kind of individual, but one who like the true Israelite of old, could never be divorced from his social relationship.'[272] It is not mystical absorption but 'identity with differences',[273] a corporate personality 'in which the individual loses himself in some larger entity, to discover himself again on a higher level'.[274] It is the heightening of the Jewish conception of the unity of Israel in which the

[269] As over against the opinion of H. Weinel, op. cit. p. 331; cf. S. Hanson, op. cit. p. 89. A. Schweitzer, *The Mysticism of Paul*, p. 21, and J. A. T. Robinson: 'In so far then as the Christian community feeds on this body and blood, it becomes the very life and personality of the risen Christ' (op. cit. p. 57). These views bring Paul too close to the Mystery-cults where the performance of physical acts in themselves produced spiritual results (cf. C. H. Dodd, *The Meaning of Paul for Today*, p. 119).

[270] See J. A. T. Robinson on Acts 26[14-15], op. cit. p. 58. Contrast A. E. J. Rawlinson who thinks Paul's conception of the Eucharist is 'superstitious' (op. cit. p. 230; cf. H. Lietzmann, *The Beginnings of the Christian Church*, pp. 124-5).

[271] E. C. Rust, op. cit. p. 116. 'To the Hebrew individuality is not in the least endangered by saying that as σῶμα, man is "part of one stupendous whole". In fact Paul deliberately substitutes a new solidarity for the old (the "body" of creation), without in any way undermining the fact of individuality' (J. A. T. Robinson, op. cit. p. 79 note 1).

[272] H. W. Robinson, 'The Group and the Individual in Israel', p. 169.

[273] Cf. Wm. Robinson, op. cit. p. 108.

[274] H. W. Robinson, *The Cross of the Servant*, p. 79; cf. L. S. Thornton, *The Incarnate Lord*, pp. 51-2, 60-1.

suffering of a member or his sinning were not private affairs, but reacted on the whole (1 Cor 12²⁶). In other words, the bond of the Community is love in its deepest sense.²⁷⁵ It is just as R. N. Flew says:

Love implies a society: 'Above all put on love, for love gives cohesion to the perfect life' (σύνδεσμος τῆς τελειότητος). The meaning here (Col 3¹⁴) is probably the perfect fellowship that ought to exist among Christian men. Love is the bond that united them in a common service.²⁷⁶

Lack of love, by the same token, destroys the society and denies the reality of the Lord who is its constituting Head.

In conclusion and summary, we may say that the object of the Supper is two-fold. It creates a realization of the solidarity of the members within the Body even as it produces fellowship with Christ, the Head of the Body. This *koinonia* is the realistic bond of the Community and corresponds to the psychic bond pervading the Hebrew kin-group as well as Israel as a whole.

The Last Supper, like baptism, applies the Jewish principles of identification with the Person of Jesus Christ and consequently involves contemporaneity, by which the participant realistically re-experiences the redemptive events which instituted the New Covenantal relationship with God.²⁷⁷ There is no real value in it apart from this participation in the realities which the symbols of the Supper represent.²⁷⁸ The main difference between the Jewish Passover and the Eucharist is found in the eschatological character of the New Covenant and the participation of the New Humanity in the 'powers of the age to come' (Phil 3¹⁰) through the Holy Spirit. In the commemorative Meal the Community confesses and shares in the spiritual benefits which the historical sacrificial death of Christ had provided as well as in the solidarity conferred upon the Community through the communication of the life of the risen Christ through the Holy Spirit. It is in the Eucharistic Meal that the assembly witnesses to and becomes a

---

²⁷⁵ Cf. F. R. Barry, *Christianity and Psychology* (5th edn, London, 1933), pp. 286-7; E. Brunner, *Man in Revolt*, pp. 290-1; J. Bright, op. cit. p. 263.
²⁷⁶ *The Idea of Perfection in Christian Theology*, p. 70.
²⁷⁷ Cf. A. Raymond George, op. cit. pp. 163-4. This author suggests that this identification led to the συν-compounds and developed into the expression 'in Christ'.
²⁷⁸ Note that it is the Jewish son who fails to re-experience contemporaneously the Exodus redemption (one might say, believe it personally) that is barred from the Jewish Communion (cf. *supra*, pp. 56-9).

'corporate personality'.[279] It is for this reason that the members of the Community who fail to show love to other members are violently judged by God for they attack the very essence of its constitution in denying its unity.

CONCLUSION

Although we have made an attempt to indicate a number of points where the conceptions of the solidarity of the race evinced by Paul correspond to those found in the Old Testament and Early Judaism, we must make a cursory assessment of a few general as well as specific conclusions.

We may say at the outset that not a single major conception or implication of solidarity found in either the Old Testament or Early Judaism is omitted from Paul's Epistles. Particularly good examples are found in Paul's deductions regarding corporate blessing or merit and corporate punishment or demerit. It is because Christ is a member of the group (albeit a chief Member) that He can represent that group, acting in and as a corporate personality. This is the basis of Paul's doctrine of atonement and redemption (cf. e.g. Rom 3^{25}, $5^{15,\,18-19}$, 2 Cor $5^{14,\,21}$). We need not repeat what is self-evident, namely, that the foundational background of this view is the characteristic Hebrew conception of man as more than an individual.[280] His actions are not private; his life is bound up in the bundle of life common to all men.

Equally important to Paul's conceptions of the solidarity of the race is the idea of an exclusive relationship within the totality of men. This totality is the counterpart to the Israel of old who were the elect people of God, united to Him by a common covenant. In Paul the primary conception of the solidarity through the covenant is displaced by the solidarity mediated through a personal relationship to the risen Christ, who is Himself the covenant of the New Israel.

A third fundamental point which must be taken into account is that for Paul the Messianic Age had dawned. This meant simply that the myriad expectations originating in the early prophets

---

[279] See J. Weiss (op. cit. p. 640) and allusion to W. R. Smith. Cf. H. A. A. Kennedy, *Theology of the Epistles*, pp. 150, 152.

[280] C. Ryder Smith, *The Bible Doctrine of Man*, pp. 218, 272, 274. Cf. A. Nygren, 'Christ and the Forces of Destruction', p. 373; H. W. Robinson, *The Cross of the Servant*, p. 85.

and expanded by apocalyptic and Rabbinic speculation had found, or soon would find, their fulfilment in the re-gathered Israel. The expected attributes of unity and holiness to characterize the eschatological nation play an important part in Paul's doctrine of the Church which is the New Israel. It is imperative that there be no division or schism in the Israel within the Messianic Age to act as counterparts to the sects of Judaism. Of course, there were many other implications, such as the giving of the Holy Spirit 'poured out upon all flesh' and the inauguration of the reign of the Davidic Messiah (Col 1[13], 1 Cor 15[24-8]).[281] We need not point again to the references made by Paul to the Messianic figures and their peculiar use to describe Christ. These basically indicate Paul's conception of the solidarity of the Church through its relationship to Christ. Involved throughout are the principles of realistic representation, oscillation, vicarious substitution, and so on.

Paul, just as the Jewish teachers, used metaphors and symbols to describe the solidarity of the Church. The metaphors need not be the same ones, but the point was unchanged; a mysterious unity pervaded the Elect Race so that the action of a member or a group implicated the whole in reward or punishment. In Paul these metaphors are often organic (i.e. a body, tree) because it is the organic structure which best describes the implications of solidarity; therefore Paul says: 'And whether one member suffereth, all members suffer with it; or one member is honoured all the members rejoice with it' (1 Cor 12[26]).

Besides this, there are the ideas of contemporaneity, and realistic identification in the experiences of another. These are so clear that we need say no more. Rather than mediation of experience through sharing in the life of the ancestor(s), the Christian shared in the experience of redemption through faith and the mediated life of Christ through the Holy Spirit. In place

---

[281] One may well ask why Paul's references to the Kingdom are so limited. H. A. A. Kennedy suggests: '. . . we are not unduly pressing the data when we assert that for Paul the conception of the Family of God, as established and knit together in Christ takes the place of the Kingdom' (*Theology of the Epistles*, p. 106; so also Wm. Robinson, op. cit. p. 50; cf. A. G. Hebert, op. cit. p. 138). But R. N. Flew is not impressed: 'The Church is not to be identified with God's Kingly Rule. Neither is it a conception substituted for that of the kingdom in the later writings of the New Testament' (*Jesus and His Church*, p. 24). 1 Corinthians 15[24-8] indicates that Paul looks forward to the Kingdom although it does exist at present in Colossians 1[13]. It may be another example of the tension between the present intermediate condition and that which is yet to come.

of the Passover, the Christian Community celebrated the Eucharistic Supper as a realistic commemorative sharing in the death of
Christ. The initiatory rite of baptism in the same manner as
proselyte immersion brought the convert into the visible fellowship of the People of God. In baptism, one shared in the death
and resurrection of Christ and received 'the law of the Spirit of
life in Christ Jesus' (Rom 8²; cf. Gal 6²).

When all is said and done, it is the Church as the 'household of
God' (Eph 2¹⁹) or the 'household of faith' (Gal 6¹⁰) which most
distinctively shows the relationship of Paul to his own background. It is the Community as a family, the 'sons of God', which
stands over against the Adamic kin-group who are the 'sons of
disobedience' (Eph 2²). Solidarity in both Judaism and the Old
Testament is based upon relationship. We noted the conception
of Israel as a family united together after the pattern of the most
closely united מִשְׁפָּחָה. In Paul, the Church, through its vital
relationship to Christ (who is the counterpart to the racial
ancestor) is a family of brethren.

Paul took this concept of brotherhood within the household
most seriously.[282] He admonishes a member of the Community to
abstain from any harmless practice such as the eating of meat if
by doing so he should offend a weaker brother (Rom 14¹⁵, 1 Cor
8¹¹⁻¹³). Just as one helps another within the family relationship,
so the Christian brotherhood must bear one another's burdens
and restore him who has been overtaken in a fault (Gal 6¹⁻²).
Adoption into the Christian Family transcends the social distinctions between a master and his slave; therefore, Paul enjoins
Philemon to receive Onesimus, 'a brother beloved . . . in the
Lord', even as he would receive Paul himself (Philem 16-17). For
the same reason, slaves are not to dishonour their Christian
masters, 'because they are brethren' (1 Tim 1¹⁻²). The mutual
love and regard within the family correspond to the mutual
regard which the members of the body have for each other
(1 Cor 12¹⁴⁻³¹). This mutual concern for one another within the
Family is summed up in Paul's varied use of *agape*. Deissmann
appropriately calls 1 Corinthians 13, 'the Song of Songs on
brotherly love'.[283]

Corresponding to the corporate involvement for good and evil
which characterized the membership of the Hebrew family is St

[282] A. Deissmann, op. cit. p. 209.   [283] Ibid. p. 210.

Paul's doctrine of the common sharing of experience within the Household of Faith. The significance of this point is clear in a statement such as this excerpt from the Second Letter to Corinth:

> For as the sufferings of Christ abound unto us, even so our comfort also aboundeth through Christ. But whether we be afflicted, it is for your comfort and salvation; or whether we be comforted, it is for your comfort, which worketh in the patient enduring of the same sufferings which we also suffer: and our hope for you is stedfast; knowing that, as ye are partakers of the sufferings, so also are ye of the comfort . . . (2 Cor 1$^{5-7}$ *RV*).[284]

The sufferings of Christ overflow into the life of the apostolic emissary; sufferings which are endured for the sake of ($\dot{\upsilon}\pi\acute{\epsilon}\rho$) the church of Colossae (1^{24}). This common sharing in the corporate suffering of the Family is further illustrated in the letter to Timothy:

> Therefore I endure all things for the elect's sake, that they also may obtain the salvation which is in Christ Jesus with eternal glory. Faithful is the saying: For if we died with him, we shall also live with him if we endure, we shall also reign with him . . . (2 Tim 2$^{10-12}$).

This suffering *with* Christ guarantees reigning with Him in His glory (Rom 8^{17}); therefore, Paul seeks to experience 'the $\kappa o\iota\nu\omega\nu\acute{\iota}\alpha$ of his (Christ's) sufferings' (Phil 3^{10}).[285]

What is true of suffering within the Family is also true of the holiness of the Community. It is a corporate ethical and psychic quality characterizing the People of God. Within the Family, the sin of a member is a direct violation of the corporate holiness of the group, issuing in the corporate judgement of the Church (cf. e.g. 1 Cor 5 *passim*, 3$^{16-17}$, 11$^{27-34}$).

Paul's conception of the Lordship of Christ within the context of his representation of the Church as the 'household of God' is noteworthy. As the New Israel acquired the title 'sons of God' through adoption into the divine Sonship of Christ,[286] so the brotherhood of members within the household is a derived relationship through Christ, the Elder Brother (Rom 8^{17}, Gal 4^{5}, Eph 1^{5}; cf. Heb 2$^{11-18}$). As the chief member of the family,

---

[284] Cf. L. S. Thornton, *The Common Life*, pp. 35-6.
[285] Cf. H. W. Robinson, *The Cross of the Servant*, pp. 79-80.
[286] Cf. Phythian-Adams, *The People and the Presence*, pp. 187-8.

Christ is the Lord (i.e. *baal*) of the household.[287] This idea of the Headship or Lordship of Christ is indicated even more directly through the designation of the Church as the Bride ('But I would have you know, that the head of every man is Christ; . . . and the head of Christ is God' is spoken in the context of this conception— 1 Cor 11³). In the Semitic conception of the family, the wife and minors were accorded a more or less equal status under the father and husband who was the *baal*. He most realistically incorporated them in himself; he was the sole cause for their existence, at once the absolute authority and provider for the family. It is this general sphere of thought which governs Paul's doctrine of Christ as the Head of the Body in distinction to His role as King over the whole creation (1 Cor 15²⁵).

We have already noted that although Ephesians and Colossians distinguish the Head from the Body while the earlier Epistles identify Christ with the Body, there is no fundamental contradiction involved. Both of them must be interpreted in the light of the designation of the Church as the Bride, the Second Eve. What is more, it is basic to the declaration that Christ is the Head of the Body to realize that Paul is thinking of either a husband-wife or father-family relationship, rather than the head as the superior organ in the body which is the seat of direction for the members. The Head is the exalted member of the Body only because it is higher, not because it rules over the other members through mental directives (note that in 1 Cor 12²¹⁻⁷, the head is but one member among others).

Once we recognize that the *baal* relationship of the chief member of the Family is what Paul is saying concerning the idea of the Head over the Body, a two-fold emphasis emerges: (1) the complete subordination of the Community under Christ,[288] (2) a vital relationship of Christ to the Family as the one who penetrates it and nourishes it.[289] In designating Christ as the Head, Paul gathers together the whole complex of the Semitic idea of

---

[287] The significance of this point is brought into relief when we remember that the earliest Christian confession or creed was 'Jesus is Lord' (cf. R. N. Flew, *Jesus and His Church*, p. 118).

[288] Cf. Eph 1²²⁻³, 5²³, ³³. C. H. Dodd, *According to the Scriptures*, pp. 121-2; W. Grossouw, *In Christ*, trans. from 2nd edn, M. W. Schoenberg (Westminster, 1952), p. 131; C. A. A. Scott, *The Fellowship of the Spirit*, p. 71.

[289] R. Asting, op. cit. p. 212. This writer correctly notes that Ephesians and Colossians do not think of the Body as an organism but in its relationship to Christ (ibid). Cf. G. Aulén, *This is the Church*, ed. A. Nygren and G. Aulén (Philadelphia, 1952), p. 10.

corporate personality centring in the chief member of the group, whether priest, king, ancestor, or a lowly *baal* over his מִשְׁפָּחָה.

For this reason, the head, for Paul, is the centre of subjection in unity.[290] Those who beguile the Colossian Christians through Gnostic teachings do not hold themselves to the Head, 'from which the whole body, being supported and held together by joints and ligaments, goes forward in the growth of God' (Col 2[18-19]; cf. Eph 4[16]). In a similar way, the Ephesian assembly is warned of the craftiness of erroneous teachers who masquerade as the 'gifts' proffered to the Church, but destroy the unity of the faith (4[10-29]). On the contrary, the Body must grow up into Him in all things, that is, Christ, who is the Head (4[15]).

The effective working of the apostles, prophets, evangelists, pastors, and teachers (Eph 4[11]) in their respective roles is the means by which the fullness of Christ is received. Paul continues to look forward to the Church's attainment of 'the unity of the faith, and of the knowledge of the Son of God, unto a fullgrown man, unto the measure of the stature of the fulness ($\pi\lambda\eta\rho\dot{\omega}\mu\alpha\tau\sigma\varsigma$) of Christ' (4[13]). This is the Church possessed of the life of Christ, mediated through the Holy Spirit, existing as an actual extension of His personality. The solidarity of the Old Testament and Early Judaism could only approximate this idea; it could only provide the type while the unity of the Church is the anti-type, the real thing. It is not a solidarity which exists *as though* the ancestor lived on in his progeny but is an actuality through the personal existence of the Holy Spirit in whom each member of the Church participates ($\kappa\sigma\iota\nu\omega\nu\epsilon\hat{\iota}$).

Our case is herewith concluded. The evidence, in our estimation, warrants the overall conclusion that Paul does apply Hebraic conceptions of the solidarity of the race or group in the orbit of major doctrines, especially Anthropology, Soteriology, and Ecclesiology. It is only in a Jewish context that Paul's propositions on human and cosmic unity can be rightly understood. Paul claims that his theology and teaching are of divine origin (Gal 1[12]). This claim we are not disposed to deny. However, the medium and context of the Apostle's inspired writing are Old Testament and Jewish conceptions, not Hellenistic thought.

[290] Cf. T. Soiron, op. cit. p. 19.

PAUL'S CONCEPTION OF THE SOLIDARITY
OF ETHNIC ISRAEL

N O extended discussion of Paul's application of Old Testament and Early Jewish conceptions of the solidarity of
the human race would be complete without the mention
of his conception of the solidarity of national or ethnic Israel as
an entity over against humanity at large as well as distinct from
the Church as the New Israel. We do not wish to retract the
conclusion at which we arrived regarding the Church as the
New Israel which replaces the old Israel after the flesh. This
point is never clouded; the necessity for Israel to be incorporated
into the Church is never controverted nor are its theological implications exempted (cf. Phil 3^{2-9}). The salvation of the individual Jew, as that of the individual Gentile, is attained only
through incorporation into the eschatological Israel through the
acceptance of the New Covenant and through faith in Jesus
Christ the Messiah. Paul's problem arises completely on the issue
of God's corporate election of national Israel.[1] How can it be
that although the promise had specific application to Israel, the
Jews have rejected the only means of obtaining the proffered
prize of salvation through faith in Christ? Although the Apostle
appears to give two answers to this question, there is in fact only
one solution and it turns on the conception of the solidarity of
Israel.

(1) *The Advantage of Israel*

Paul was most reluctant to entertain the view that Israel as
a people had been rejected by God. To be sure, this divine
reaction was warranted because of Israel's stubborn refusal to
heed the gospel invitation (cf. Acts 28^{25-31} with Rom 11^1). With
passionate sincerity Paul deliberates on the results of his missionary labour among the Jews; he would willingly exchange his

[1] Cf. G. F. Moore, *Judaism*, I.542; M. M. Bourke, *A Study of the Metaphor of the
Olive Tree*, p. 24.

own salvation for that of his own race if it were but feasible (Rom 9³).²

When Paul considers the benefits which are Israel's by prerogative, two opposing conclusions are drawn. In one sense there is no advantage whatsoever to being a Jew, while in another there are most consequential benefits. Thus, in answer to the questions: 'What advantage has the Jew? Or what is the value of circumcision?' (Rom 3¹), Paul asserts: 'Much in every way.' To begin with, the Jews are entrusted with the oracles of God. What if some were unfaithful (εἰ ἠπίστησάν τινες)? Does their faithlessness nullify the faithfulness of God? 'By no means' (3²⁻⁴). With this incomplete statement, the Apostle breaks off only to resume this line of thought in Chapter 9.³ Here there is an extensive list of benefits which belong to ethnic Israel:

They are Israelites, and to them belong the sonship, the glory, the covenants, the giving of the law, the worship, and the promises; to them belong the patriarchs, and of their race, according to the flesh is the Christ. God who is over all be blessed for ever. Amen (Rom 9⁴⁻⁵ *RSV*).

This passage clearly shows that Paul is thinking of Israel's solidarity in terms current in the Judaism of his day (cf. *supra* Chap. 2). Here there is no consideration of the individual apart from the group. The sonship (ἡ υἱοθεσία), the covenants, or the giving of the law (ἡ νομοθεσία) belong to Israel as a whole. These privileges belong to the group and are mediated by it to the individual. It is of further significance for us to note that Paul did not break with the Jewish conception of ancestral merit in that the phrase, ὧν οἱ πατέρες, designates one among Israel's most prominent blessings. Elsewhere, Paul says explicitly that Israel is beloved for the sake of the forefathers (Rom 11²⁸). Thinking in terms of contemporary solidarity, Paul assumes that

---

² A. D. Nock notes that this passage embodies the idea of corporate salvation. There is no salvation for the individual apart from the group (*St Paul*, pp. 241, 244). Of course, Paul does not go that far, but the idea may not have been far removed from his mind. For a brief but acceptable appraisal and refutation of F. C. Baur's and Harnack's reconstruction of the framework of the particularism and universalism of both Paul and the Early Church, see J. Munck, *JTS*, Vol. II (1951), pp. 3ff. Paul never completely divorced his doctrine of the salvation of the Gentiles from the salvation of Israel (Rom 1¹⁶). It is for this reason that his imprisonment is 'because of the hope of Israel' (Acts 28²⁰), even though he is the missionary to the Gentiles.

³ Sanday and Headlam, *Romans*, p. 69.

it would be more natural that the merit of Christ provided in His vicarious atonement should implicate Israel, because He came of that race according to the flesh.[4]

When Paul is thinking of Israel in these corporate terms, the main point is that the rejection of the gospel by *some* Jews is not the last word nor the end of the matter. There remains, no matter what individuals may do, the unshakable promise of God which guarantees the salvation of all Israel:

Lest you be wise in your own conceits, I want you to understand this mystery, brethren: a hardening has come upon part of Israel, until the full number of the Gentiles come in, and so all Israel will be saved; as it is written, 'The Deliverer will come from Zion, he will banish ungodliness from Jacob; 'and this will be my covenant with them when I take away their sins.' As regards the gospel they are enemies of God, for your [Gentiles] sake; but as regards election they are beloved for the sake of their forefathers. For the gifts and the call of God are irrevocable (Rom 11[25-9] *RSV*).

Since the unit which Paul has in mind is the totality of Israel, any number of individuals, even a majority, may turn from the truth, but such an attitude cannot change the unconditional promises of God regarding the salvation and the restoration of Israel. God has the power to engraft again the natural broken branches of Israel; that is less remarkable or objectionable than the engrafting of wild slips (Rom 11[23-4]).

In this corporate sense the salvation of all Israel is assured. πᾶς 'Ισραήλ is to be understood in Paul's thought-context of representative universalism.[5] That generation which turns to the Lord will stand representatively for the whole of Israel stretching back to the call of Abraham.[6] In this representative sense, the continuity of Israel cannot be abrogated. Ethnic Israel is still embraced in the irrevocable election which is founded on the immutability of God. This is what Paul means when he says: 'If the dough offered as first fruits is holy, so is the whole

[4] Cf. G. A. Danell, 'The Idea of God's People in the Bible', pp. 35ff. This idea arises out of the recognition of the closer solidarity within the national family relationship as over against the totality of the race. It is more natural that the atonement should be applied to Israel because Jesus Christ comes from that family group, than to the whole race where the solidarity originating in Adam is more widely diffused.

[5] This is a Semitic idea and does not refer to individual opportunity but to the continuity of the nation represented by one generation or one segment (cf. J. Munck, op. cit. p. 8).

[6] Cf. K. Stendahl, 'The Called and the Chosen', p. 69.

lump [note the parallel figure which he applies to the Church in 1 Cor 5⁶⁻⁸]; and if the root is holy, so are the branches' (Rom 11¹⁶).

By turning to the Old Testament, Paul finds a parallel situation. Although the major part of the nation had rejected the covenant, there remained still the remnant, 'the seven thousand who had not bowed their knee to Baal' (Rom 11²⁻⁶). It is with relief and conviction that Paul recognizes that even in his own day there is a representative 'remnant chosen by grace' out of Israel, the elect who have garnered the reward of the promise (Rom 11⁵⁻⁶).[7]

(2) The rejection of Israel

In quite another sense, a temporary and individualistic sense, Israel has been rejected. This is clearly brought out in Paul's statement to the Jews of Rome:

'The Holy Spirit was right in saying to your fathers through Isaiah the prophet: "Go to this people, and say, You shall indeed hear but never understand, and you shall indeed see but never perceive. For this people's heart has grown dull, and their ears are heavy of hearing, and their eyes they have closed; lest they should perceive with their eyes, and hear with their ears, and understand with their heart, and turn for me to heal them." Let it be known to you then that this salvation of God has been sent to the Gentiles; they will listen' (Acts 28²⁵⁻⁸ RSV).

In this individualistic and temporary context, there is absolutely no difference whatever between the Jews and the Gentiles (Rom 10¹²). Although Israel has been rejected by God, individuals continue to come from among the Jews to trust in Christ and to have the veil removed from their understanding of the Scripture (2 Cor 3¹⁴⁻¹⁶).

Now, this hardening of Israel is itself the result of the operation of the principle of representative universalism. By applying it to his own generation, Paul deduces that the gospel has gone out into the whole earth (Rom 10¹⁴⁻²⁰. Note the quotation of Psalm 19 and Isaiah 53). In this connexion, J. Munck points out:

---

[7] M. M. Bourke thinks that Rom 9⁶ ('. . . not all who are descended from Israel belong to Israel') is another reference to this remnant rather than to the spiritual children of Abraham. It is therefore not a parallel to Rom 4¹¹, as it has often been thought—op. cit. p. 24.

If however the words of the quotation (Ps 19, 'Their sound went out into all the earth, and their words unto the end of the world') are taken literally, they mean that the apostles who were sent forth to the Jews have now finished their task. . . . The parts to which they have preached stand for the whole, the Jewish people. Therefore Paul is able to assert that Israel is unbelieving and stubborn as he does in the passage which follows.[8]

Those that have had the opportunity to hear the gospel have made the decision which binds the whole of Israel under the judgement of the hardening of God.

This hardening is, however, only a temporary expedient that the Gentiles might be given a share in the dispensation of the grace of God (Rom 11[10-11]). It could never mean the complete and irrevocable by-passing of the Jewish mission, for the salvation of the Gentiles is itself integrally related to the restoration of all Israel (Rom 11[12]). The gospel is offered first of all to the Jew (Rom 1[16]) 'in order to win them and Jerusalem, and thus through representative universalism, the whole'.[9]

(3) *Conclusion*

Although Paul by no means accepted a very common and current Jewish opinion that every single Israelite would be saved, and be included in the eschatological Age of blessing (cf. *supra* p. 47), he faithfully maintains the conception of the solidarity of Israel. In applying the idea of representative universalism it is possible for him to say, 'all Israel will be saved'. There is furthermore the additional factor of the continuity of Israel seen in the remnant of Jews who have believed the gospel. This thread of continuity will not be broken nor the promises of God abrogated. In its corporate application, the culmination of the continuity of Israel will be the incorporation of all Israel into the true People of God. In fine, for Paul, the bond of Israel's solid-

---

[8] Op. cit. p. 8.

[9] J. Munck, op. cit. p. 10. On the surface, this point would seem to warrant the conclusion that preaching to the Gentiles was a waste of time and effort as long as the salvation of Israel was the decisive event which would (as the Old Testament prophecy maintained) be the means of winning the Gentiles. But the hardness of Israel's heart in their rejection of Christ and His apostles, meant a turning to the Gentiles that the Jews might be enticed through jealousy to turn to the Lord (Rom 11[14]) (cf. J. Munck, op. cit. pp. 10-11). Thus, the reversal of the original programme of God is one of expediency.

arity is no longer determined by the Old Covenant of Sinai which was abrogated by Christ (2 Cor 3[4-18], Gal 3[13-14]),[10] but rather by the corporate election of Israel which has been sealed by the prophetic promises of God. The fulfilment of this election is therefore eschatological (Rom 11[26]).

[10] Cf. F. Prat, *The Theology of St Paul*, II.205-6.

INDEX TO AUTHORS